Between the Old and the New World

Migration - Ethnicity - Nation: Cracow Studies in Culture, Society and Politics

Edited by Dorota Praszałowicz

Editorial Advisory Board:
Grzegorz Babiński
Marcin Kula
Zdzisław Mach
Adam Walaszek

Reviewer:
Prof. Grzegorz Babiński

Volume 1

PETER LANG
Frankfurt am Main · Berlin · Bern · Bruxelles · New York · Oxford · Warszawa · Wien

Agnieszka Małek
Dorota Praszałowicz
(eds.)

Between the Old and the New World

Studies in the History
of Overseas Migrations

PETER LANG
Internationaler Verlag der Wissenschaften

Bibliographic Information published by the Deutsche Nationalbibliothek
The Deutsche Nationalbibliothek lists this publication in the Deutsche Nationalbibliografie; detailed bibliographic data is available in the internet at http://dnb.d-nb.de.

Cover Design:
© Olaf Gloeckler, Atelier Platen, Friedberg

The publication of this volume was supported by
the Jagiellonian University - Faculty
of International and Political Studies.

Typesetting by **motivex**

ISSN 2191-3285
ISBN 978-3-631-61757-1
© Peter Lang GmbH
Internationaler Verlag der Wissenschaften
Frankfurt am Main 2012
All rights reserved.

All parts of this publication are protected by copyright. Any utilisation outside the strict limits of the copyright law, without the permission of the publisher, is forbidden and liable to prosecution. This applies in particular to reproductions, translations, microfilming, and storage and processing in electronic retrieval systems.

www.peterlang.de

Table of contents

Introduction 7
Dorota Praszałowicz

I Research Agenda Old and New

Sending Money 'Home': Toward a Transnational History of Migrant
Remittances 11
*Barbara M. Posadas (Northern Illinois University, DeKalb) and Roland L. Guyotte
(University of Minnesota, Morris)*

Ethnicity, Inclusion, and Exclusion: Poles in France and Bretons in Paris 27
Leslie Page Moch (Michigan State University)

European Immigrant Poverty in America 37
Stan Nadel (University of Portland, Salzburg Austria Center)

Love in All the Wrong Places: Relating Migration Patterns and Marriage
in U.S. Immigration, 1945-2000 55
Suzanne M. Sinke (Florida State University)

II Multicultural Places

Polish Immigrants and Chicago's Progressive Parks: Creating Public Space
in the City 65
Dominic A. Pacyga (Columbia College)

The Pitfalls of Macrohistory: The Case of Waterloo, Québec 75
Wolfgang Helbich (Ruhr Universität Bochum)

III The Jewish Experience

Different. Polish and Post-Soviet Jewish Immigrants in New York City 89
Anna Sosnowska (University of Warsaw)

From Oświęcim to Ellis Island: Jewish and Other Transmigrants and the
Evolution of Border Controls Along Germany's Eastern Border, 1885-1914 109
Tobias Brinkmann (Penn State University)

Before "The Holocaust": American Jews Confront Catastrophe, 1945-1962 125
Hasia Diner (New York University)

IV Local Immigrant Communities: Polish-American Perspective

Neighbourhood on a Hill: the Traditional Polish American Neighbourhood: Has it Changed Forever? Has it a Future? The Examples of Worcester and Webster, Massachusetts 159
David A. Jones (University of Warsaw)

The Role of Religious Institutions in Building the Polish Community in Windsor, Ontario 169
Agata Rajski (Jagiellonian University)

Introduction
Dorota Praszałowicz (Jagiellonian University)

> Americans have built a global society
> whose peoples' origins
> have come to look much like the world itself.
>
> (David Gerber, 2011: 134)

This volume contains papers presented at the Fourth Workshop "American Ethnicity: Rethinking Old Issues, Asking New Questions". The workshop was organized in Kraków, Poland, on May 24th–25th, 2010. It was hosted by the Institute of American Studies and Polish Diaspora of the Jagiellonian University, and supported by the (American) Immigration and Ethnic History Society. The event was made possible thanks to the generous support of the United States General Consulate in Kraków, the Faculty of International and Political Studies of the Jagiellonian University, the Doctorate Students' Society of the Jagiellonian University, and the Kraków Chapter of the Stowarzyszenie "Wspólnota Polska" (a non-governmental organization in Poland whose aim is to stay in touch with Polish diaspora).

There is a tradition of organizing bi-annual workshops "American Ethnicity: Rethinking Old Issues, Asking New Questions" which take place in Kraków. The First Workshop (under the same title) took place at the Jagiellonian University in October 2004. It gathered eminent scholars from the US, Germany, Austria and Poland. Among the participants there were Hasia Diner, David Gerber, Victor Greene, Hartmut Keil, Dominic Pacyga, Suzanne M. Sinke, and Annemarie Steidl. Most of the participants returned to Kraków for the next workshops. The workshop proceedings were published as a special English language volume of the quarterly of the Polish Academy of Sciences: *Przegląd Polonijny* ("Polonia Review"), vol. 31, 2005, No 4. The texts in the 2005 volume deal with (among others): "Wandering Jews: Peddlers, Immigrants, and the Discovery of the <New Worlds>" (Hasia Diner), "Young, Unwed, Mobile and Female. Women on Their Way from the Habsburg Monarchy to the United States of America" (Annemarie Steidl), "Love, Sex, and Bureaucracy: The U.S. Military and Marriage to <Foreigners>" (Suzanne M. Sinke).

The Second Workshop took place in May 2006, and the third one in May 2008. Most of the participants are social historians who focus their research on the past as well as on the present migration issues, therefore the workshop presentations deal with both historical and contemporary perspective. For example, due to the presidential election of 2008, the Third Workshop (May 2008) was started with David Gerber's comments on this subject (*Ethnicity and the 2008 Elections, At This Moment, Mid-May 2008*) and Victor Greene's presentation entitled *Offering a Refuge or Refusal? : American Immigration Policy, Past & Present*. Their comments were followed by a lively discussion.

The proceedings of the third workshop were also published as a special issue of the *Studia Migracyjne – Przegląd Polonijny* ("Polonia Review"), vol. 35, 2009, No 3. The list of texts included "Another Look at Whiteness: The Persistence of Ethnicity in American Life" (Ronald Bayor), and "Immigration, Development, and Assimilation in the United States in a Global Perspective, 1850-1930" (Jose Moya).

A group of people who feel attached to the workshops is increasing. The first meeting, somehow improvised, was modest in comparison to the following ones. In the course of time the workshops have won a reputation and became supported by prestigious diplomatic and academic institutions. Ronald Bayor (who attended the third workshop) and Barbara Posadas (who participated in the fourth workshop, and contributed to this volume) are the leaders of the Immigration and Ethnic History Society. The Society was founded in 1965 as the Immigration History Group, and it publishes a quarterly *Journal of American Ethnic History*.

> *The Society's stated purpose is to promote the study of the history of immigration to the United States and Canada from all parts of the world, including studies of the background of emigration in the countries of origin; to promote the study of ethnic groups in the United States, including regional groups, native Americans and forced immigrants; to promote understanding of the processes of acculturation and of conflict (...)* (www.iehs.org/mission)

The Kraków workshops' objectives are consistent with the above quoted purposes. Generally speaking, the meetings gather leading scholars of American ethnic and migration studies who share basic theoretical and methodological assumptions. The aim is to give an opportunity to discuss ongoing research, and to examine new research perspectives. Most of the workshops' participants are historians, who study societies "from the bottom up", and adopt a "longue durée" perspective". American immigration, ethnicity, assimilation – the very basic notions in this field of studies – are discussed, and sometimes redefined. Most participants accept the research paradigms which inform classical immigration studies (authored among others by: Barkan 1996, Brettel 2000, Foner 2000, Gerber 2011, Hoerder 2002), and they agree, that there is a need to apply again the concept of assimilation, however in its new revised version (Morawska 1994, Barkan 1995, Alba & Nee 2003).

Moreover, the workshops provide atmosphere in which scholars feel challenged to seek a broader context. For example while discussing American immigration, Jose Moya situated the American experience in a global perspective, and asserted that *migration is a basic feature of the human species rather than an American or modern phenomenon*. (Moya 2009). Moya pointed to the level of *separation and continuity* of Arabs in East Africa, Volga Germans in Russia, and Chinese in Malaysia; the analysis led him to a conclusion that: *ethnic persistence in the U.S. and the other Neo-Europes seems, particularly after the third generation, less consequential, to put it mildly* (Moya 2009). Different, but not opposite position was taken by Ronald Bayor, who questioned the idea (popular in some studies of the 1990's) that American immigrants from Europe have adopted identity of the white group. In his talk, Bayor gave abundant evidence to *the persistence of ethnicity in American life* (Bayor 2009). Clearly, both presentations were followed by a discussion.

Many presentations focused on the forgotten aspects of immigrants' trajectories, for instance a story of the German liberal intellectual Francis Lieber and his experience in the US South (1835-56) where he witnessed slavery (Keil 2008); Polish American youth as members of mixed-ethnic gangs in Chicago (Dominic Pacyga 2004); or the German convicts who had agreed to banishment to America as an alternative to detention in Germany (Wolfgang Helbich & Walter Kamphoefner 2008).

The discussions which start during the sessions are usually continued in private conversations during the workshops. In contrast to large conferences, which consists of many parallel sessions or huge plenary sessions, the workshops give the participants the chance to meet and hold discussions face to face. There is enough time for presentations and for comments.

The workshops are attended by the local scholars and students, especially by the students of American Studies, as well as the students of MA Migration and Ethnic Studies (both programs are carried on at the Jagiellonian University). The sessions give the students an opportunity to meet the authors of the classic works on American immigration and ethnicity. Moreover, the Fourth Workshop featured a doctorate students' session, and one of the presented papers is published in this volume (Rajski).

The current volume contains texts which provide a comparative context to immigration studies (Leslie Page Moch, Wolfgang Helbich), contribute to the gender perspective (Suzanne M. Sinke), bring up new issues like the Chicago *parks programs where* [immigrant] *youth could obtain healthful physical training* (Dominic Pacyga), and remind the most important aspects of migrants' life, eg. the remittances (Barbara Posadas & Roland Guyotte), or poverty (Stan Nadel). There is also a set of three texts on American Jewish experience, studied from a variety of angles (Hasia Diner, Tobias Brinkmann, Anna Sosnowska). The Polish-American section presents texts on local immigrant communities and their collective memories (David Jones, Agata Rajski).

The Fourth Workshop was inaugurated in the medieval building of the Jagiellonian University – the Collegium Maius – by Mr. Allan Greenberg, the United States General Consul in Kraków; Prof. Andrzej Mania, Deputy Rector of the Jagiellonian University; and Prof. Adam Walaszek, Director of the Institute of American Studies and Polish Diaspora (of the Jagiellonian University). The introductory speech was given by Prof. Barbara Posadas, the President of the Immigration and Ethnic History Society who noticed that *small conferences such as this workshop provide the very best opportunities for significant scholarly dialog across nation-state boundaries.*

References

Alba, Richard, and Victor Nee. *Remaking the American Mainstream. Assimilation and Contemporary Immigration.* Cambridge, Massachusetts: Harvard University Press, 2003.

Barkan, Elliot Robert. *And Still They Come. Immigrants and American Society 1920 to the 1990's*. Wheeling: Harlan Davidson, 1996.
Barkan, Elliot Robert. "Race, Religion and Nationality in American Society: A Model of Ethnicity – From Contact to Assimilation." *Journal of American Ethnic History*, vol. 14, no 2 (1995).
Bayor, Ronald H. "Another Look at "Whiteness": The Persistence of Ethnicity in American Life." *Studia Migracyjne. Przegląd Polonijny*, no 3 (2009).
Brettell, Caroline B., and James F. Hollifield, ed. *Migration Theory. Talking Across Disciplines*. New York: Routledge, 2000.
Foner, Nancy. *From Ellis Island to JFK: New York's Two Great Waves of Immigration*. New Haven and London: Yale University Press, 2000.
Gerber, David. *American Immigration: A Very Short Introduction*. Oxford: Oxford University Press, 2011.
Hoerder, Dirk. *Cultures in Contact. World Migrations in the Second Millennium*. Durham: Duke University Press, 2002.
Kraut, Alan M. *The Huddled Masses. The Immigrant in American Society, 1880-1921*. Wheeeling: Harlan Davidson, 1982.
Morawska, Ewa. "In Defense of the Assimilation Model." *Journal of American Ethnic History*, vol. 13, No 2. (1994).
Moya, Jose. 2009. "Immigration, Development, and Assimilation in the United States in a Global Perspective, 1850-1930." *Studia Migracyjne - Przegląd Polonijny*, no 3. (2009).
Moya, Jose C. *Cousins and Strangers. Spanish Immigrants in Buenos Aires, 1850-1930*. Berkeley: University of California Press, 1998.
Walaszek, Adam, ed. "Mass Migrations: Their Economic, Political and Cultural Implications." *Przegląd Polonijny*, vol. 31, no 1 (A Special Issue: Proceedings of the Migration Session at the International Congress of Historical Sciences, Sydney, Australia (July 2005).

Sending Money 'Home': Toward a Transnational History of Migrant Remittances

Barbara M. Posadas *(Northern Illinois University, DeKalb)* and
Roland L. Guyotte *(University of Minnesota, Morris)*

On January 13, 2007, in its online edition, the *Milwaukee Journal Sentinel* posted excerpts of letters written from Milwaukee over nearly twenty years by Irma Martinez to her family in the rural Philippines.[1] Nineteen years old when she arrived in the United States in 1985, ostensibly for medical treatment, Irma observed during her first winter: "I'm lonely, but thankfully we are sharing letters to talk to one another. No matter what I say, ma, I'm stuck in this life. . . . " Irma Martinez had been brought illegally to the United States to work as a domestic in the suburban Milwaukee home of Drs. Jefferson and Elnora Calimlim, an immigrant Filipino physician couple with three children. She initially agreed to stay for five years in return for $150 per month, and began sending remittances to her parents. Almost two years later, in September 1987, she wrote: " . . . Ma, you asked when I'm coming home. I am not sure. It could be in December 1990. I know I am going home sometime. . . . Ma, read this to Nonoy Kie and tell him what I am saying. Sing to him for me. Comfort him and say that sometime I will come home. . . ." In an undated missive written later, Irma expressed her hope for a future with her family in the Philippines, in a home paid for with her labor: "Mom, is it possible to make sure that when I go home that we will have a new house already? I want a big living room with two levels. I want the living room upstairs next to the kitchen. I will send the money in December. Please take care of the rest. Plan that the house has a gate and a fence around it, if possible." In September 2002, after a brief telephone call from her parents, Irma wrote to explain her situation:

> "I'm glad that you and papa called. Sorry if it was a short conversation. Ms. Nora is not giving me enough time. She stands and watches beside me. You might think I don't want to talk to you, but I was working when you called and I was also tired. The house is too large [actually, a massive 8,600 square feet] and I am the only servant. . . The visa that they promised me has not been arranged. . . . If I go home there without my visa, I will never be able to return here. If I go home there now, you will not have anybody to help you educate the others."

During almost two decades, Irma's remittances, estimated at about $20,000, helped to lift her impoverished farm family's economic circumstances. Ever the dutiful daughter, over time she paid for her siblings educations, her father's medicines, her mother's surgery, plots of land, a carabao, and later a Honda tractor. Letters from home pressured her with more requests for money or goods—a watch for her father and jewelry for her mother. Throughout, the

---

[1] "A Life Wasted Waiting: Irma Martinez's Letters to Her Family," *JSOnline* [*Milwaukee Journal Sentinel*], January 13, 2007, www.jsonline.com (accessed 4/3/2007).

Calimlims kept Irma's identity as an undocumented alien a secret by passing her off as a visiting relative or hiding her in a locked basement bedroom when others were in their home. They took her Philippine passport, forbade her to leave the house by herself, and told her to answer the telephone only after ten rings which indicated that a family member was calling. When she attended religious services with the Calimlim family, they made her sit apart from them, on the other side of the church. The Calimlims' threats—that she would be deported, that the remittances to her family would end, and that everyone would be in serious legal trouble—hung over Irma's head like a sword. How could she possibly sacrifice her family's future by contesting her plight? How could she betray the Calimlims by telephoning for help when no one else was at home?

In the end, Irma did not initiate her own rescue. Instead, Sherry Bantug, a young Filipina American who grew up in the Milwaukee area and had graduated from Marquette University, revealed Irma's plight. While dating a Calimlim son, Sherry puzzled over the identity of the Filipina "visitor" who was always there. After she became closer to the family and married young Calimlim, she learned the truth. With her marriage in shambles in less than a year, Sherry made an anonymous call to the authorities. In September 2004, federal agents and local police raided the Calimlim home, found Irma Martinez cowering in a basement closet, and arrested the physicians.[2] Brought by the government to the United States to testify at the trial, Irma's parents revealed that in nineteen years, they had spoken with their daughter four or five times in very brief telephone conversations. The Calimlims were convicted of four felony counts of human trafficking, imposing forced labor, and harboring an illegal alien, sentenced to four years in prison—which was later increased to six years—and ordered to pay Irma $934,420 in restitution.[3] They face almost certain deportation after their release.[4]

And what of Irma? In the months that followed, she received almost $700,000 of the money that the court ordered the Calimlims to pay, was spared deportation and received a T visa enabling her to apply for a green card in three years.[5] Almost forty years old and no longer the young girl who had hoped for a family of her own, Irma relocated to the Chicago area where she found employment in a cosmetics store, the regular hours a welcome relief from the fifteen plus hour days that she worked as a virtual slave. One wonders whether she has

---

2   Joseph Lariosa, "Doctor Couple Goes to Two Federal Prisons," *The Filipino Express Online* March 19-25, 2007 (Vol. 21, #12). http://www.filipinoexpress.com/21/12_news.html (Accessed 6-23-09)

3   "Maid Lived 20 Years in Quiet Struggle," *JSOnline* [Milwaukee Journal Sentinel], January 14, 2007, (accessed 4/3/2007).

4   "Best of the Blogs www.jsonline.com/blogs," *JSOnline* [*Milwaukee Journal Sentinel*], June 14, 2009, www.jsonline.com (accessed 6/16/2009).

5   Jane Huckerby, "United States of America (USA)," *Collateral Damage: The Impact of Anti-Trafficking Measures on Human Rights Around the World*, (Bangkok, Thailand: Global Alliance Against Traffic in Women, 2007), 230-253. http://www.antislavery.org/homepage/resources/PDF/CollateralDamage_2007.pdf (Accessed 6-20-2009).

visited the rest of her family in the Philippines, including six siblings born after she left her homeland.[6]

Within the context of United States history, the Irma Martinez case shocks precisely because it seems so extremely atypical; it evokes incredulity and contempt despite our certain knowledge that remittances constitute a vital element in contemporary migration. Remittances sent by those who migrate to those who remain at home enrich not only individuals and families, but also the communities and the nations to which they flow. Remittances have become essential to governments that rely on them to constitute a substantial element of GDP. Consequently, remittances have also become of increasing interest to historians of immigration. This essay considers immigrant remittances sent from the United States in the context of immigrant motivation and behavior, state policies of both the sending and receiving countries, and the social consequences of the contemporary remittance stream.

* * * * *

Have remittances always loomed large, or have they generally been ignored in the scholarly literature? A brief review of historians' treatment of remittances over time can prove instructive. What does their work on remittances reveal about the development of U.S. immigration and ethnicity as a field? On most occasions when historians have written about immigrants of earlier eras sending money to the folks at home, remittances appear as positive and benign, rather than as coercive. Sending remittances suggests persistent bonds based on love and obligation, despite great distance. While they remained unmarried, Hasia Diner's devoted daughters of Erin sent money home to parents across the Atlantic in Ireland and helped siblings to join them in America. Roger Daniels pointed out that Greeks and Italians sent young men to work in Turkey or Switzerland, while the money they sent home helped sustain the impoverished villagers and peasants, a pattern repeated when Greeks and Italians migrated to the United States. As early as 1939, Carl Wittke noted: "In the eight years before 1927, it has been estimated that $5,000,000 a year were sent back to Mexico by postal money orders."[7]

But most of these historians paid rather cursory attention to remittances. For decades, historians typically emphasized instead the nature, the means, and the extent of adjustment to *life in the United States*. To be sure, most historians termed the "new social historians" have underscored the immigrants' *active* role in forging their American ethnicities in communities, work places, and families. Immigrants, despite the constraints that they faced, were *not* passive victims, as they were more likely to "transplant" than be "uprooted." Some of these historians, as well as a few of their predecessors, have highlighted ways in which im-

---

6 "Maid Lived 20 Years in Quiet Struggle," January 14, 2007.
7 Carl Wittke, *We Who Built America: The Saga of the Immigrant* (NY: Prentice Hall, Inc., 1939), 467.

migrants remained involved both with kin left behind and with the lands of their birth.[8]

In one instance, Josef Hasiak, Barbara Posadas's Polish grandfather, migrated to Chicago from Rzeszów in Galicia Poland in 1903, intending like many others to return eventually to his homeland. Not long after his arrival, he married Apolonia Kemp, a young Polish woman from near Łódź, and they began raising a family while saving money to purchase more farm land near his father's in the homeland. In early 1912, he sent his pregnant wife and their three children back to Poland to do just that. Certainly, he remitted money to his wife for the family's support while they were in Poland, but instead of joining his family after a couple more years of work in the Windy City, as he had originally intended, he called his family back to Chicago in 1913. Rumors of war in Europe and the threat of his being drafted into the military changed his original plan forever. As his family in Chicago grew, his remittances to family members who remained in Poland diminished, and ceased altogether after his parents died. Neither Josef nor Apolonia Hasiak, nor any of their six children, ever visited Poland again, nor did any of their eight grandchildren—until, almost a hundred years later, when Barbara Posadas came to Krakow in 2010 to deliver the paper that has become this article.

In this account of Josef Hasiak, remittances are implicit, but they are never central to the story of the Hasiak family's life that takes place *in the United States*. Then-partitioned Poland shaped Josef and Apolonia before they arrived—social customs, cultural practices, religious beliefs, family relationships, gendered norms and behaviors, and economic skills—all of these factors affected their acculturation and adjustment, their rearing of their children, and their understanding of ethnicity—what it meant to be Polish in America. For many historians of immigration, concern with the "old country" similarly receded into the background, as did the nature and extent of ties to family and friends back "at home."

In the 1980s and 1990s, this began to change. **First**, the sweeping overhaul of U. S. immigration policy in 1965 began to be felt across the nation. Not only did immigration surge and show no sign of slowing, but also immigrants began arriving in record numbers from nations that had not previously contributed nearly so much of the migration stream. Between 1981 and 2000 almost 16.5 million immigrants came to the United States, half again as many as had arrived in the previous thirty-five years. In both decades, the Americas, excluding Canada,

---

8   The first synthesis of the "new social historians'" work was John Bodnar, *The Transplanted: A History of Immigrants in Urban America* (Bloomington, IN: Indiana University Press, 1985). Works that have paid substantial attention to remittances include Robert F. Foerster, *The Italian Immigration of Our Times* (Cambridge, MA: Harvard University Press, 1919), Arnold Schrier, *Ireland and the American Emigration, 1850-1900* (Minneapolis, MN: University of Minnesota Press, 1958), Charlotte Erickson, *Invisible Immigrants: The Adaptation of English and Scottish Immigrants in Nineteenth-Century America* (Coral Gables, FL: University of Miami Press, 1972), and Roger Daniels, *Coming to America: A History of Immigration and Ethnicity in American Life*, 2nd edition (New York: Perennial Books, 2002).

provided approximately 49 per cent, with Mexicans constituting 22.6 per cent of all immigrants in the 1980s and 24.7 per cent in the 1990s. In the 1980s, immigrants from Asia constituted 37.3 per cent of all immigrants, in the 1990s 30.7 per cent. **Second**, changes in the technology of travel reworked the process of migration, making it far easier to come—and to return. Jet planes replaced transoceanic vessels, and although being stuck like a sardine in an eight-across seat in the middle section of an economy class cabin on a 747 is no fun, it is not comparable to passage in steerage. Nor does it take weeks, as it did in 1926, when the voyage of Barbara Posadas's father Alipio Posadas from Manila to Vancouver consumed twenty-one days. **Third**, technology also revolutionized the means of keeping in touch across space. Earlier, personal letters and photographs limited contact between immigrants and kin in the homeland to paper, and even telegraph messages sent in emergencies also arrived on paper. Later, telephone calls reintroduced the nuances of verbal communication: love, anger, or sorrow in voices across the miles. Now, communication has become increasingly instantaneous, varied, and global. Cell phones are ubiquitous. In a commercial broadcast with nauseating regularity on CNN, a man rejects two cents in change—"Keep it." But the savvy clerk responds, "With two cents, I can call my brother in Argentina!" Others chime in: "For two cents, I can talk to my granddaughter in Hong Kong," "I can talk to my brother. He's stationed in Germany." With internet, computers, video cameras, and social networking sites, communication takes place in real time.

Remitting money from one country to another has also become an electronic transaction. A quick "google" search of the terms "Philippines" and "send money," yielded 338,000 hits in .26 seconds, among them:

> Send Money to Philippines for $10 Flat at remithome.com flat fee, high exchange rate, and first transfer free when you send money to Philippines online! Better Business Bureau accredited. www.remithome.com

Another online transfer service, www.xoom.com, and the Philippine National Bank announced a partnership that simplifies the remittance process: "[Overseas Filipino Workers] . . . all over the world can send money to their beneficiaries' PNB bank accounts hassle-free and at very affordable rates." When the money comes from a U.S. bank account, the fee for transferring up to $2,000 is a flat $7.99. "In addition to bank deposits in minutes, Xoom.com also provides cash pickup in over 1,900 locations in the Philippines, and home delivery in major cities and home provinces."[9]

In the early 1990s, a concept of more specific relevance to the topic of contemporary remittances—"transnationalism"—began to take center stage among anthropologists and sociologists studying migration. In 1992, Nina Glick Schiller, Linda Basch, and Cristina Blanc-Szanton published "Transnationalism: A

---

9 "Xoom.com and PNB Launch Innovative Online Remittance Service," https://www.xoom.com/sendmoneynow/news/xoom-and-pnb-launch-innovative-online-remittance-service-11102008 (Accessed 6-21-09).

New Analytic Framework for Understanding Migration," in the *Annals of the New York Academy of Sciences*.[10] They argued:

> Our earlier conceptions of immigrant and migrant no longer suffice. . . . Now, a new kind of migrating population is emerging, composed of those whose networks activities and patterns of life encompass both their host and home societies. Their lives cut across national boundaries and bring two societies into a single social field. . . . Transmigrants develop and maintain multiple relations—familial, economic, social, organizational, religious, and political that span borders. Transmigrants take actions, make decisions, and feel concerns and develop identities within social networks that connect them to two or more societies simultaneously.

Based on their observations of Haitians, Grenadians, and Filipinos living in New York, Schiller, Basch, and Blanc-Szanton concluded that contemporary migrants—"transmigrants"—"actively manipulate their identities and thus both accommodate to and resist their subordination within a global capitalist system."[11] As transmigrants cross borders, they deal with the limits imposed by nation-states, but they live their lives simultaneously in both places. This, the authors argued, was fundamentally new and a reaction to the global economic demands not present in the past, either for individuals, for their families, and for their countries of origin.

While recognizing the utility of this concept and the need for a global perspective, many historians have since questioned whether transnationalism surfaced only in the late twentieth century. Were all migrants and immigrants of the past so fundamentally different from the "transmigrants" of the present?

In 2000, in *Dreaming of Gold, Dreaming of Home: Transnationalism and Migration Between the United States and South China, 1882-1943*, historian Madeline Hsu vigorously refuted the claim that transnationalism had appeared only among recent migrants. Chinese husbands and wives who lived for years on opposite sides of the Pacific created transnational families despite time apart and distance between. Because U.S. law prevented Chinese laborers from having their wives join them in the United States and restricted the men's movement back and forth across the Pacific, the Chinese from Taishan Province developed elaborate means for keeping contact with and supporting their families and home communities in China throughout the 1882 to 1943 "exclusion" period. Gold Mountain firms handled the sending of letters and the transfer of money, usually for a two percent commission. Remittances became the life blood of prosperity in South China: "Dependence upon remittances and declining productivity produced a society that could not do without foreign money."[12]

---

10 Nina Glick Schiller, Linda Basch, and Cristina Blanc-Szanton, "Transnationalism: A New Analytic Framework for Understanding Migration," *Annals of the New York Academy of Sciences* (645: 1992): 1-24, reprinted in Steven Vertovec and Robin Cohen, eds., *Migration, Diasporas and Transnationalism* (Northampton, MA: Edward Elgar Publishing, Inc., 1999): 26-49.
11 Schiller, Basch, and Blanc-Szanton, 37.
12 Madeline Y. Hsu, *Dreaming of Gold, Dreaming of Home: Transnationalism and Migration Between the United States and South China, 1882-1943* (Stanford, CA: Stanford University Press, 2000), 42.

Wives left in China, "Gold Mountain widows," became more powerful as decisions concerning expenditures and children's education fell to them. Husbands and fathers supported their families out of obligation, knowing that if they succeeded in amassing a considerable sum—at least $10,000—they could retire in comfort, at least so long as the money lasted. Their communities in South China also benefited from the money sent by overseas Chinese. Magazines directed toward the overseas population successfully targeted them for contributions to projects such as school construction, and the money they sent helped to educate poorer children. Of course, split families endured much pain and sorrow as well. We cannot do full justice here to Hsu's rich portrait of Chinese living transnationally in the late nineteenth and early twentieth centuries. However, it should be clear that she has made a convincing case for the existence of transnationalism before the closing decades of the twentieth century. Indeed, her work and that of Adam McKeown in *Chinese Migrant Networks and Cultural Change* (2001) both make abundantly clear that economic necessity drove the goals of Chinese migrants long before the arrival of the "global capitalist economy." McKeown's Chinese created interwoven networks that incorporated Hawaii, Peru, and Chicago with China.

* * * * *

Remittances can be thought about is several ways. At their most basic, they are monetary payments to family members in the country of origin. This form of remittance is clearly linked to the absence of those family members from the destination country. Government policies, "there" and "here" often have influenced who comes and goes. In the case of the Chinese during the exclusion era, families remained split because of discriminatory policies enacted by the United States. Indeed, the exclusion era really begins in 1875 when the Page Act codified measures intended to keep Chinese women—ostensibly only "prostitutes" but in reality virtually all Chinese women who were not merchants' wives—from migrating to the United States. Hence, the married Chinese working men studied by Hsu had no choice about becoming transnational, and their remittances continued so long as they lived apart from their families.

Restrictions applied to the Chinese also targeted other Asians in the early twentieth century. In 1917, the United States enacted a geographically-defined Asiatic Barred Zone and forbade the immigration of Asians from within these bounds, exempting only Japanese who were not laborers, and Filipinos who were from an American colony and defined as U.S. nationals. In 1924, under terms of the National Origins Act, all Japanese also came under the total ban. Filipinos became the last Asian group to be restricted. The Tydings-McDuffie Act of 1934, which promised the Philippines independence in ten years, reduced immigration from the Islands to a fifty-per-year quota during the transition to independence, to be followed by a total prohibition once Philippine independence became reality. Those Asians who had come legally were denied naturalization and family reunification, and no doubt sent remittances home as they were able. To illustrate, from the late 1920s through the 1940s, life-long bachelor

Philip Vera Cruz, a leader in the 1960s of the California farm workers movement, sent regular remittances to his mother that helped to educate his younger siblings in the Philippines.[13]

By contrast to Asians, immigrants whom the government permitted to enter and become naturalized citizens had more control over whether they would send remittances *or* send for their wives and children and encourage other family members to join them. Of course, remittances might still flow when those working in the United States sent money to parents, siblings, and other kin. But faced with the needs of their own families in the United States, it is rather likely that married immigrants who lived with their spouses typically sent less in remittances to parents and siblings than married immigrants sent to spouses and children living abroad. Hasia Diner notes that Irish women stopped working outside the home after they married and began having children. Their remittances back to Ireland likely contracted.

To a great extent, such strictures still govern migration to the United States and the flow of remittances. Think about their implications with respect to both legal and illegal migration to contemporary America. Policies and laws relating to immigration define *who* may come, who may *not*, and, very importantly, *when and if* they may be joined by other family members. Under *occupational* preferences in force since 1965, immigrants whose skills the United States needs have been able to qualify for admission. Numerous Filipino physicians (such as the Calimlims) and nurses have migrated legally because the United States has sought their medical skills. These immigrants have been able to utilize *family* preferences to bring spouses, children, parents, and siblings—newcomers who then become the next links in that family's migration chain. In the last quarter of the twentieth century, skillful use of the preference system enabled Filipinos to become the second largest group of newly naturalizing citizens.

The eagerness of Philippine, Mexican, South Asian, and Mainland Chinese nationals to immigrate has already put great strains on the preference system's annual numerical quotas and helped keep alive the remittance stream as successful immigrants try to help kin to live more comfortably in the homeland, even as some wait to migrate. Of these groups, Filipinos had the longest standing interest in using government policy to promote the chain migration of family members. Those Filipinos who had come to the United States by 1934 became eligible for naturalized citizenship in 1946.[14] They, along with the Filipina wives that some married after World War II, could also file immigrant visa petitions for their brothers and sisters after 1965. Early on, the wait to bring adult children and brother and sisters from the Philippines to the United States was relatively short. Now, family reunification can take many years. In June 2009, the Filipino

---

13   Craig Scharlin and Lilia V. Villanueva, *Philip Vera Cruz: A Personal History of Filipino Immigrants the the Farmworkers Movement* (Seattle, WA: University of Washington Press, 2000), 69-70

14   Filipinos already living in the United States who served in the military during World War II became eligible for naturalization in 1943. Earlier, Filipinos who served during World War I were permitted a very brief period of time during which they could naturalize.

brothers and sisters of U.S. citizens whose petitions were filed *prior to August 1, 1986* finally became eligible for immigrant visas after waiting for *almost twenty-three years*. The comparable date for Mexican brothers and sisters was May 22, 1995, about fourteen years; for brothers and sisters born in India or mainland China, the comparable date was August 15, 1998, about eleven years. Mexicans wait *seventeen years* for both married and unmarried adult sons and daughters. For brothers and sisters of naturalized citizens from *all* other countries, the wait is eleven years.[15] Thus, successfully beginning a new migration chain offers no guarantee of swift family reunification. Although considerably shorter than the time required for obtaining family preference visas, the current backlog of visa petitions for third preference occupational visas for college graduates and skilled workers will also result in delays. In November 2010, such workers from mainland China, India, Mexico, and the Philippines would have waited from five to nine years before their visa applications began to be processed.[16] Consequently, those who wish to come legally often seek temporary work visas that are numerically capped and never plentiful enough to meet demand.

Such conditions in the United States and in other countries that have their own migration controls affect the worldwide remittance streams and have prompted scrutiny of remittances by scholars, policy analysts, and governments that carefully track their flow and their impact on senders, receivers, and the countries in which they are located. In 2007, the four top nations receiving remittances garnered 94.7 billion dollars from migrants living either temporarily or permanently outside their homeland. Remittances have been particularly significant to the Philippine economy which derived thirteen percent of its GDP from remittances in 2006. Encouraging temporary migration and the sending of remittances became official policy in the Philippines in the early 1970s. After the imposition of martial law by President Ferdinand Marcos in 1972, the government actively encouraged the migration of its workers in the face of an exploding population, increasing landlessness, rising rural to urban migration, and unemployment. In 1974, Presidential Decree No. 442 established a 'Labor Code of the Philippines,' under which the Philippine government assumed an active role in promoting and regulating overseas employment: "For more than a quarter of a century, through various government agencies such as the Philippine Overseas Employment Administration [POEA] and the Overseas Workers Welfare Administration, the Philippine state has aggressively and successfully fostered the dispersal of its population as contract workers."[17] In 2007, an average of 2,952

---

15   United States, Department of State, *Visa Bulletin for June 2009*, IX:9 (Washington, D.C.: Department of State, 2009). http://travel.state.gov/visa/frvi/bulletin/bulletin_4497.html?css=print (Accessed 6-22-09)

16   United States, Department of State, *Visa Bulletin for November 2010*, IX:26 (Washington, D.C.: Department of State, 2010). http://travel.state.gov/visa/bulletin/bulletin_5172.html (Accessed 11-30-10)

17   Barbara M. Posadas and Roland L. Guyotte, "Life Is a Gamble": State Policies, Gender, and the Global Context of Filipino Migration to the United States," in *Remapping Asian American History*, ed. Sucheng Chan (Walnut Creek, CA: Alta Mira Press, 2003), 155.

Filipinos left the country *each day* to work overseas.[18] The POEA licenses and regulates more than thirty-three hundred recruitment agencies operating in the Philippines and makes their current status—in good standing, delisted, cancelled, forever banned—available to prospective workers; informs overseas employers about procedures for recruiting workers; sets and seeks to enforce minimum terms of employment; registers workers seeking initial and subsequent overseas employment; assists in the adjudication of disputes between OFWs and employers; and attempts to ease the situation of OFWs forced back to the Philippines by declining economic conditions abroad.

While most of its work deals with nations other than the United States, POEA does play a critical role in the migration of temporary workers to the United States. In 2009, the last year for which complete data is available, the United States admitted 19,350 Filipinos and their families under the non-immigrant temporary worker classification. Among these were 6,387 Filipinos holding H1B visas for professional workers.[19] These figures are *only* for a single year and do *not* include temporary workers who arrived in prior years, including those whose three-year visas have two more years to run or have been extended for another three-year period, or those who have adjusted their status from temporary worker to permanent resident. Remittances to the Philippines sent by these temporary workers are vital to the support of their families.

Nurses are among the occupational groups most heavily recruited to the United States in the early twenty-first century. From 2000 through 2007, 1,904 Filipino nurses left for the United States—approximately twenty-one percent of nurses leaving their homeland during these years.[20] Nurses remain in such demand and are so well paid overseas by contrast with what nurses *and doctors* earn in the Philippines that some physicians now regularly choose to re-tool and earn a nursing credential after completing their medical training. In 2005, according to the Philippine Secretary of Health, 6,000 Filipino physicians had enrolled in nursing schools, migration to pastures greener than the Philippines their obvious goal.[21]

Nonetheless, bettering the lives of their family members can come at a heavy cost to all those concerned. Emotional and physical longing plague

---

18 Republic of the Philippines, Department of Labor and Employment, Philippine Overseas Employment Administration, "2007 Annual Report," 7. http://www.poea.gov.ph/stats/stats2007.pdf (Accessed 6-22-09)

19 United States, Department of Homeland Security, Office of Immigration Statistics, *Yearbook of Immigration Statistics: 2009* (Washington, D.C.: Department of Homeland Security, 2010), 78, 86. http://www.dhs.gov/xlibrary/assets/statistics/yearbook/2009/ois_yb_2009.pdf (Accessed 11-30-10)

20 Republic of the Philippines, Department of Labor and Employment, Philippine Overseas Employment Administration, "2007 Overseas Employment Statistics," 33. http://www.poea.gov.ph/stats/stats2007.pdf (Accessed 6-20-09)

21 Sol Jose Vanzi, "6,000 Pinoy Doctors Want To Become Nurses To Get Jobs Abroad," *PinoyProfessionals.com*, September 12, 2005. http://www.pinoyprofessionals.com/pinoy/doctors/6,000-pinoy-doctors-want-to-become-nurses-to-get-jobs-abroad/ (Accessed 6-26-09)

spouses who must live apart for months and years at a time. Will spouses be faithful to their marriage vows? Mothers and fathers who leave their children behind experience sadness and guilt when they are not present to tend their needs, comfort their sorrows, and share in their joys. Disconsolate when their children see them as strangers after years away, they must leave again on their next labor contract, knowing that the breach cannot be mended in so short a time. Wives working abroad worry about how well their husbands are coping with the responsibilities of being not only father, but mother as well. Mothers without husbands on whom they can rely agonize about burdening their children's grandmothers and aunts with the day-to-day care of their offspring while they are gone. Children may relish newly purchased comforts—better food, new clothing, consumer goods, and improved housing—even as they feel abandoned. All fear that while they are apart, some sickness, danger, or abuse will harm their loved ones. When disaster or death strikes, they ask what they might have done to prevent it. After learning of her little brother's death, a grief-stricken Irma Martinez wondered if better medicines that she might have sent could have saved him.

Other tensions can arise when loyalties to different sides of a family come into conflict. As they raise their own children in the United States, couples may differ on what is owed to kin who remain in the homeland. How much should be sent to each spouse's relatives? One's own parents, of course, take precedence because of their enduring claim upon the loyalty of a child, but after their passing, how much should whose siblings receive? Spouses may have to negotiate the competing claims of their relatives. What proportion of a couple's disposable income should be sent to those in the Philippines, especially when one spouse believes that the needs of their own children should take precedence? Should money be saved for their children's college years, or sent home to alleviate the poverty of their kin? Should money be invested in the purchase of land and the building of a house in the Philippines when one's children have been born or raised in the United States and retiring back home would mean leaving offspring and grandchildren behind? Resentments may also grow when kin in the Philippines ask for more and more—seemingly as an entitlement—from those in the United States. While earlier generations of immigrants seem to have linked remittance aid to the prospect of other relatives' eventual migration, the continued poverty of the homeland exacts an ongoing financial pull.

* * * * *

Not only families, but also nations with workers laboring outside the borders of their homelands have an ongoing interest in remittances. Worldwide, ". . . recent studies estimate that international remittances exceed US$100 billion per year, approximately twice the amount of official aid-related income to developing countries."[22] In Mexico, only oil and tourism are more economically im-

---

22 Jim Airola, "The Use of Remittance Income in Mexico," *International Migration Review* 41:4 (Winter 2007): 850.

portant to the nation than remittances. Hence, both the Mexican and Philippine governments celebrate remittance-senders. In the late 1990s, Mexico altered its Constitution to create a Mexican 'nationality' for emigrants who have become citizens of foreign countries.[23] Traveling to the United States on a two-day tour of the border after his election in 2000, Mexican President Vicente Fox urged Mexico's "heroes" in the United States "not to forget their homeland – and to invest money in their hometowns."[24] By 2000, "[t]he 8.5 million Mexicans in the United States . . . formed about 1,500 hometown clubs, and some of these clubs channel remittances into job creating investments at home. . . . A 2001 'godfather program' also encourages Mexican Americans to make job-creating investments in Mexico."[25] In 2001, the Mexican government began issuing consular identification cards to its nationals whether or not they were in the United States with proper documents;[26] a year later, Wells Fargo, a bank with a presence in almost half the United States, began accepting these cards as sufficient identification for opening bank accounts. Having a bank account has since enabled millions of Mexicans "to send money home cheaply," rather than through middlemen who charged high commissions.[27] Recent research on the impact of migrant remittances argues that they serve as a "development mechanism" in Mexico, enabling remittance-receiving families to keep their children in school longer and to spend more of their total income on durable goods, healthcare, and housing than comparable families without such support. In addition, remittances supply about twenty percent of the capital for investment in small business start-ups.[28]

From the Marcos era to the recent administration of President Gloria Macapagal Arroyo, Philippine government programs supporting and honoring overseas workers far surpass Mexico's efforts. The Overseas Workers Welfare Administration [OWWA], established in 1977, seeks to protect the interests and provide for the welfare of OFWs and their families. For $25.00 per contract term, the OWWA provides workers with life insurance, disability and dismemberment benefits, and a burial benefit from a fund that covered almost 1.1 million OFWs in 2007.[29] The OWWA awards primary and secondary school schol-

---

[23] "Mexican President Praises Migrant 'Heroes,'", April 22, 2007. *The New York Times*, December 13, 2000, A13. http://www.nytimes.com/2000/12/13/world/mexican-president-praises-migrant-heroes.html (Accessed 6-28-09)

[24] "Fox Tours Border, Courting Immigrants," *Eugene Register-Guard*, 4. http://news.google.com/newspapers?id=53UVAAAAIBAJ&sjid=nsDAAAAIBAJ&pg=4734,3670991&dq=heroes+vicente-fox (Accessed 6-28-09)

[25] Philip Martin, "Remittances," *Immigration and Asylum: From 1900 to the Present*, ed. Matthew J. Gibney and Randall Hansen (Santa Barbara, CA: ABC-Clio, 2005), 513.

[26] David M. Reimers, *Other Immigrants: The Global Origins of the American People* (NY: New York University Press, 2005), 111.

[27] Reimers, *Other Immigrants*, 111.

[28] "The Use of Remittance Income in Mexico," 850, 852.

[29] Republic of the Philippines, Department of Labor and Employment, Overseas Workers Welfare Administration, "About OWWA." http://www.owwa.gov.ph/index.php?page=

arships to the poorest children of OFWs, holds Christmas parties through out the nation for OFW families.[30] Each year, Arroyo offered "rice cakes and red carpet to those she calls `modern heroes.'" Bleary from an eight-hour flight back to the Philippines, a few hundred workers from Abu Dhabi swapped puzzled looks for presidential handshakes on their way to baggage claim. One, too dazed to offer much reaction, received a 'livelihood package' that included a jeepney, life insurance, one thousand Philippine pesos, and a karaoke machine.

Critics charge that by praising overseas workers as heroes because of their remittances, successive Philippine governments have sought to divert attention from the nation's fundamental problems and their inability to solve them. Export labor has become institutionalized because the Philippines cannot provide sufficient employment for a burgeoning population. Reliance on export agriculture has thrown small farmers off the land and fueled a rural to urban internal migration, but, stymied by foreign imports, domestic industries remain too weak to absorb new workers. As remittance money flows into the Philippines, the country's dollar reserves increase and can be used as collateral for new loans from the IMF, but without remittances, prospects for paying these loans will diminish.[31] In 1992, the Philippines allocated 30.7 percent of its budget to debt service, and only 7.7 percent to social services.[32]

The recent and persistent economic downturn is likely to have a chilling effect on overseas worker remittances. Remittances from Filipinos working in virtually all nations dropped perceptibly in the first quarter of 2009 by comparison to 2008: Kuwait, down 58.6 percent; Taiwan, 37.5 percent; Italy, 23.2 percent; South Korea, 22.8 percent; and Hong Kong, 15.9%. By comparison, the 9.1 percent decline in remittances from the United States looks small—until one remembers that Filipinos in the United States provide more than half of all remittances.[33] Similarly, Mexico's central bank, which keeps track of money sent home by Mexicans living abroad, announced that funds sent back to Mexico had dropped by more than 18 percent from $2.19 billion in April 2008 to $1.78 billion in April 2009.[34] Many Mexicans send less money back to Mexico because they

---

about-owwa#; "2007 Performance Highlights." http://www.owwa.gov.ph/index.php?page=2007-performance-highlights (Accessed 6-28-09)

30 Republic of the Philippines, Department of Labor and Employment, Overseas Workers Welfare Administration, "OWWA Marks Migrant Workers Day." http://www.owwa.gov.ph/news/2009/06/owwa-marks-migrant-workers-day/#more-132 (Accessed 6-28-09)

31 Lualhati Roque, "The Impact of OFWs' Remittances on the Philippine Economy," *Bulatlat* V:22 (July 10-16, 2005). http://www.bulatlat.com/news/5-22/5-22-remittances.htm (Accessed 6-28-09)

32 "Strategic Instantiations of Gendering in the Global Economy," 49.

33 Falling Remittances Foretell Gloomier Consumption, Growth," *Bulatlat*, June 16, 2009. http://www.bulatlat.com/main/2009/06/16/falling-remittances-foretell-gloomier-consumption-growth (Accessed 6-28-09)

34 Gina Potthoff, "Remittances to Mexico Decrease," HispanicBusiness.com, June 17, 2009. http://www.hispanicbusiness.com/news/2009/6/17/remittances_to_mexico_decrease.htm (Accessed 7-8-09)

have lost their jobs or experienced a cutback in hours.[35] Paying their own bills now takes a greater share of their income, leaving less money to remit.[36] The impact on the economy in Mexican towns has been noticeable. Twelve months ago, declining remittances were already "threatening businesses, stalling construction and choking cash flow to hamlets where as much as half the population works in the United States."[37]

* * * * *

Finally, let us turn to the social and cultural change accompanies transmigration and affects places that send and receive migrants. In the small, western Minnesota town of Morris, population about 5,000, where the University of Minnesota's liberal arts campus is located and Roland Guyotte teaches, Willie's SuperValu, the town's only full-service grocery, caters to its expanding Hispanic clientele by stocking a variety of Mexican food items. Until recently, a large sign in Willie's window called out: *"Cambiar su dinero,"* but handling large remittance transactions got to be too much for Willie's son Paul, who now owns the store, so he convinced a local bank that the practice would flourish because one of the bank's employees is fluent in Spanish.

In all of this, long-time community businesses compete with La Tienda, a small store on the town's main street opened by local resident Nancy Huot in May 2007 and "intended as an `outreach store, not just a retail store.'" In addition to selling and doing what Willie's and the bank do, La Tienda stocks devotional candles and other religious items, offers an extensive supply of work clothing, carries Spanish-language DVDs, music, and magazines, helps with mailing, wire transfers, and check cashing, and provides second-floor space for community-sponsored ESL classes, mostly serving Mexicans from Puebla who come on temporary work visas and are employed on commercial pig farms in the area. As Huot put it, "Most of the people who work here have families and they would love to have their families with them. It's economics – they can make here in a year what it takes maybe five years to make at their homes. Most of them are here to give their families a better life.'"[38]

If change has come **to** communities throughout the United States because of the arrival of new immigrants, so too change has come to the places that they have left—communities **in** Mexico, the Philippines, and other nations that send workers, receive remittances, and also find that their cultures are being altered in a variety of ways. Perhaps most fundamentally, migration extends horizons for those who go **and** for those who stay. As David Reimers recounts in *Other*

---

35 Jesse Bogan, "Tough Times for Mexican Immigrants," Forbes.com, July 2, 2009. http://www.forbes.com/2009/07/02/illegal-immigration-unemployment-business-mexico-remittances.html (Accessed 7-8-09)
36 Potthoff, "Remittances to Mexico Decrease." (Accessed 7-8-09)
37 Mark Stevenson, "Layoffs in U.S. Mean Trouble For Mexico," abcnews.com, July 30, 2008. http://media.abcnews.com/m/screen?id=5483410&pid=76 (Accessed 7-8-09)
38 "La Tienda." http://www.geocities.com/goodnewsmorris/latienda.html (Accessed 6-28-09)

Immigrants, in Villa Juarez, a Mexican town of about 5,000, "half of the population had been to the United States." Just as remittances funded families in Villa Juarez, remitters supplied information on conditions in the United States, and their remittances also provided the money necessary for others to follow those who had gone before.[39] Women who have been to *El Norte* claim prerogatives unfamiliar to women who have never left home—driving a car, working outside the home, demanding help from their husbands with household chores—thus indicating that altered gender roles observed and experienced while living in the North can also transmigrate home.

In the twenty-first century, remittances are a global phenomenon present whenever and wherever migration occurs.[40] Remittances alter, even as they perpetuate, pre-existing bonds and forge complex linkages across space for people here and there and between. The economic element—the transfer of money—dominates, especially when considered at the national level. Nonetheless, the social and cultural consequences of remittances intertwine with the economic to change both senders and receivers. What occurs in the United States cannot be separated from what takes place back in the homeland; both aspects are essential to our understanding of how remittances shape the lives of the immigrants whom we study.

References

Airola, Jim. "The Use of Remittance Income in Mexico." *International Migration Review* 41:4 (Winter 2007)
Bodnar, John. *The Transplanted: A History of Immigrants in Urban America*. Bloomington: Indiana University Press, 1985.
Daniels, Roger. *Coming to America: A History of Immigration and Ethnicity in American Life*. 2nd edition New York: Perennial Books, 2002.
Erickson, Charlotte. *Invisible Immigrants: The Adaptation of English and Scottish Immigrants in Nineteenth-Century America*. Coral Gables: University of Miami Press, 1972.
Foerster, Robert F. *The Italian Immigration of Our Times*. Cambridge, Massachusetts: Harvard University Press, 1919.
Glick Schiller, Nina, Linda Basch, and Cristina Blanc-Szanton. "Transnationalism: A New Analytic Framework for Understanding Migration," *Annals of the New York Academy of Sciences* (1992) reprinted in *Migration, Diasporas and Transnationalism*. Ed. Steven Vertovec and Robin Cohen. Northampton: Edward Elgar Publishing, Inc., 1999.
Hsu, Madeline Y. *Dreaming of Gold, Dreaming of Home: Transnationalism and Migration Between the United States and South China, 1882-1943*. Stanford: Stanford University Press, 2000.
Martin, Philip. "Remittances," in *Immigration and Asylum: From 1900 to the Present*. Ed. Matthew J. Gibney and Randall Hansen. Santa Barbara: ABC-Clio, 2005.

---

39 Reimers, *Other Immigrants*, 110.
40 Although they do so with difficulty, even workers from the repressive state of Myanmar find ways to remit money home from Thailand. (Nwet Kay Khine, "Remittance Flows from Thailand to Mawlamyine, Mon State, Myanmar," M.A. Thesis, Program in International Development Studies, Human Security Conference, Chulalongkorn University, 2007).

Posadas, Barbara M., and Roland L. Guyotte. "'Life Is a Gamble': State Policies, Gender, and the Global Context of Filipino Migration to the United States," in *Remapping Asian American History*. Ed. Sucheng Chan. Walnut Creek, CA: Alta Mira Press, 2003

Reimers, David M. *Other Immigrants: The Global Origins of the American People*. NY: New York University Press, 2005.

Scharlin, Craig, and Lilia V. Villanueva. *Philip Vera Cruz: A Personal History of Filipino Immigrants and the Farmworkers Movement*. Seattle: University of Washington Press, 2000.

Schrier, Arnold. *Ireland and the American Emigration, 1850-1900*. Minneapolis: University of Minnesota Press, 1958.

Wittke, Carl. *We Who Built America: The Saga of the Immigrant*. NY: Prentice Hall, Inc., 1939.

Ethnicity, Inclusion, and Exclusion: Poles in France and Bretons in Paris

Leslie Page Moch (Michigan State University)

This paper considers the relationship between two elements of the immigrant experience: the dynamics of inclusion and exclusion on the part of the state, on one hand, and of migrants' own impulses of acculturation as revealed in the choice of a life partner, on the other. I am comparing the workings of these elements for two groups of migrants – Poles in France and Bretons in Paris, an ill-regarded native-born group from the western French peninsula of Brittany. Migrants from Poland had a longstanding presence in France, as did Bretons in Paris, but each group also arrived a sort of mass migration for which it is well known.

Poles came to Paris in what is called the "great immigration" following the 1830 revolt against Czarist Russia, and understanding themselves to be "moldering in exile."[1] This immigration became rooted in an elite community that is remembered for the likes of romantic composer Fryderyk Chopin and Maria Skłodowska – daughter of a Warsaw physicist who came to France and subsequently married Pierre Curie and became a Nobel Prize-winning physicist and chemist. Nonetheless, this is the movement to France that anchored Polish immigration.

In the age of Polish mass migrations to the U.S. from the 1880s, most Poles resisted attempts to recruit workers to France, having better places to go – to the Ruhr valley in Western Germany (which had more modern mining, and better working conditions) and the United States. But this changed dramatically after the Great War, when the U.S. began to close its doors and Germany hardened its attitude toward Poles (which was never generous), and demanded German citizenship of Poles in the Ruhr. These immigrants had a strong sense of Polish national identity and were not attracted to German citizenship, but would prefer to be citizens of the new Polish nation state.[2] By contrast, France was eager for Polish workers and did not demand naturalization. At this time, then, the great forces of changes in immigration law in the U.S., continuing war conditions in Poland, and a France that was eager for labor aligned to bring on a

---

1 This was the phrase used by Alexandre de Kronowski in his preface to *Almanach historique ou souvenir de l'emigration polonaise* (Paris: Bourgogne et Martinet, 1837-1838), cited in Pierre Nora, ed., *Realms of Memory: The Construction of the French Past*, vol. 1 (New York: Columbia University Press, 1992), 166.
2 Jeanine Ponty, "Les Polonais," in Laurent Gervereau, Pierre Milza and Emile Temime, eds., *Toute la France: Histoire de l'immigration en France au XXe siècle* (Paris: Bibliothèque de Documentation Internationale Contemporaine, 1998), 105-106; Gary Cross, *Immigrant Workers in Industrial France: The Making of a New Laboring Class* (Philadelphia: Temple University Press, 1983), 27, 92.

mass migration to France. By 1921, 46,000 Poles were in France – and 508,000 a decade later.[3]

The French perceived Poles as a group apart. Why was this? First of all, these newcomers did not speak French. More important, they were not loyal to France, but rather to the new nation state of Poland, to which they planned to return. Indeed, Poles were less likely than any other group of immigrants to become naturalized citizens of France in the 1920s – the second largest group of immigrants, they were only 3.2 percent of the naturalized newcomers.[4] Scholars have pointed out that both French authorities and Polish communities encouraged the separation of Poles from French nationals: Poles concentrated in the mining communities of northern France, where they were lodged in company housing and encouraged to remain in Polish-speaking communities; the church encouraged Polish parishes with their distinct ritualistic qualities; finally all sorts of Polish sport and cultural societies provided "an important alternative to assimilation into the culture of the French miner."[5] Poles had a well-deserved reputation for poverty because wages were not high. Despite the fact that host societies often perceive newcomers as lazy, the French did not have this perception of Poles – on the contrary, Poles had the reputation of being excellent workers. Nonetheless this reputation for good work did not prevent the schoolyard jibes of "sale Polak" to which their children were exposed.[6]

Like the Poles in France, Bretons could claim distinguished forerunners like thenineteenth-century geniuses Jules Verne – the father of science fiction with works such as *Twenty thousand leagues under the sea* – and the founder of French romanticism, poet François-René Chateaubriand. More ordinary Bretons came to Paris *en masse* at the turn of the twentieth century. By 1900 there were over 87,000 people from Brittany in the city limits alone and nearly 110,000 a decade later when Bretons garnered the concern of the clergy, the police, and the welfare state.[7] What was perceived to be wrong with Bretons? Most important, they did not speak French or even a dialect of French, but rather the Celtic Breton language. In the early years of the III Republic, non-French languages were forbidden in the public school and Breton children were shamed if they spoke it.[8] Furthermore, Bretons did not look like the French because, as a

---

3   Gerard Noiriel, *Population, immigration et identité nationale en France, XIX-XXe siècle* (Paris: Hachette, 1992), 70.
4   Christoph Klessmann, "Comparative Immigrant History: Polish Workers in the Ruhr Area and the North of France," *Journal of Social History* 20 (1986) 348.
5   Cross, *Immigrant Workers in Industrial France*, 89-93.
6   Mary Lewis, *The boundaries of the Republic: Migrant rights and the limits of universalism in France* (Stanford, California: Stanford University Press, 2007); Cross, *Immigrant Workers*; Ponty, "Les polonais," 105-107.
7   Leslie Page Moch, *The Pariahs of Yesterday: Bretons in Paris* (Durham, North Carolina: Duke University Press, forthcoming/in press), chap. 2.
8   Pierre-Hakez Hélias, *The Horse of pride: Life in a Breton village* (New Haven, Connecticut: Yale University Press, 1978), 131-176; Eugen Weber, *Peasants into Frenchmen: The Modernization of Rural France, 1870-1914* (Stanford, California: Stanford University Press, 1976), 67-94, 303-338.

Celtic people, their coloring was more fair that that of most French; "hair the color of dirty hemp" was how the novelists put it, beginning with Emile Zola in 1882.[9] Third, Bretons were known as country bumpkins, unsophisticated if not stupid, a fact that reverberated in Parisian jokes and stories. And like many migrants, Bretons were characterized as drunks and alcoholics. Bretons were also undeniably poor – men relegated to unskilled laboring positions, for the most part. The women of Brittany became a significant presence in the Parisian maternity hospital for the indigent in the 1890s; this was a sign of poverty and need for support in an age when French women preferred the safety of giving birth at home assisted by a midwife.[10] Many Breton women worked as domestic servants, so that the *bonne bretonne*, the Breton maid, became a stock figure. Even worse, the Breton maid was pictured as the cartoon character Bécassine in a popular children's magazine beginning in 1905 and Bécassine was profoundly, spectacularly stupid.[11] Although Breton women were in the majority in the city, Breton men lived and worked in the city as well, many as transport workers. More Breton men gathered in the industrial suburbs in the outskirts like the so-called "French Manchester" of St. Denis, where they found employment as day-laborers.[12]

These are the outlines of reputations of Poles in France and of Bretons in Paris, but of course neither all Bretons nor all Poles were alike; middle-class and educated elites arrived among them, and important distinctions ran through these two communities. The Bretons from cities were distinct from peasant Bretons – but the most important was the difference between people from Upper and Lower Brittany. Lower Brittany was farther from Paris and it was here that Breton was spoken while in Upper Brittany a dialect of French was the norm. Places like the industrial suburb of St. Denis attracted people from Lower Brittany almost exclusively, and more men than women; the city itself attracted those Bretons who hailed from Upper Brittany, where women outnumbered men. The distinction among Bretons was one of language.[13]

The distinction among Poles in France was their point of origin. Most new workers in French fields, factories, and mines were those who came directly from the Polish countryside – but they were joined by a smaller, distinct group of Poles who had previously worked in the mines of the Ruhr Valley of Germany; these were called the "Westphalians." Although they numbered only one in seven among the Poles who entered the mines between the wars, the Westphalians bore extraordinary influence in the Polish community. It was they who opened the first shops with Polish goods and who, in 1924, transferred two

---

9   Emile Zola, *Piping-Hot*, trans. Percy Pinkerton (New York: Boni and Liveright, 1924), 44; Moch, *The Pariahs of Yesterday*, chap. 1.
10 Rachel Fuchs and Leslie Page Moch, "Pregnant, single, and far from home," *American Historical Review* 95 (1990), 1025-1027.
11 Moch, *The Pariahs of yesterday*, chap. 2.
12 Jean-Claude Farcy and Alain Faure, *La mobilité d'une génération de français* (Paris: INED, 2003); Moch, *The Pariahs of Yesterday*, chaps. 2-3.
13 Moch, *The Pariahs of yesterday*, chaps. 1-2.

Polish language daily newspapers from the Ruhr to France.[14] The Westphalians' social conservatism and nationalism came from years of defending their national identity in Imperial Germany, where they had developed an autonomous ethnic culture and religious nationalism.[15] Of course, not all Poles in France worked in the mines, or even the factories, and not all were men: many were hired for agricultural work, many women among them. Indeed over a third of Polish workers (37 percent) who came to work on French farms were women – a high figure in comparison with Italians and Belgians; Polish woman farm-workers who arrived in the five years between 1921 and 1926 numbered nearly 30,000. Polish men and women were valued for their strength and skill. Yet the farm-workers among them were not prized for their loyalty because, like French farm workers, they did not want to stay on the farm, where conditions were poor and wages low. Many would decamp to urban areas where there were Polish communities in order to escape the loneliness and isolation of farm life and find factory work.[16]

These two groups of migrants – one international and the other internal – shared similar experiences in the France of the 1920s. In this period, both groups of migrants included organizers who formed sports teams, home area associations, mutual help societies, and social clubs. The French *Loi des Associations* of 1901 had legalized and facilitated these formal ties that strengthened the community. This law encouraged associations that fundamentally are stimulated by the migration process itself, which, because it displaces people, "intensifies and sharpens collective identities based on national, ethnic constructs."[17] Not everyone joined such groups, but associations strengthened collective identity for those who did so.

Hundreds of thousands of Poles found work in the industrial areas of central France and the mines, factories, and fields of the north. Between 600,000 and 700,000 workers and their family members arrived, and over 500,000 remained in 1931.[18] Poles formed large, thriving, tightly knit communities of workers. In those prosperous times, the French recruited and manipulated Poles strictly in order to serve the French economy; as one scholar put it, "the migration of Polish labor to the coal basins of the French northeast was a clear example of an effort of organized capital to shape a workforce to suit its specific needs." French entrepreneurs wanted a docile labor force and they were able to

---

14   Less that 20,000 of the 139,000 Poles were Westphalians; Ponty, "Les Polonais," 106-107; the papers were *Wiarus Polski* which went to Lille (until 1944) and *Narodowiec* which went to the heart of the coalfields of the Pas-de-Calais (until 1989).
15   Cross, *Immigrant workers*, 92; Klessmann, "Comparative immigrant history," 335.
16   Cross, *Immigrant workers*, 79-80, 244; Philip Slaby, "Paris, the Prefecture and Immigrant Poles," paper presented at the Social Science History Association Annual Conference, Miami, November 2008.
17   Jose Moya, "Immigrants and Associations: A Global and Historical Perspective," *Journal of Ethnic and Migration Studies* 31 (2005), 839.
18   Ponty, "Les Polonais," 107.

encourage "a class of anti-left Catholic miners organized around a paternalistic cultural nationalism, profoundly divided from the radical French milieu."[19]

Just as jobs were plentiful for Polish immigrant workers, the Bretons thrived, found work, and founded social and home-town associations in greater Paris. The men found better jobs than before, often as transportation workers and sometimes as postal employees, for example. Most Breton women in the labor force continued with the profession that other French women had come to avoid – domestic service.[20]

But the prosperity of the 1920s gave way to the economic crisis of the 1930s – the decade in which France transformed itself from a nation that welcomed foreign labor to a hostile state that expelled foreign workers, excluded newcomers, and withdrew naturalizations.[21] During the Great Depression, many Bretons lost their jobs in the Paris area and went back to Brittany – and others stayed at home rather than try city life. However, Bretons were not forced out of France. By contrast, Poles, in the words of scholar Jeanine Ponty, suffered from the "conjunctural xenophobia" that heightened French prejudices and cost people their jobs and right to live in France.[22]

Expulsions outnumbered new entries. Although in 1930, 55,000 Poles entered France and 10,000 had departed the country, by 1932, 6,000 entered and 37,000 left France.[23] In 1934, coal-mining companies organized and financed special trains to repatriate unwanted Polish families, sending home over 7600 miners (and nearly 19,000 Poles, when family members are included) in 1933 and 1934. Most people left quietly, but some miners waved the red flag and shouted "down with France" as their trains left the station. Those families that remained suffered from denials of unemployment benefits and work permit renewals.[24] With the Vichy collaborationist government during World War II naturalization of foreigners plummeted, but it was especially low for Poles, partly because Vichy would not naturalize Jews, but also because the "hierarchy of assimilability that was in fashion at the time" did not have high regard for Slavic Poles. Moreover, of those who had their naturalizations revoked under Vichy, nearly one in five was a Pole.[25]

If I close this comparison with the collapse of the French III Republic and the German invasion of June 1940, it provides a simple contrast between a classic history of national integration, on one hand, and a classic history of welcome and expulsion on the part of a manipulative state, on the other. But of course, as every scholar knows, things are more complex and multifaceted than such a so-

---

19 Cross, *Immigrant workers*, 97-98.
20 Moch, *Pariahs of yesterday*, chap. 3.
21 Weber, *The Hollow Years: France in the 1930s* (New York: Norton and Co., 1994), 87-110
22 Jeanine Ponty, *Polonias méconnus: Histoire des travailleurs immigrés en France dans l'entre-deux-guerres* (Paris: Publications de la Sorbonne, 1988), 319.
23 Weber, *The Hollow Years: France in the 1930s* (New York: Norton and Co., 1994), 90.
24 Cross, *Immigrant workers*, 200-201.
25 Patrick Weil, *How to be French: Nationality in the Making since 1789* (Durham, N.C.: Duke University Press, 2008), 105, 114.

called classic story – and this is certainly true of both the Bretons and the Polish community.

Bretons came to Paris in droves after World War II, where they counted one in six of new arrivals between 1945 and 1960.[26] Bretons continued to face prejudice in work and housing, and needed help in Paris. At this time the Father Elie Gautier founded the Breton Mission near the Montparnasse Railroad Station where Bretons disembarked – the mission provided a community, helped with employment searches, and offered French lessons; these were the same services that had been offered by a similar and important church organization called the Breton Parish from before 1900 into the 1920s.

Marriage records relate a tale that contradicts stories of exclusion and adds nuance to the Breton history because the choice of a spouse for any migrant is an important indicator of social location and plans for the future. On the outskirts of Paris, in the industrial suburb of St. Denis, Bretons had married fellow Bretons almost exclusively well into the Belle Epoque and they began to marry out only in the 1920s; the majority of these Bretons were men. In the *arrondissement* of Paris near the Montparnasse station, by contrast, the great majority of Breton marriage partners were women, and they did not marry a fellow Breton, for the most part, but married other newcomers who were skilled laborers, white-collar workers, and fellow nurses. Since Breton men could get better jobs in the 1920s, a few more Breton women married men from their home area, but these marriages pointed to an urban future, and the jobs of these marriage partners clearly aimed to avoid replicating their parents' lives. The women in the city married at an older age than those in St. Denis, were more literate, and were more likely to have borne a child out of wedlock before their marriage.[27]

Nonetheless, Bretons are still remarked upon as unlike other French or Parisians. To cite one very recent example, the 2008 film "Paris" starring Juliette Binoche features a small-minded bakery owner who will not hire Bretons because she believes they do not work, but who is very positive about her North African clerk. There is a Breton couple in the film that consists of two hard-living fishmongers who went to the top of the Montparnasse tower to see the view of Paris as soon as they got off the train – they remained village folk in the city.[28]

As for the Poles, although France expelled many Poles in the 1930s, others remained in France, saving, in many cases, to return to Poland. After the end of World War II, these plans changed for many people, whose permanent home became France at least partly for political reasons.[29] Then, as the labor force changed after the war, their children were able in some cases to access the kinds

---

26 Moch, *The Pariahs of Yesterday*, chapter 4.
27 Moch, *The Pariahs of Yesterday*, chapter 4.
28 "Paris," director Cedric Klapisch, 2008.
29 Philippe Rygiel, "Dissolution d'une groupe ethnique. Origines des temoins et des conjoints des enfants des familles polonaises implantées dans le Cher, 1940-1975," *Le Mouvement Sociale* 191 (2000), 78-79.

of skilled and white-collar jobs that had been inaccessible to immigrants in the 1920s and 30s.

Here, too, marriage records tell a complex tale. Polish workers were more likely to be married when they arrived in France than other immigrant workers, encouraged by employers to bring their families in order to stabilize the labor force.[30] Consequently, it is not their, but their children's marital choices that tell us a good deal about the ongoing history of the Polish community. Historian Janine Ponty described many children when she wrote, "Francophones outside, Polophones at home, biculturals, attracted by French values but held back by those of their fathers, namely, filial respect and marriage inside the community."[31] Miner's children usually married the children of other Poles – three quarters in the case of the district of the Pas-de-Calais. The children of agricultural workers, who were more isolated from Polish worker communities and lived among the French, were more likely to marry non-Poles – more than half (55 percent) in the case of the northern department of the Aisne. With the marriages of children born in France of Polish parents between 1923 and 1945 (and married between 1940 and 1975) for the central French department of the Cher, a different picture emerges. These are later marriages of children who were born and socialized in France and overall, only one in five married into a Polish family.[32] This depended on the cohort – children born in the 1930s were much more likely to marry into a Polish family, while those born in the after 1935 were much less likely to do so. When family plans changed – in other words, when the project of return was abandoned after World War II – children became more likely to marry a non-Polish spouse. The core of French Polish culture remained in urban worker communities, and children from these communities were most likely to marry into another Polish family.[33] Upward mobility, in other words, acted against endogamy.

Consequently, when Gérard Noiriel famously surprised the French over twenty years ago with the fact that every third French person has a foreign-born grandparent, some of those grandparents were the very Poles who came in the 1920s. In many families, Polish identity had faded and for this reason Philippe Rygiel asked "where are the immigrants of yester year?" in his study of intermarriage.[34]

Polish immigrants and their descendants in France have had considerable intermarriage and upward mobility since World War II; in the present, European immigrants are perceived as much less a threat than Muslim Africans or oth-

---

30   Family migration was encouraged by the automatic granting of work authorization to wives and children of new miners, and only 27 per cent of the Polish miners in the Pas-de-Calais were unmarried in 1931, compared with 42 per cent of the total immigrant population; Cross, *Immigrant workers*, 89-90.
31   Ponty, "Les Polonais," 109.
32   Rygiel, "Dissolution d'une groupe ethnique," 75.
33   Rygiel, "Dissolution d'une groupe ethnique," 79-84.
34   Gerard Noiriel, *Le creuset francais*; Rygiel, "La dissolution d'un group ethnique," 69-89. Rygiel echoes the interrogative refrain "mais ou sont les neiges d'antan?" from Francois Villon, "Ballade des dames du temps jadis."

er non-European newcomers. Nonetheless, the Polish immigrant in France is viewed as somewhat distinct – and as willing to work. This view has been reawakened since the end of socialism in Poland in 1989. Indeed, during the election campaign of 2005, the "Polish Plumber" was offered as a stand-in for inexpensive labor just as the French were set to vote for or against the European Union Constitution. The constitution was rejected at the polls. Thus, despite years of migration and participation in the labor force and integration into French society, both Poles and Bretons are perceived as distinct when it suits the French or Parisian occasion.

In conclusion, this comparison demonstrates that state forces of inclusion (be it the rough inclusion by forcing the French language in the classroom or making French-born sons of immigrants eligible for military service) along with exclusion (be it expulsion or job loss) make a powerful pair of engines in migrant life. In addition, newcomers to the city, like immigrants' children, make choices of life partner that change the fabric of community life. Acculturation and inclusion are also a choice.

In addition, this comparison suggests that in some respects the French were true to their identity as an inclusive nation – they did not exclude on the basis of ethnicity, as the United States was to do in the 1920s, and had done earlier in the case of Chinese exclusion. Rather, the French excluded foreigners for economic and above all political reasons. That is, although many Polish workers lost their jobs, many Polish immigrants were not expelled in the early 1930s – it was rather the political radicals, and more especially the communists and militant trade unionists who most keenly felt the French impulse for order. Moreover, the mechanisms and means by which immigrants were rejected or expelled from France during the Great Depression varied not only by national origin, but also by region of France.[35]

Finally, this essay demonstrates that the processes of migration, settlement, and acculturation lend themselves to comparison. More pointedly, migration across national borders does not represent a phenomenon distinct from that of migration across regions; consequently the comparison between international and internal migrants elucidates the role of the state, local economies, and migrant culture in the migration process. Indeed, the more conceptually oriented and clear our comparisons, the more they reveal about human movement.

References

Cross, Gary. *Immigrant Workers in Industrial France: The Making of a New Laboring Class.* Philadelphia: Temple University Press, 1983.

Farcy, Jean-Claude, and Alain Faure. *La mobilité d'une génération de français.* Paris: INED, 2003.

Fuchs, Rachel, and Leslie Page Moch. "Pregnant, single, and far from home," *American Historical Review* 95 (1990).

---

35 Lewis, *The Boundaries of the Republic.*

Hélias, Pierre-Hakez. *The Horse of pride: Life in a Breton village*. New Haven: Yale University Press, 1978.
Klessmann, Christoph. "Comparative Immigrant History: Polish Workers in the Ruhr Area and the North of France," *Journal of Social History* 20 (1986).
Lewis, Mary. *The boundaries of the Republic: Migrant rights and the limits of universalism in France*. Stanford: Stanford University Press, 2007
Moch, Leslie Page. *The Pariahs of Yesterday: Bretons in Paris*. Durham, North Carolina: Duke University Press, 2012.
Moya, Jose. "Immigrants and Associations: A Global and Historical Perspective." *Journal of Ethnic and Migration Studies* 31 (2005).
Noiriel, Gerard. *Population, immigration et identité nationale en France, XIX-XXe siècle*. Paris: Hachette, 1992.
Ponty, Jeanine. *Polonias méconnus: Histoire des travailleurs immigrés en France dans l'entre-deux-guerres,*. Paris: Publications de la Sorbonne, 1988.
Ponty, Jeanine. "Les Polonais," in *Toute la France: Histoire de l'immigration en France au XXe siècle*. Ed. Laurent Gervereau, Pierre Milza and Emile Temime. Paris: Bibliothèque de Documentation Internationale Contemporaine, 1998.
Rygiel, Philippe. "Dissolution d'une groupe ethnique. Origines des temoins et des conjoints des enfants des familles polonaises implantées dans le Cher, 1940-1975," *Le Mouvement Sociale* 191 (2000).
Slaby, Philip. "Paris, the Prefecture and Immigrant Poles," paper presented at the Social Science History Association Annual Conference, Miami, November 2008.
Weber, Eugen. *Peasants into Frenchmen: The Modernization of Rural France, 1870-1914*. Stanford: Stanford University Press, 1976.
Weber, Eugen. *The Hollow Years: France in the 1930s*. New York: Norton and Co., 1994.
Weil, Patrick. *How to be French: Nationality in the Making since 1789*. Durham: Duke University Press, 2008.
Zola, Emile. *Piping-Hot*. New York: Boni and Liveright, 1924.

European Immigrant Poverty in America
Stan Nadel (University of Portland, Salzburg Austria Center)

In the Fall of 1855 Celia and Wanda S. gave up. Three years earlier the two young unmarried German sisters had migrated to America along with Wanda's illegitimate son Edward. The only skills they had involved sewing so they made their living as embroiderers in New York City. But despite putting in long hours at their craft they found that they could hardly get by on the miniscule wages paid to women for such work in America. Sometimes they had to borrow money from friends to survive and after two years of increasing desperation they told a friend that "if things grew much worse" they would send the boy to his father in Germany and take poison. In the fall of 1855 things did grow worse. Their employer went out of business and the two sisters were unable to find work. Soon the rent was due and the larder was empty. They had already borrowed all that they could, their money was gone, and they were unwilling to turn to prostitution. By September 4th they had reached the end of their rope. They got their landlady to give them another day to pay the rent and they used their last few pennies to buy some flowers. Setting out the flowers to cheer up the bare room, they got into their one bed with six year old Edward. Settled in bed with the flowers in front of them, each of the three took a drink from a bottle of prussic acid—and their troubles were soon over (Nadel, 1990: 76).

Like millions of other Europeans Celia and Wanda had gone to America seeking a better life. Sophisticated citizens of the twenty-first century treat the notion that the streets in America were paved with gold as a pleasant fable, but the dominant narrative of European migration to America still caries a strong whiff of that myth. It is engraved on the Statue of Liberty in the words "Give me your tired, your poor...The wretched refuse of your teeming shore. Send these...to me, I lift my lamp beside the golden door!" The poor of Europe came by the millions and if the streets were not paved with gold, they worked hard and made better lives for themselves and their children. That's the received wisdom and that was indeed the experience of many immigrants and their children. But, as we saw with Cecelia, Wanda, and Edward, that wasn't always the case. The American national myth is powerful because of its strong basis on reality, but it is only a very partial reality. Here we will focus on another part of that reality, the continued poverty of millions of immigrants after their arrival in America.

Poverty and hardship among new arrivals in America is an old story that goes back to the 17th century when poor English men and women were lured to Virginia by the prospect of getting land after five years of service—and were then worked to death or allowed to starve by their employers in the first few years after their arrival (Morgan, 1975: 71-130, 158-179, 215-234). Of course conditions improved over time and by the middle of the 18th century Pennsylvania was known as "the best poor man's country" (Lemon, 1972). Would-be immigrants too poor to pay for their passage to America could sign labor contracts with ship captains in exchange for transportation and the captains would then make a profit by selling the contracts to Pennsylvanians in need of labor. Unlike their 17th century predecessors, these immigrants were only rarely abused severely—most of them survived their period of indentured servitude with ease and went on to enjoy relatively decent lives. We could examine their experiences more closely and ask about those who didn't fare so well, but here we will pass over them quickly and focus on the experiences of 19th and 20th century European immigrants instead.

The Irish

The great nineteenth century migrations to America began with Ireland where a rapidly increasing and impoverished peasant population provided surplus labor to a rapidly developing and labor short U.S.A. Then the Great Irish Famine of the late 1840s set off a flood of emigration as millions of Irish men and women gave up on their devastated homeland. Many of them never made it to America as unseaworthy ships pressed into service sank in the Atlantic. Many others died en route and were tossed overboard as famine related epidemics followed them on board the ships or died soon after arrival in the quarantine stations set up to keep them from bringing the epidemics into America. Many of those admitted to the New York City quarantine hospital in 1847 with only minor illnesses died from smallpox, typhus or cholera contracted in the hospital—the Commissioners of Emigration concluded that their admission tickets proved to be their death warrants (Commissioners of Emigration, 1861). Altogether in 1847 at least 17,465 would be immigrants died en route to British North America or on arrival in quarantine, while another 1,879 died en route to New York and many more died en route to other ports (Coleman, 1973: 157-163, 183). Of course that was the worst year and conditions improved immensely after that, but the voyages and quarantines continued to claim the lives of poor emigrants over the decades. In 1852, for example, more than one sixth of those admitted to the New York quarantine hospital died there (Commissioners of Emigration, 1861: Table 11).

Those who made it to the next stage often found that life in America could be very harsh as well. The Irish poor moved into the poorest districts like New York City's notoriously overcrowded Five Points, or the similarly notorious slums of Boston's North-End and Fort Hill. Five Points was located on swampy ground and three to five families were crowded into single family houses while others lived in large tenements buildings that housed over a hundred families—in 1856 one tenement called Manhattan Place had 96 rooms housing 145 different families including 577 people, i.e. six people per room (*Wochenblatt der New Yorker Staats-Zeitung*, April 19, 1856; Handlin, 1972: 100-108). Most notorious of these was the Old Brewery, a former brewery partitioned into a hive of criminality and disease. Worst of all were the damp and unsanitary cellar apartments. In 1850 Boston's Fort Hill had 586 of these frequently flooded quarters that had 5-15 residents in each and sometimes squeezed as many as 14 residents into less than 2 square meters of windowless space (Handlin, 1972: 109-110). Speaking of shoemakers living and working in cellars like these in New York, the Tribune reported in 1845:

> The floor is made of a rough plank laid loosely down, the ceiling is not quite so high as a tall man. The walls are dark and damp, and a wide desolate fireplace yawns in the centre, to the right of the entrance. There is no outlet back and of course no yard privileges of any kind [i.e. no water or toilet facilities]...In this apartment often live the man with his workbench, his wife and five or six children of all ages...and perhaps a palsied grandfather or grandmother and often both. In one corner is a squalid bed, and the room elsewhere is occupied by the work-bench, a cradle made from a dry-goods box, two or three broken and seatless chairs, a stewpan and a kettle (September 9, 1845).

The cellars were particularly hard hit by what one historian summarized as periodic infestations of cholera and yellow fever, and the almost chronic typhoid and typhus that devastated poor Irish immigrant neighborhoods in Boston, New York and Philadelphia. In Boston more than 500 of the 700 deaths in the cholera epidemic of 1849 were Irish immigrants or their children. While the cholera epidemic soon passed, high infant mortality and high death rates from tuberculosis continued to coincide with Irish immigrant settlements over the following decades. Conditions were so bad in the Irish districts that it was said that an Irish immigrant had a life expectancy of only 14 years after arriving in Boston (Groneman Pernicone, 1973: 34 & 59; Handlin, 1972: 114-116).

In New York City poor immigrants who became ill were entitled to admission to a special hospital established for them several miles from the city on Ward's Island. The hospital accommodated thousands of patients who sometimes outnumbered the inmates of the quarantine hospital by 5:1. Sick patients were crowded into barracks, 150-200 at a time. The first warden of the hospital was a man who had begun his career as a butcher before becoming a policeman, and he ran a hospital that would have been closed down as a health menace if it had been a butcher shop. One of the doctors employed there, Dr. Thomas Emmet, told an investigating committee that the hospital was so crowded that sometimes he had to put 5 patients in 3 beds put together, though fever patients were generally put in separate beds—when they weren't just put on the floor for lack of beds (New York Assembly Document No. 34, 1852: Dr. Thomas Emmet). Another doctor said many patients left in worse condition than they had arrived in, and that beds in which patients were dying of typhus were sometimes covered with snow coming through the closed windows. He also said that the meat for the patients' meals was delivered in a garbage cart and was often covered with dirt and horse manure (New York Assembly Document No. 34, 1852: Dr. Alexander Hosack). A different witness reported that immigrants in need dreaded being sent there for good reason:

> I recollect a case where an Englishman had a wife and five children who were destitute; his wife and children were sent to Ward's Island; before many days, the woman and four of the children died of a fever they took there...; the man went there and found his only remaining child, then sick, carrying wood... New York Assembly Document No. 34, 1852: Charles H. Webb).

Conditions improved somewhat on Ward's Island after 1852, but death rates for the immigrant poor remained high there and in the other city hospitals.

Irish immigrant poverty remained conspicuous in the 1850s as winter unemployment regularly drove "thousands of hungry starving poor [to] apply daily for food" at Philadelphia's Moyamensing Soup Society (Clark, 1973: 47). The Irish weren't the only immigrants threatened with starvation and in New York an outraged German immigrant journalist named Wilhelm Weitling wrote "Need pounds with heavy fist on the door of public attention, which has offered only beggars-soup in response. Beggars-soup! Beggars-soup!! In America it has already come to that" (Schlüter, 1907: 156). But it was the Irish immigrants who often suffered the worst in hard times. When a Philadelphia paper reported in 1855 that over 2/3 of the inhabitants of the Blockley Almshouse were Irish born, it was striking an already familiar theme about Irish-American poverty that would be repeated by news reports in many cities over the next few decades (Clark, 1973: 47).

The arrival of hundreds of thousands of immigrants aroused massive opposition and the 1850s saw the rise of a powerful anti-immigrant and anti-Catholic political party that won control of the state government in Massachusetts in 1855. Massachusetts then deported nearly 700 poor immigrants and their children across the Atlantic. Among them was Irish immigrant Mary Williams who cried and begged to be allowed to stay—along with her baby daughter Bridget who was also deported even though she was an American citizen (Coleman, 1973: 248-249). Anti-immigrant riots by American nativists in the 1840s and 1850s devastated immigrant neighborhoods in many cities and took dozens of lives. These riots most often targeted Irish Catholics, but sometimes they targeted Germans—as in Cincinnati Ohio where there was a major anti-German riot in 1855.

The Germans

German immigrants were generally better off than Irish immigrants, often arriving with money to buy farmland or with skills in short supply in America. But as we saw with the fate of Celia and Wanda S., that wasn't always the case. Single women and families solely dependent on women's earnings were often immersed in direst poverty. Those like Celia and Wanda who worked in the sewing trades found it took the full wages of two women to provide enough to live on—and even that was sometimes not enough. Taking in washing was the major alternative for German immigrant women over forty, but that too failed to provide more than minimal subsistence, and not always even that. In cities young and attractive women had the option of waitressing in the numerous respectable beer halls, the less respectable dance halls, and the even lower class cellar saloons. Even in the best of these wages were often insufficient and the waitresses supplemented them with occasional prostitution. In New York the police counted them all as prostitutes, but reported that "the girls employed to dance do not consider themselves prostitutes" (Nadel, 1990: 77-78; New York *Tribune*, 11/11/1863). Prostitution often provided a decent standard of living for some of its practitioners and many full time and part time prostitutes probably married or moved on to other occupations as opportunities arose. But it was a hard life and prostitutes turned up all too often in the coroner's suicide reports (Nadel, n.d.: 12-13).

Then there were the marginal poor, like those who lived in the squatter colonies of "German rag pickers" in New York City whose tents and shacks made of scraps were scattered through the waste lands along the East River. Most of the city's rag pickers were "German women living on the sale of the rags and bones which they and their children gather all the day long through the streets of the City" (New York Times, 3/21/1855). "From the bones and scraps of meat, certain portions are selected wherewith to prepare soups and ragouts. The rags are ... washed ... the bones ... are boiled, after which rags and bones are sold" (Bretting, 1981: 99).

Some German immigrant men with traditional artisanal skills sometimes did far better than this of course, but the reality of degraded trade standards in America and periodic economic crises often brought them to, or over, the brink of poverty—especially in the sewing trades. Wilhelm Weitling was a highly skilled tailor and with the added skilled labor of his wife and sister-in-law they achieved a solidly middle-class income in the late 1860s. But it didn't last, and by the annual slow season in the winter of 1870 even with three skilled adults prepared to work full time their income had fallen by 80% and they were threatened with starvation (Nadel, 1990: 69). The annual slow seasons were always the harbingers of hard times in the sewing trades and the rise of the tenement sweatshop was a mark of the increasing pauperization of clothing production in America. By the 1880s German immigrants had largely abandoned the trade to more desperate immigrants from Eastern Europe.

If the sweatshops were notorious producers of poverty, they paled before the scenes in many urban bakeries where German immigrant workers toiled for long hours and dismally poor wages. They "were in many respects in a state of absolute slavery, having not only to work late in the hot bakehouses of the city, but afterwards to carry heavy loads of bread at an early hour of the morning, until many of them had become stooped and round shouldered from the practice" (New York Daily News, 7/24/1864). One newspaper reported in 1863 that "there is scarcely a trade in existence whose members are worked as hard as this, the hours being usually sixteen and in many instances twenty-four for a day's work" (NY Sun, 4/14/1863). In 1872, when other workers in New York struck for the eight-hour day, the bakers struck for a twelve-hour day—and lost (NY Sun, 5/27/1872).

Of course German immigrants rapidly took over the beer brewing trade in America and some brewery owners became very rich in the process. In the 1850s and '60s brewery workers toiled fourteen to eighteen hours a day—often prodded by the brewmasters' fists if they slacked off. Room and board were provided by the employer, though often the room was a hop sack on the brewery floor and the board amounted to little more than "all the beer you can drink" (NY Tribune, 5/7/1853; NY Daily News, 11/17/1865; Schlüter,1910: 90-94).

The urban bakers and brewers had their rural counterparts among the proletarians who cut timber in the north woods in the summers and ice from the northern lakes in the winters. German immigrants predominated in this work until late in the nineteenth century, when they became outnumbered by Scandinavian immigrants. Some amassed enough savings to establish small farms on the frontier but others remained desperately poor and as they aged or became too badly injured to continue this hard and dangerous work they populated the skid row districts of the cities of the Upper Midwest. They were joined by immigrant farm workers who had also failed to accumulate enough resources to buy their own farms—or who had lost their farms in the increasingly severe agricultural depressions of the late 19th and early 20th centuries.

Of course one of the basic questions about immigrant success or their lack thereof relates to the children of the immigrants rather than the immigrants themselves. We have very few studies that track the intergenerational mobility of German and Irish immigrants in the mid nineteenth century, but we can get a partial picture based on the limited evidence that we do have. The tailor Wilhelm Weitling and his family may have verged on starvation in 1870, but his eldest son became a corporate executive and a banker while his younger son became an export manager and his daughter became a teacher (Nadel, 1990: 86). The success of the two sons was unusual (especially that of the elder), but like their sister a substantial minority of the children of German immigrant made it into white-collar occupations and the professions—perhaps a third of those in New York and around a quarter in Philadelphia (Nadel, 1990: 66, 190-91). Of course the other side of this coin is that the majority of the children of German immigrant workers remained workers and some unknown proportion of them remained poor.

A much larger proportion of the Irish immigrants was immersed in poverty in the first place and while some of their children too moved up the social ladder it is clear that many did not. Some of the more notorious slums of the late nineteenth and early twentieth century, like New York's Tenderloin district and Hell's Kitchen, contained large numbers of second and third generation Irish Americans along with more recent arrivals from the Emerald Isle. Indeed, the majority of petty and not so petty criminals who populated urban America's criminal underworld before the 1920s were American born descendents of Irish Immigrants. American born daughters of Irish immigrants were reported to predominate among the prostitutes of New York, Boston and Philadelphia for many decades, while their brothers filled the ranks of the criminal gangs like the Whyos, the Five Pointers, and the Gophers—just to name a few of the more notorious Irish American gangs (Asbury, 1927: 225-59). And in the 1920s it was American gangsters with Irish names like Madden, Curry, Coll, O'Leary and Sullivan—not to mention Al Capone's Chicago rival Dion O'Banion—who pioneered in the bootlegging trade that turned organized crime into big business in the Prohibition era (Clark, 1973: 155; Nelli, 1976: 150, 164). Of course these infamous men were mostly the successful gang bosses who got rich for a while, not the poor. But they and the large numbers of their foot soldiers who stayed poor, all came from the substantial ranks of the Irish American poor.

One of the characteristic occupations of Jewish immigrants was peddling, and the mythology of American immigration is enhanced with true stories of Jewish peddlers who started out carrying packs through rural America but then moved on to peddling from wagons, keeping shops, and then to banking—the Seligmans, Guggenheims, Lehmans, Wertheims and their like. Far more often successful peddlers only got as far as owning their own shops, but that too was a great success. Still, far from all achieved even this level of success and many peddlers spent their entire lives tramping through the countryside or through the cities with heavy packs filled with goods acquired on credit—credit whose terms may be inferred from the nickname peddlers gave to their creditors, "Hershel Ganef," Hershel the thief (Diner, 1992: 69). Carrying a pack was hard work at best and both hot sunshine and cold rain or snow could make it miserable. With little English and little contact with their fellows it was a lonely life at best, while lone peddlers sometimes suffered severely from accidents and they were easy prey for robbers. A worst case scenario played out in Woodville Mississippi in 1849 when the peddlers Jacob Cohen and Jacob Schwartz bought a small plot of land to bury a fellow peddler who had died on the road (Diner, 1992: 58). If some succeeded as peddlers, others found the life so hard and unrewarding that they abandoned it and turned to factory work—sometimes even the desperately poor sewing trades (Diner, 1992: 73-74).

When the great wave of Eastern European Jews migrating to America swelled after 1880 they too often took up peddling, but in an increasingly modern American economy the prospects for peddlers were far worse than they had been a generation earlier. At the same time, the rapid expansion of the ready made clothing industry created tens of thousands of new jobs for new immigrants. By 1890 the sewing trades provided Eastern European Jews with their greatest opportunity for employment and 60% of employed Jews in New York City worked in the garment industry—at a time when an ever larger majority of America's Jews lived in New York City. But if working conditions and wages had been poor in mid-century they were now even worse at the century's end. The introduction of noisy sewing machines drove production out of the immigrants' homes into the overcrowded and unpleasant workplaces known as sweatshops.

The classic description of these sweatshops, accompanied by photographs, can be found in an 1890 book by Jacob Riis called How the Other Half Lives.

> Five men and a woman, two young girls, not fifteen, and a boy who says unasked that he is fifteen, and lies in saying it, are at the machines sewing knickerbockers, "knee-pants" in the Ludlow Street dialect. The floor is littered ankle-deep with half sewn garments. ... The faces, hands, and arms to the elbows of everyone in the room are black with the color of the cloth... They work no longer than to nine o'clock at night, from daybreak. There are ten machines in the room ... (Riis, 1971: 96-107).

Tuberculosis was rampant, the social worker Lillian Wald said "We see so much of it we call it the tailor's disease" (Howe/Libo, 1976: 81).

Of course it wasn't only tailors who suffered from what was called the "White Plague." The old German immigrant neighborhood of Kleindeutschland centered on the Tenth Ward had been rapidly transformed into the ever more crowded Jewish Lower East Side. By 1890 the overcrowded Tenth Ward, with 523.6 residents per acre, was being described as more crowded than the notorious Black Hole of Calcutta. A decade later the Tenth was up to over 700 per acre and by 1910 there were over half a million impoverished Jewish immigrants and their children crowded into the tenements of the Lower East Side (Rischin, 1970: 79-93).

Poverty was especially hard on women without men—widows, women with children whose husbands had fled from their overwhelming responsibilities and abandoned them to their fates, or just young single women whose wages were never more than a fraction of those of their male co-workers. Poverty like this had driven Celia and Wanda S. to suicide and their later counterparts fared no better. Prostitution had been almost unknown among Jews in Eastern Europe, but conditions in America drove increasing numbers of Jewish women to adopt the course rejected by Celia and Wanda (Diner, 1992: 63). A pair of investigations sponsored by the NY State legislature in the 1890s uncovered widespread prostitution on the Lower East Side (Howe/Libo, 1976: 97-98). In 1896 the 28 year old Lena Meyers not only supported herself, she regularly sent money back to her parents in Krakow. But after she got a letter from her mother asking her why she didn't get married: "do you want to be an old maid?" she too took her own life (NY *World*, April 23, 1896).

The creation of communal institutions and labor unions, combined with strengthened tenement house and public health laws gradually alleviated the worst conditions for Jewish immigrants, but that was too late for those who had arrived before 1900. A New York Times reporter described them as "attenuated creatures, clad in old, faded, greasy, often tattered clothing...men and youths whose cheeks are pinched and pale and hollow, whose lungs yield to the first advance of the Autumn cold and fill the air with incessant coughing; whose sad, lustrous eyes ...[are] like the eyes of hunted and captured animals that press up to the bars of their cages" (November 13, 1894). Later arrivals called them the "farloyrene menshn" —the lost ones (Howe/Libo, 1976: 77). Given the conditions we have reviewed for the early waves of Irish and German immigrants we might well apply the same term to many of these as well. It is virtually a constant in the history of suicide that male suicides greatly outnumber those of their female counterparts, but when New York was first flooded with European immigrants the suicide rates for adolescent girls and young women actually exceeded those of their male cohorts (Nadel, n.d.: 11-12). This pattern of mass misery for especially large portions of the first waves of immigrants from each part of Europe would be repeated by later immigrants as well.

Despite their reputation for upward mobility, Jews too had an American born population of poor. Michael Gold's novel Jews Without Money provided a devastating portrait of his childhood neighborhood:

SUMMER. Everywhere the garbage. Plop, bung, and another fat, spreading bundle dropped from a tenement window. Many of the East Side women had this horrible custom. To save walking downstairs, they wrapped their garbage in newspapers and flung it in the street. In summer the East Side heavens rained with potato peelings, coffee grounds, herring heads and dangerous soup bones. Bang, went a bundle, and the people in the street ducked as if a machine gun sounded (Gold 1930: 7).

And as with the Irish-American poor, these sorts of conditions spawned generations of hardened criminals. The early Jewish gangsters of the mid nineteenth century like "Sheeny" Mike Kurtz were no match for their Irish American contemporaries, but by the end of the century American born Jewish hoodlums filled the ranks of Brooklyn born Monk Eastman's gang. Eastman's mobsters took on Paul Kelly's Five Pointers and won, becoming the leading gang in New York's turn of the century underworld (Asbury, 1927: 225-259; Joselit, 1983). Poor, American born, Jewish gangsters specialized in gambling, prostitution, and protection rackets for decades, but they too got in on the ground floor of big time operations during Prohibition. Charles "King" Solomon's gang dominated the early bootlegging [liquor smuggling] business in Boston while "Dutch Schultz" [Arthur Flegenheimer, the son of German Jewish immigrants] ran a major bootlegging operation in New York before he was murdered by rivals. At the same time Moses "Moe" Dalitz' gang did the same in Cleveland, and Sammy "Purple" Cohen's Purple Gang not only ran Detroit, they also provided Al Capone's organization with its major source of smuggled booze (Nelli, 1976: 168-179: Rockaway, 1993). Out West it was Benjamin "Bugsy" Siegel who took over organized crime in Los Angeles and then set up the first Las Vegas casino for the mob—before his partners had him killed for shortchanging them in 1947. Siegel's associate, Brooklyn born but Los Angeles raised Mickey Cohen got his start with the Capone organization in Chicago before he joined Siegel's organization. Cohen took over Siegel's Las Vegas and Los Angeles operations after Siegel's murder and along with Meyer Lansky he was one of the last two major Jewish gangsters—remaining active until the 1970s. The supply of poor young Jewish thugs seems to have dried up after the 1930s and the Jewish American gangster gradually receded into myth, but there had been a substantial population of poor American born Jews from immigrant families spawning them for over three quarters of a century before that happened. In the 1970s a new wave of Jewish immigrants arrived from the Ukraine and Russia, and once more there was a pool of poor, tough young Jews ready to kill for a living. Evesi Agron, who arrived in 1975, set up the first of the new gangs in New York City's Little Odessa—starting with a protection racket preying on fellow Jewish immigrants, and then moving on to bigger and more profitable criminal enterprises (Orleck, 2001: 131-132).

Of course not all poor immigrants crowded into the big cities. By the late nineteenth century plantation owners in some of the southern US states began to look for a docile new labor force to compete with the former slaves and their descendants who worked their plantations. Some of them imported Chinese "coolies" while others imported thousands of the "Chinese of Europe," Italian agricultural laborers. The Italians found themselves toiling in the sugar cane fields and cotton plantations of Louisiana for even less pay than that given to the former slaves. Working conditions in the American South were even worse than they had been for agricultural laborers back in Italy and the new immigrants sometimes found themselves classified with their fellow field workers in the racial hierarchy of their new home –as when Italian children were forced into segregated schools with Black children or when eleven Italians were lynched in New Orleans in 1891 (Dinnerstein/Reimers, 1975: 40, 64). The family of Gabriella Antolini spent five miserable years living in shacks and slaving in the fields of Louisiana (where the children working the fields along with their parents were spared the experience of segregated schools by not being sent to any schools) before they were able to scrape up the resources in 1912 to flee back to the poverty of rural Italy (Avrich, 1991: 107).

While tens of thousands of Italian immigrants worked in the cane and cotton fields of the South, the vast majority of the more than four million Italians who went to the US between 1880 and 1920 went to the cities and towns of the northern states. In 1890 Jacob Riis wrote that "the Italian comes in at the bottom, and in the generation that came over the sea he stays there" (Riis, 1971: 43). Riis was hardly an objective observer, but that was indeed the case for large numbers of Italians. The tenements of New York's Little Italy rivaled those of the Lower East side for crowding and were often dirtier and in even worse condition. Young Italian women often sewed alongside young Jewish women in the sweatshops, but they were also concentrated in the least skilled, lowest paid, occupations in the shops.

As for the men, there were so many Italian immigrant men that their variety of occupations and career paths was enormous. But a very large proportion of them filled the American economy's hunger for unskilled and semi-skilled labor, often transient and highly mobile. In doing so they often joined other recent immigrants from southern and eastern Europe—Greeks, Romanians, Slavs, Hungarians, and Balts.

Bartolomeo Vanzetti's early experience in the US could be taken as a typical case for many Italians. Arriving in New York at the age of twenty in 1908 he started off as a dishwasher, working 12-14 hour days—six days a week plus half days on Sundays—all for less than the dollar a day that New York laborers had been paid sixty years earlier. Fearing for his health after eight months of working in a hot and damp windowless kitchen (he had already suffered from a lung ailment when he had been a pastry maker in Italy) he quit and looked for outdoor work—roaming the city's streets for months and taking day labor work whenever he could find it. Then he teamed up to seek work outside the city with a paisan [fellow Italian] who hadn't eaten for days. They tramped the countryside begging for work at farms and factories until they landed jobs working in a brick factory. Less than a year later Vanzetti was on the search for work again and found it in a stone quarry, cutting wood, digging ditches, and selling fruit and ice cream (Avrich, 1991: 31-33). Virtually all of these were stereotypical jobs for Italian immigrants.

Large number of Italians found work in the rapidly expanding coal mines of America along with other recent immigrants. They worked the mines from Pennsylvania and West Virginia in the east, to Illinois and Colorado in the west. Mostly unskilled except with a pick and shovel they came into the mines as helpers and laborers at the bottom of a notoriously poor pay scale—and often stayed there. Coal miners generally lived in company housing, often in company towns where the company was the law as well as the landlord and the employer. There the Italians lived among miners from other parts of Europe and of other races—Black and white together at the bottom of the heap. Literally Black and white together in the smaller camps, but in the larger mining towns like Matewan West Virginia they sorted out by nationality and part of Matewan was called "Little Italy." The company housing in the mining camps was so bad that some new arrivals thought the miners' shacks were chicken coops (Corbin, 1981: 69). They were often paid in company scrip rather than cash, which meant they could only shop at the company store with its excessive prices where the miners sometimes found themselves forced into a form of debt servitude (Corbin, 1981: 10). They (or at least their children) sang:

> You load sixteen tons and what do you get?
> Another day older and deeper in debt
> Saint Peter, don't you call me, 'cause I can't go;
> I owe my soul to the company store.
>   (Merle Travis, *Folk Songs of the Hills*, 1947)

Working conditions were even worse than living conditions, and the early 20th century mine accident death rate was as much as five times that of any European country (in West Virginia during World War I it even exceeded the combat death rate of American soldiers in Europe) (Corbin, 1981: 10).

Pushed to the limit, they joined multiethnic strikes in virtually every coal field —only to be crushed in most contests by heavily armed company gun men who were backed by State militias and even US troops when needed. The massacre in Ludlow Colorado was only one of the best known of these confrontations which sometimes escalated into open warfare between armed miners and the armed forces at the companies' command (Corbin, 1981: 87-101, 116-117, 195-224; Greene, 1968; Gorn, 2001). After company gunmen killed an Italian immigrant organizer named George Lippiatt in the streets of Trinidad Colorado in 1913, the striking Italian, Greek and Slavic immigrant miners and their families moved a few miles away to a tent colony in a field near Ludlow. On the morning of April 20, 1914 the tent colony was surrounded by militia men and heavily armed guards from the Rockefeller owned Colorado Fuel and Iron Co.. The guards and militia men attacked the camp in force and after driving off most of the camp's defenders they shot up the striker's tents and burned them to the ground—over the heads of the women and children taking shelter in holes dug under the tents. Two women and twelve children were among the dead, along with a handful of strikers and a Greek immigrant union organizer named Louis Tikas who was summarily executed by the victorious company gunmen (Andrews, 2008; Gorn 2001: 213).

A similar mix of immigrants filled the ranks of American steel workers, with Italians and Poles again concentrated overwhelmingly among the unskilled. At the beginning of the 20th century around 90% of the Russian and Austrian Poles and about three-quarters of the Italians in Pittsburgh were counted as unskilled. And around two-thirds of the city's Poles and Italians were still counted that way in 1940 (Bodner/Simon/Weber, 1982: 64, 107, 139, 145, 252). Wages for unskilled steel workers were dismal, their dollar or two per 12 hour day was worth less than the dollar a day their Irish immigrant predecessors had been paid in 1850 for ten hours (Bodner/Simon/Weber, 1982: 17, 19).

Work in the steel mills may not have been quite as dangerous as work in the coal mines, but it was still very dangerous. Men were injured and killed when molten metal splattered on workers or poured onto them from cracked containers. Others were caught in boiler explosions, and sometimes workers exhausted from long hours working in the heat with molten steel simply slipped and fell into the vats of liquid metal. The steel companies refused to give out the numbers of severe accidents, but the Pittsburgh newspapers ran frequent stories about accidents killing and wounding up to a couple of dozen workers at a time. According to a study of hospitalizations by Crystal Eastman in 1906-1907, the accident toll was around 500 cripples and 200 deaths a year in the Pittsburgh mills alone (Bukowczyk, 1986: 26-27; Bodner/Simon/Weber, 1982: 17-18).

Steelworkers' annual incomes generally averaged less than the cost of maintaining a household, so even in good times a steelworker household generally needed more than one wage earner to survive—either borders adding to the income of small families or working children in larger ones (Byington, 1910: 35-106). Unemployment during economic downturns or sickness on the part of a key wage earner often pushed family economies into crisis—and serious injury or death put their very survival in question. But as we have seen, serious injury or death was not an infrequent experience and substantial numbers of immigrant wives and widows with young children were forced into the most extreme poverty every year in the coal fields and steel towns of America.

Another arena of mixed ethnic labor in America was in the meat packing industry that was concentrated in Chicago in the first half of the twentieth century. In 1906 its notoriously bad conditions were publicized in Upton Sinclair's novel The Jungle.

> The people had come in hordes; and old Durham had squeezed them tighter and tighter, speeding them up and grinding them to pieces and sending for new ones. The Poles, who had come by tens of thousands, had been driven to the wall by the Lithuanians, and now the Lithuanians were giving way to the Slovaks. Who there was poorer and more miserable than the Slovaks, Grandmother Majauszkiene had no idea, but the packers would find them, never fear. (Sinclair, 1906: 95)

Sinclair's graphic descriptions of the brutal and dangerous conditions on the killing floors and the horrible living conditions of the packinghouse workers have become iconic, but the investigations of historians like James Barrett (1987) and Rick Halpern (1997) have found that Sinclair's descriptions were not exaggerated. Like the coal mines and the steel mills, the meat packing plants generated a large class of impoverished immigrants, with disease and accidents wreaking an enormous toll of devastation and misery upon them.

Numerous studies have shown that there was some upward mobility on the part of a significant portion of Italian immigrants even as the majority remained immersed in so-called unskilled labor at the bottom of the wage scale (Bukowczyk, 1986: 32; Bodner/Simon/Weber, 1982; Kessner, 1977; Perlmann, 2005; Covello, 1967). Polish immigrants, on the other hand, generally remained in "unskilled" occupations for their entire working lives. For many former Polish peasants this meant they had succeeded, as Joseph K. put it:

> I don't know what anybody else thinks about it. I didn't get into trouble. I worked pretty good. I was fortunate. I was healthy. I was never sick or anything. I worked steady, that was the main thing, you know. As far as I think myself, I did [succeed]. (Bodner/Simon/Weber, 1982: 143)

Of course those who did get into trouble, got sick, or failed to "work steady" failed even in these terms and fell into extreme poverty. But it is striking that the children of these southern and eastern European immigrants rarely advanced further up the occupational ladder than had their parents.

Part of the problem resulted from the family economy culture of the southern and eastern European peasants, combined with their desperate need for additional wage earners in America. Children, especially sons, were expected to contribute to the family income from an early age—meaning that they were withdrawn from school as soon as possible or even kept out of school altogether (Covello, 1967: 275-329; Bukowczyk, 1986: 77-78). Pushed into the work force at a very young age by both family pressure and cultural norms these youngsters were rarely able to get enough education or vocational training to escape the trap of a career of unskilled labor—with all the risks of ensuing poverty that were enhanced by such a career path.

Given the fame of Italian-American criminal enterprises, the Mafia or Cosa Nostra, Al Capone, Lucky Luciano, Tony Anastasio, Joe Colombo, John Gotti and so on right up to the fictional Tony Soprano, it hardly seems necessary to discuss the criminal underworld spawned by poor Italian-American communities. The main thing that seems to have distinguished them from the other sources of organized crime is the multi-generational character of the Italian gangs and their persistence—but even here the gradual shrinkage of the pool of poor young Italian-Americans after the 1950s seems to have forced these classic organizations to open major sectors of their business to groups of newer, poorer, and tougher immigrants.

What is far more striking in a way than the Italian-American crime organizations is the paucity of them among Polish immigrants and their children. Even poorer than the Italians, reputed to be physically stronger, and even less upwardly mobile, poor Polish immigrants would seem to be natural sources for the production of at least two generations of gangsters. Polish communities did produce large numbers of juvenile delinquents and youth gangs as we might expect from such conditions, but they didn't produce much of a significant criminal underworld and their only really famous gangster is generally known by a Jewish sounding alias, "Hymie Weiss" (Radzilowski, 2002: 18).

After the Second World War the spread of labor unions combined with increasing American prosperity to greatly reduce poverty among these European immigrants and their children. But even into the later part of the twentieth century poverty remained a major problem for the sick and elderly among them—and especially for older widows if they couldn't count on help from their children.

New immigration laws passed in the 1920s greatly changed the situation. National origin quotas were designed to exclude all but a few southern and eastern Europeans, while even northern and western Europeans were strictly limited by declining quotas. Regardless of national origin, any would be immigrant held to be "likely to become a public charge" was refused entry (a limitation that in the depression conditions of the 1930s kept out even well educated professionals and formerly prosperous businessmen who had been stripped of their property by Nazi Germany). In fact, further European immigrant poverty in America was largely avoided through the simple expediency of practically ending European immigration altogether. Some exceptions were created by various refugee acts, like the Displaced Persons immigration acts of the late 1940s, the law permitting thousands of Hungarian refugees to enter the US after the failed revolution of 1956, and the 1970s Jackson Vanik law allowing for the admission of thousands of Jews from the Soviet Union. These laws often gave priority to the young and healthy or the well educated, factors which helped reduce poverty among those allowed to immigrate, and private organizations often had to guarantee the well being of those let in. Even so there were some who suffered from difficulties making the adjustment to the US or who developed serious health problems after they arrived. The American social safety net created by Franklin Roosevelt's New Deal and expanded by Lyndon Johnson's Great Society kept some of these from suffering the worst forms of poverty, but the American safety net always had gaps that allowed many to fall into poverty and the exclusion of non-citizens from access to most of these programs after 1996 has exposed many more to the danger of poverty.

Because of the strong institutional structure of the American Jewish community and its support for research on the subject we have some good data that demonstrates the persistence of poverty among recent immigrants from Europe. Nearly half of the Jewish immigrants from the Former Soviet Union who arrived between 1991 and 2000 ended up in New York City and nearly half of the city's Russian speaking Jews were reported to be living in poverty in 2002—that is, there were 100,600 poor Russian speaking Jews living in New York that year along with an unknown number of others in the rest of the US. (Metropolitan Council on Jewish Poverty/UJA-Federation of New York, 2004: 22). As with the earlier generations of European immigrants the elderly are particularly likely to have ended up in poverty:

> Especially important in this regard has been the fact that many of the refugees from the FSU were elderly and many were in ill health; these circumstances added immeasurably to their difficulties in escaping from poverty... 85% of the people in Rus-

sian-speaking households who are age 65 or older are poor...[and] even in Russian-speaking households where the heads of households are in their 50's or early 60's, many of the issues associated with old age may be present – such as poor health and an inability to work. (Metropolitan Council on Jewish Poverty/UJA-Federation of New York, 2004: 17, 18)

These figures are important not only because of the perhaps unexpectedly large number of poor Jewish immigrants they feature, but also because the figures for other groups of recent immigrants from Europe may well be similar—especially for immigrants from Albania, the Former Yugoslavia, and other parts of Eastern Europe. We don't really know much about these immigrants because their numbers in recent decades have been dwarfed by immigrants from outside of Europe who have been the focus of most of the research on recent immigrants.

What we do know is that the shrinking American welfare state has provided them with only minimal benefits, only $674 a month for a single person and $1,011 a month for a married couple. And we also know that as part of the welfare reform law of 1996 (as amended later) these benefits will no longer be provided to non US citizens after October 1, 2010. Several thousand refugees who have been unable to gain citizenship because of their age, poor health or mental condition will be cut off from all government aid and reduced to dependence on private charity or face starvation (http://www.nytimes.com/2010/08/09/opinion/09mon4.html).

What is clear it that what really kept the numbers of poor European immigrants down was the strict limits that allowed only very small numbers of Europeans to immigrate since 1921, along with an increasing prosperity in Europe that has provided other places to go for most of the sorts of European migrants who used to become poor immigrants in America.

Reviewing all of this historical material has led me to conclude that there is a serious problem with the approach to immigration history that predominates in today's scholarship.

For many decades immigrants were mostly ignored when it came to the writing of American history. Then they were written about by representatives of the various immigrant groups or their descendants with an eye to raising the status of the group or to flatter its members—an airbrushed, if not outright falsified history. When professional historians finally turned to the task they often adopted a model of immigrant communities that is best summarized by the title of Oscar Handlin's classic *The Uprooted*. This was a model of migration as social disruption and disintegration. Migrants were torn from their roots and subjected to severe anomie; they were disoriented and lost in their new homes. They created and perpetuated what anthropologist Oscar Lewis called "a culture of poverty."

Later generations of migration historians reacted strongly against this model. We rejected the image of a mass of individual immigrants who were lost, isolated and demoralized. Instead we treated immigrants with more respect—as active agents who created their own lives and built institutions and communities to make them tolerable. This was an enormous stride forward and has produced an impressive and important literature that shouldn't be ignored.

But this approach which has now dominated the writing of American immigration history for over a generation has its weaknesses. By its very nature it tends to focus on long term successes—families, institutions and communities created and maintained. It leads to a narrative of success and even celebration—one taken up as the focus of most of the immigration history written in the past forty years.

Now that's putting it a bit strongly and those of us who work in the field know that we were always aware of those who didn't do so well and have even included some of their experiences in our work—just as I included the story of Cecelia, Wanda and Edward in my own study of German immigrants in New York City. But somehow the overall balance is clear, we were interested in what was created—families, communities and ethnic groups—and we tended to pay less attention to failures—especially those rapidly removed from the historical narrative by early death. The result is a body of literature that is easily fit - or at least easily squeezed—into a celebratory version of American history that is popular in the US and is widely accepted abroad. If we are to correct that version, and we should, we have to focus clearly on the experiences of losers like Cecelia, Wanda and Edward. We need to reintegrate them into our story of the immigrant experience in ways that give them the prominence they deserve as representatives of what was at least a large minority of immigrants—if not an actual majority.

References

Andrews, Thomas G. *Killing for Coal: America's Deadliest Labor War*. Cambridge: Harvard University Press, 2008.
Asbury, Herbert. *The Gangs of New York*. New York: Alfred A Knopf Inc., 1927.
Avrich, Paul. *Sacco and Vanzetti: The Anarchist Background*. Princeton: Princeton University Press, 1991.
Barrett, James R. *Work and Community in the Jungle: Chicago's Packinghouse Workers 1894-1922*. Urbana: University of Illinois Press, 1987.
Bodner, John, Roger Simon, and Michael P. Weber. *Lives of Their Own: Blacks, Italians, and Poles in Pittsburgh, 1900-1960*. Urbana: University of Illinois Press, 1982.
Bretting, Agnes. *Soziale Probleme deutscher Einwanderer in New York City, 1800-1860*. Wiesbaden: Steiner Verlag, 1981.
Bukowczyk, John. *And My Children Did Not Know Me: A History of the Polish-Americans*. Bloomington: Indiana University Press, 1986.
Byington, Margaret F. *Homestead: The Households of a Mill Town*. New York: Charities Publication, 1910.
Clark, Dennis. *The Irish in Philadelphia: ten generations of urban experience*. Philadelphia: Temple University Press, 1973.
Coleman, Terry. *Going to America*. New York: Anchor/Doubleday, 1973.
Commissioners of Emigration of the State of New York, Annual Report 1848—in *Annual Reports of the Commissioners of Emigration of the State of New York 1847-60*. New York, 1861.
Corbin, David Alan. *Life, work and Rebellion in the Coal Fields*. Urbana: University of Illinois Press, 1981.
Covello, Leonard. *The Social Background of the Italo-American School Child*. Leiden: Brill, 1967.

Diner, Hasia R. *A time for Gathering: The Second Migration, 1820-1880.* Baltimore: Johns Hopkins University Press, 1992.

Dinnerstein, Leonard, and David M. Reimers. *Ethnic Americans: A History of Immigration and Assimilation.* New York: Harper & Row, 1975.

Gold, Michael. *Jews Without Money.* London: Noel Douglas, 1930.

Gorn, Elliot J. *Mother Jones: The Most Dangerous Woman in America.* New York: Hill and Wang, 2001.

Greene, Victor R. *The Slavic Community on Strike: Immigrant Labor in Pennsylvania Anthracite.* South Bend: University of Notre Dame Press, 1968.

Halpern, Rick. *Down on the Killing Floor: Black and White Workers in Chicago's Packinghouses, 1904-54.* Urbana: University of Illinois Press, 1997.

Handlin, Oscar. *Boston's Immigrants: A study in Acculturation* (reprinted.) New York: Atheneum, 1972.

Howe, Irving, and Kenneth Libo. *World of Our Fathers.* New York: Harcourt Brace Jovanovich, 1976.

Joselit, Jenna Weissman. *Our Gang: Jewish Crime and the New York Jewish Community, 1900-1940.* Bloomington: Indiana University Press, 1983.

Kessner, Thomas. *The Golden Door: Italian and Jewish Immigrant Mobility in New York City, 1880-1915.* New York: Oxford University Press, 1977.

Lemon, James T. *The Best Poor Man's Country: Early Southeastern Pennsylvania.* Baltimore: Johns Hopkins University Press, 1972.

Metropolitan Council on Jewish Poverty/UJA-Federation of New York. *Report on Jewish Poverty* (New York, 2004).

Morgan, Edmund S. *American Slavery American Freedom: The Ordeal of Colonial Virginia.* New York: W.W. Norton, 1975.

Nadel, Stanley. "Choosing Death in the Victorian Metropolis: Gender and Suicide in New York and London" (unpublished paper, n.d.).

Nadel, Stanley. *Little Germany: Ethnicity, Religion, and Class in New York City, 1845-80.* Urbana and Chicago: University of Illinois Press, 1990.

Nelli, Humbert. *The Business of Crime.* New York: Oxford University Press, 1976.

Orleck, Annelise (2001): "Soviet Jews: The City's Newest Immigrants Transform New York Jewish Life," in *New Immigrants in New York.* Ed. Nancy Foner. New York: Columbia University Press, 2001.

Perlmann, Joel. *Italians then, Mexicans Now: Immigrant Origins and Second-Generation Progress, 1890-2000.* New York: Russell Sage Foundation, 2005.

Pernicone, Carol Groneman. *The "Bloody Ould Sixth": A Social Analysis of a New York City Working-Class Community in the Mid Nineteenth-century,* unpublished Ph.D. dissertation, University of Rochester, 1973.

Radzilowski, John. *Crime, Delinquency, Deviance, and Reform in Polish Chicago, 1890s-1940s.* New Britain: Polish Studies Program Central Connecticut State University, 2002.

Report of the select committee to examine into the condition, business accounts, and management of the trusts under the charge of the commissioners of Emigration, New York Assembly Document No. 34, 1852.

Riis, Jacob A. *How the Other Half Lives.* New York: Dover Publications, 1971.

Rischin, Moses. *The Promised City: New York's Jews, 1870-1914.* New York: Harper & Row, 1970.

Rockaway, Robert A. *But He Was Good to His Mother: The Lives and Crimes of Jewish Gangsters.*(Jerusalem: Gefen Publishing House, 1993.

Schlüter, Hermann. *Die Anfänge der Deutschen Arbeiterbewegung in Amerika.* Stuttgart: J.H.W. Dietz, 1907.

Schlüter, Hermann. *The Brewing Industry and the Brewery Worker's Movement in America.* Cincinnati: United Brewery Workers of America, 1910.

Sinclair, Upton. *The Jungle.* New York: Doubleday, Page & Company, 1906.

Love in All the Wrong Places: Relating Migration Patterns and Marriage in U.S. Immigration, 1945-2000

Suzanne M. Sinke (Florida State University)

When people move around, relationships develop in unexpected locations. At times those relationships transform into long-term commitments. At times they involve people of different national backgrounds. Proximity, physical as well as virtual, allows for interpersonal relations of a one-on-one international variety. Mobility provides opportunities.

When we think of the relationship of marriage and migration in the late twentieth century United States we may think first of "foreign brides," recruited from other countries in order to marry U.S. men. They get a great deal of (typically negative) press.[1] They tend to obscure the larger group of marriages tied to migration, which remain between those of the same background. Yet they also herald a shift, an increase in the proportion of marriages between those of different nationalities over the course of recent decades. The broadening of the cartography of desire, to borrow another scholar's phrase, links in part to improvements in communications and technology, as well as a shift in key identity markers.[2] Nationality and ethnicity remain salient in some cases, but increasingly other categories play larger roles in marital choices.[3]

When marriages mix nationalities it is most typically between those who met while engaged in migration for other reasons. The individuals explore commonalities, and nuptial choices can (though they will not necessarily) overcome the differences. This paper examines a few of the key categories of migration of the educated and relatively affluent, a major component of the migration stream in the late twentieth century. It offers four key migration scenarios that contribute to the marital mixing of populations: military service, study, work, and travel. None of these are new in the literature. It is their combination that needs more stress as they blend individual identities. The classic "wife or worker" needs more and multifaceted counterparts such as "soldier *and* spouse,"

---

1 Note the reluctance of men to allow a researcher to write about the phenomenon due to these stereotypes in Nicole Constable, *Romance on a Global Stage: Pen Pals, Virtual Ethnography, and "Mail order" Marriages* (Berkeley: University of California Press, 2003). One element of late twentieth century trends in migration related to marriage appears in Guillermina Jasso, Douglas S. Massey, Mark R. Rosenzweig, and James P. Smith, "Assortative Mating among Married New Legal Immigrants to the United States: Evidence from the New Immigrant Survey Plot, "*International Migration Review*, 34/2 (Summer 2000): 443-459.

2 Gregory M. Pflugfelder, (1999) *Cartographies of Desire: Male-Male Sexuality in Japanese Discourse, 1600-1950* (Berkeley: University of California Press, 1999).

3 This finding echoes Johanna Leinonen, "Elite Migration, Transnational Families, and the Nation State: International Marriages between Finns and Americans across the Atlantic, 1960-present" Ph.D. Dissertation, University of Minnesota, 2011.

"student, traveler, suitor, *and* engineer."⁴ Visa categories notwithstanding, most people live their lives in multiple roles simultaneously, and models of either migration or marriage become more robust when they include a greater degree of that complexity. Already in early studies of migration from the late nineteenth century, marriage loomed large as a cause of local migration, but the two demographic forces link in many more complex ways, reflecting global trends in realms such as labor, transportation and communications, military alliances, and leisure.⁵

Factors Promoting Personal Connections Across Borders

If we can make a case that some people look beyond their own borders and beyond the limits of their own nationalities for personal connections in the late twentieth century—and we can make that case—then the question is why. Here I will deal with five factors, all of which assumed greater significance as the twentieth century progressed, which made it more likely that U.S. citizen "X" would meet and marry non-U.S. citizen "Y" to form a personal equation of one plus one. Their graph of love not only existed, but drew an upward trend-line because courtship practices, scientific models of ethnicity, communications and transportation, and immigration restrictions changed just as the global reach of business and military connections opened opportunities for extended stay in another land. Let us deal with each factor individually.

First, increasing emphasis on individualism led to shifts in courtship on a large-scale basis. This shift could be local or individual, specific to an ethnic group, or national, or even world regional. As various cultural groups moved away from arranged marriage to veto-controlled and then independent choices by potential spouses, it made it more likely that people would believe in love, would act on this emotion, and would receive support for wanting to love a spouse, even if they faced challenges to the choice on other levels. Within the U.S. movies like "Guess who's coming to dinner" emphasized the ability of people to choose their own spouses even across barriers that previously would have prevented such matches.⁶ Courtship conditions also contributed to this in the United States, as more people turned to dating in the early twentieth century.⁷ By the late twentieth century, love matches were the norm, if not for all groups,

---

4 One key example is Nicola Piper and Mina Roces, eds., *Wife or Worker: Asian Women and Migration* (Oxford: Rowman and Littlefield, 2003). On military service and migration see my "Love, Sex, and Bureaucracy: The U.S. military and marriage to foreigners" *Przegląd Polonijny* 4 (2005): 119-128.

5 For one of the early studies of migration motivations and distances see E.G. Ravenstein, "The Laws of Migration. *Journal of the Statistical Society of London*. 48/ no. 2 (1885): 167-235.

6 The 1967 Stanley Kramer film portrayed a young white woman bringing home her cultured and likeable black fiancé to meet her parents. Though black-white relationships were gaining some acceptance, the racial barrier still remained a major hurdle.

7 Beth L. Bailey, *From front porch to back seat* (Baltimore: Johns Hopkins University Press, 1988).

then at least in popular cultural parlance. And with that emphasis on love came an expectation that a marriage without love was not one to sustain. Divorce rates in the United States rose to around half of all marriages. Sheer numbers meant greater acceptance of second and later marriages.

A second major cultural shift related to this first. Increasing numbers of people began to consider those of different nationalities as possible spouses. Within the U.S. this grew in part at mid-century as citizens of different nationality backgrounds but the same race (and one would assume religion, though that is a bit harder to chart), intermarried. This set the stage for those of different nationalities but similar backgrounds to consider one another as reasonable potential spouses. More over after World War II the forms of science related to ethnicity and race, which had undergirded the eugenics movements to the extreme of extermination of people in Nazi Germany, lost credibility. This too helped shift perceptions, so that when those of different backgrounds met, they would be less likely to view one another as physically different.

Third, improvements in communications and transportation made it more likely that people would think of travel and staying in touch across distances as easier than in the past. Just as the steamship revolutionized travel and communications for the nineteenth century, airplanes, the spread of telephones, and computer connections changed the expectations of how often people would and could contact one another. Though these developments came at an uneven pace both within the U.S. and elsewhere, in total they added to connectivity.[8] What intensified this was the spread of English as an international lingua franca in the late twentieth century. This meant it was much more likely that people from the U.S. could find people, at least young adults, who could communicate with them. The images of the United States that came with the language also promoted a familiarity with U.S. culture and at times a positive image of life in the United States. Numbers of foreign students in U.S. universities attested to both the strength of U.S. schools and the linguistic preparation of many young adults.[9] Programs such as Fulbright exchanges embodied a form of internationalism, with students engaging in their own versions of international relations on a personal level.[10]

A fourth factor involved legal shifts. The U.S. shifted from openly racialized policies after the second World War, but retained quotas and familial preferences. In that system, marriage remained one of the easiest ways to migrate. "War brides" acts made it possible for some of the relationships that those in military service began to turn into marriage and then migration. Later, particularly under the Hart-Cellar Act of 1965, spouses remained outside quota limits,

---

[8] I explore this in "Marriage through the Mail: North American Correspondence Marriage from Early Print to the Web." In *Letters Across Borders* (New York: Palgrave Macmillan), Bruce Elliott, David Gerber, and Suzanne M. Sinke, eds., pp. 75-94.

[9] See for example Liping Bu, *Making the World Like Us: Education, Cultural Expansion, and the American Century* (Westport, Conn.: Praeger, 2004).

[10] Randall Bennett Woods, "Fulbright Internationalism," *Annals of the American Academy of Political & Social Science*, 491 (May 1987): 22-35.

and marriage became one of the official key components in immigration law.[11] The immigration authorities granted green cards (which are pink in the last decades), allowing temporary and then permanent residence and work options to those married to US citizens. Fiancée visas also joined the list of possible immigration categories.

The final factor I want to mention is an increase in both occupations that required foreign travel as well as other activities, particularly tourism, that took U.S. citizens to other countries.[12] Like many other things, these existed in earlier times as well. The shift was less in pattern than in scale. Whether engineers or sales personnel, the globalization of many economic activities also meant increasing movement of people connected with those economic activities across borders. Tourism to other countries was largely a pastime for the wealthy in the early twentieth century. Over a half million U.S. Americans went to another country in the mid-1930s, a number that doubled and then continued to grow in the mid-1950s.[13] By late century, millions of individuals took their holidays elsewhere.

Part of my research for a book on marriage and migration entailed interviewing people who were or had been in marriages that combined a U.S. citizen with a spouse of another nationality. Four examples from those interviews demonstrate the factors on a more personal level. These interviews, at a location chosen by the interviewee, typically lasted at least one hour. I use pseudonyms here where requested to ensure privacy. Their stories appear roughly chronologically in terms of the relationships. Though each couple mixed a U.S. citizen with a foreign national, other identities of the individuals meshed: a romance based on mutual World War II military service; a businessman who found love with a woman in another office while overseas; two globetrotting cosmopolitan types who discovered one another while travelling; and a U.S. student who encountered an international student at least partly via computer.

Audrey and Howard Wilson[14]

Audrey Wilson, from London, met her U.S. American husband Howard when he was stationed in England during World War II. She was serving in a British corps listening for German radio messages, and though she recalled no anti-

---

[11] On the relationship of marriage to law, including some attention to migration, see Nancy Cott, *Public Vows: A History of Marriage and the Nation* (Cambridge: Harvard University Press, 2000).

[12] An initial statement of this linkage appeared in Cynthia Enloe, *Bananas, Beaches and Bases: Making Feminist Sense of International Politics*, (Berkeley: University of California Press, 2000).

[13] David Engerman, "Research agenda for the history of tourism: Towards an international social history," *American Studies International*, 32/ no. 2 (1994): 3f.

[14] The author carried out all interviews for this paper. The Audrey Wilson interview took place in March 2002, in the Wilson home in Tallahassee, Florida. She agreed to use of her name and other information for this project. Tapes in author's possession. Another tape of her war recollections is housed in the World War II Institute at Florida State University.

fraternization policies, she had some misgivings about U.S. soldiers based on what others told her. Dances and other gatherings with military men stood out as highlights in her social calendar. At one of these dances she met Howard. Unlike many of the roughly 70,000 war brides of this period, however, this was not a rapid romance.[15] The two lost touch for a time as he was stationed elsewhere and Audrey's mother moved after being bombed out. Shortly after the war, however, Howard went looking for Audrey, and a combination of diligence and contacts with other family members paid off. The romance bloomed; the couple married in a small ceremony not long thereafter. While many English women who married U.S. servicemen headed for the States immediately, Audrey remained in London where Howard used his GI benefits to get a PhD.

According to Audrey, the couple would have liked to stay in England or even move to Germany, but the glut of academic people, in large part due to huge numbers of highly trained refugees, meant few opportunities. Hence they headed for the States. A friend from the Air Force put them in contact with his family in Kansas City, which made their adjustment much easier, though Audrey still had many difficulties. Audrey went back and forth to Europe a number of times, though there were many years without such trips and without visits from family members. Writing was her primary form of contact across the Atlantic—she wrote twice a week to her sister. By the time Howard died in 1964 the couple had three children and Audrey chose to stay where she was and pursue her own education. She maintained her transatlantic correspondence, however.

Howard and Audrey's life history reflected one of the most common means for U.S. men to meet women from other countries: military service. From the time of World War I, the U.S. military tried to control romantic and sexual relationships of military personnel, never fully successfully.[16] Because England and the U.S. were allies during the war, and both Howard and Audrey engaged in war work, the couple did not face the difficulties seen by those who dated "enemies." Howard and Audrey also had fewer problems than some, marrying at a time after the war when the U.S. military had already handled some of the greatest logistical challenges of moving thousands of military spouses overseas. Because Howard stayed in England, it could be a "normal" marriage. And because Audrey and Howard were both white, and U.S. and English society considered them reasonable possible spouses in terms of ethnicity, they did not face the obstacles that white U.S. men who wanted to marry women in Asia, or black U.S. servicemen who wanted to marry either white or Asian women faced.

From World War II onwards, military service was a common way for U.S. men of many backgrounds to move internationally for significant periods of time, and because most of them were young adults, of an age when marriage might be a normal consideration, significant numbers of them would engage in

---

15 Jenel Virden, *Good-bye, Piccadilly: British War Brides In America* (Urbana: University of Illinois Press, 1996).
16 See for example Maria Höhn, *GIs and Fräuleins: The German-American Encounter in 1950s West Germany* (Chapel Hill: University of North Carolina Press, 2002).

relationships with women they met. This was less true for women in military service. The imbalanced sex ratio in military service meant that heterosexual women typically were in contact with many more U.S. men than vice versa. Military service could also tie to later occupational mobility, as seen in my next case, that of

Sophie and Richard (Rick) Morelli[17]

Rick Morelli, the grandchild of Italian immigrants, grew up in the area around New York City. After earning a degree in engineering, he got pulled into military service during the Korean War. He traveled extensively while in the military, and then switched into government service, gaining a couple of promotions over time. Still, the pay did not match private industry, so eventually he switched his project management skills out of government service and into a private firm. As a young man Rick still reveled in the travel this entailed: Korea, Japan, the Middle East, Morocco, many European countries. During this time he met and married his first wife. Travel continued, however, and as that marriage dissolved he looked for other romantic options. Along came news of Sophie.

Sophie was ethnically Greek and lived in Greece when Rick met her. Her parents, both from families of refugees, found themselves in trouble once again during World War II. They lost everything and fled during the civil war. Instead of affluence and a good education, as expected, Sophie ended up moving around and working at a paralegal job.

Like so many engineers, Rick sojourned in other locations for extended periods of time for various projects. He was on one such project in Greece when he heard there was a woman who spoke English who was a friend of a friend. He called and asked for a date. She accepted under the condition that it was a double date—going with a strange man just wasn't something she thought was right, even at age thirty. The two hit it off, and Rick started writing regularly. He also called at times, though back in the states he seemed to mix up the time difference often, calling in the middle of the night.

Sophie used her next vacation to meet his family and travel a bit in the United States. Because Rick's divorce was in process the two went back and forth with immigration authorities, trying to keep her status legal. The couple moved to Washington in order to have a better chance of getting through the permitting process without Sophie being deported. Business contacts and lawyers worked through the paperwork jungle, setting up an employment identity for Sophie that would help her remain. When his divorce was final, the couple married in a civil ceremony. Meanwhile Rick was getting ready for a trip to Pakistan, and Sophie came with him despite the official bureaucratic impossibilities of travelling during status adjustment. As part of that trip they stopped in Greece and went through a big Orthodox church wedding, one Sophie's family

---

17 The author carried out this interview in December 2003 in the informants' home. The names are pseudonyms. Tapes in author's possession.

attended. Immigration categories may have set the legal standard, but obscured the interplay of work and family motivations.

Rick exemplified a business traveler with projects keeping him out of the country for weeks or even months at a time. That both his marriages resulted from meetings in these settings was not that unusual. After marrying Sophie Rick eventually took another job in a different state that required less international travel. Sophie convinced him to quit that and join her in a business venture that involved no official travel at all. When I interviewed them Rick and Sophie had been together enough years that their daughter, born early in the marriage, was in high school. The couple completed one another's sentences when together. So the business traveler brought a spouse back to the U.S., someone who already had some English language skills when he met her, and who was used to being in touch with a cosmopolitan group of people based on life prior to meeting him. Communications made the continuation of their relationship possible at a time when he was often underway. Travel related to work both brought Rick together with his spouses, and contributed to the dissolution of his first marriage. Travel in another form was crucial for the next couple I want to consider.

Jim and Teresa Martinez Corazon[18]

Love of travel brought Jim and Teresa Corazon together. Life had been rough recently for Jim, whose spouse had succumbed to cancer at a young middle age. Part of getting out of mourning was to get back to traveling. As a Spanish speaker from his days as a exchange student in Mexico as a child, this U.S. citizen often chose Spanish-speaking locations for his vacations. In Spain one summer in the 1990s he encountered Teresa, a middle-aged never-married Mexican woman who shared his love of travel, his profession, and who found she enjoyed his company as well. The two stayed in touch, and met when he went to her hometown, Mexico City, for work. After four years the two decided to make a joint trip to Australia. Other joint trips in Latin America as well as to Toronto followed. When their careers were coming to an end they married, moving back and forth between their two countries of origin and going to other locations as their health and finances allowed. Teresa spoke English well, though felt less comfortable in that linguistic world than in Spanish, the language of their home.

Though work, language skills, and communication contributed to the attraction of Jim and Teresa, it was a shared interest in travel that actually brought them together and kept them together initially (at least as they told the story). Jim and Teresa knew of email, and used it for contact with relatives in Mexico, but their own contacts remained primarily by phone, or sometimes letter. The shift in communications technology that went from letters and sporadic personal visits for Audrey and Howard; to letters, visits, and phone calls for Rick

---

18 The author carried out this interview in December 2003 in the informants' home. The names are pseudonyms. Tapes in author's possession.

and Sophie; to mainly phone calls and a few letters and fairly regular visits for Teresa and Jim, took on another dimension for the next couple in my set of examples.

Judy Porter and Michael Sieger[19]

Late one night Judy, an undergraduate at a small Midwestern college, "fingered" into the computer communications network at a U.S. university where Michael, a German graduate student, was working, and they began electronic correspondence. Judy had heard about titillating exchanges in the anonymity of cyberspace, and decided to try meeting someone this way. It was the early 1990s, before e-mail was common, and Michael was sufficiently impressed both by Judy's technological knowledge and her on-line repartee that he corresponded with her not only that night, but with increasing frequency over the coming weeks. Judy was glad to have found someone who was not only computer-savvy, but who could help her learn German, in which she was enrolled at that time. After a couple of months they started telephoning in addition to their computer contacts, and a number of months later they met in person. Computer correspondence would remain important to their relationship in subsequent years, as she spent time in Europe and he moved to a job in another U.S. city. By the time they were married in 2003 they had logged many hours together on-line. And so a chance meeting in cyberspace created a relationship.

Communications spurred this relationship, but without Michael's status as a student in the United States, the chances that the couple would meet and marry would have decreased significantly. Study abroad brought tens of thousands of international students to the U.S. as well as thousands of U.S. students to other lands. Like most students, Judy and Michael were at appropriate ages in their cultures for marriage. Though Judy's family, like a significant minority of the U.S. population, included people of German background, and they were both white, there were a few questions about ethnicity. Like many U.S. families, this one associated "German" with Nazism, a result in part of an overabundance of German villains and World War II themes on U.S. television and film. A little reassurance on Judy's part and meeting Michael in person reassured the family that he did not harbor those kinds of tendencies. Michael spoke fluent English when he met Judy, much better than did Sophie when she met Rick, or Teresa when she met Jim, so that facilitated communication as well. The trends were not just teleological, but for white immigrants of the relatively well to do, the increase in likelihood of marriage played out clearly in the lives of these couples.

******

Military service, work, travel, study: each of these areas brings people from one country into contact with those from other countries. The late twentieth century made these activities conduits for courtship and sometimes marriage as well.

---

19   This interview took place in September 2003 n the informants' home. The names are pseudonyms. Tapes in author's possession.

Communications made it easier over time to remain in touch, but it served to facilitate rather than create these interpersonal relationships. This demonstrates some of the patterns of more elite migrants, a major part of the late twentieth century migration, and also manifests how migration and marriage may be related in "serendipitous" ways that nonetheless relate strongly to larger sociocultural and economic forces.

References

Bailey, Beth L. *From front porch to back seat*. Baltimore: Johns Hopkins University Press, 1988.

Bennett Woods, Randall. "Fulbright Internationalism." *Annals of the American Academy of Political & Social Science*, 491 (May 1987).

Bu, Liping. *Making the World Like Us: Education, Cultural Expansion, and the American Century*. Westport: Praeger, 2004.

Constable, Nicole. *Romance on a Global Stage: Pen Pals, Virtual Ethnography, and "Mail order" Marriages*. Berkeley: University of California Press, 2003.

Cott, Nancy. *Public Vows: A History of Marriage and the Nation*. Cambridge, Massachusetts: Harvard University Press, 2000.

Engerman, David. "Research agenda for the history of tourism: Towards an international social history." *American Studies International*, 32 no. 2 (1994).

Enloe, Cynthia. *Bananas, Beaches and Bases: Making Feminist Sense of International Politics*. Berkeley: University of California Press, 2000.

Höhn, Maria. *GIs and Fräuleins: The German-American Encounter in 1950s West Germany*. Chapel Hill: University of North Carolina Press, 2002.

Jasso, Guillermina, Douglas S. Massey, Mark R. Rosenzweig, and James P. Smith. "Assortative Mating among Married New Legal Immigrants to the United States: Evidence from the New Immigrant Survey Plot ." *International Migration Review* 34/2 (Summer 2000).

Leinonen, Johanna. "Elite Migration, Transnational Families, and the Nation State: International Marriages between Finns and Americans across the Atlantic, 1960 – present." Ph.D. Dissertation, University of Minnesota, 2011.

Pflugfelder, Gregory M. *Cartographies of Desire: Male-Male Sexuality in Japanese Discourse, 1600-1950*. Berkeley: University of California Press, 1999.

Piper, Nicola and Mina Roces, eds. *Wife or Worker: Asian Women and Migration*. Oxford: Rowman and Littlefield, 2003.

Ravenstein, Ernst G. "The Laws of Migration." *Journal of the Statistical Society of London* 48 no. 2 (1885).

Sinke, Suzanne M. "Marriage through the Mail: North American Correspondence Marriage from Early Print to the Web," in *Letters Across Borders*. Ed. Bruce Elliott, David Gerber, and Suzanne M. Sinke. New York: Palgrave Macmillan.

Sinke, Suzanne M. "Love, Sex, and Bureaucracy: The U.S. military and marriage to foreigners." *Przeglad Polonijny* 4 (2005).

Virden, Jenel. *Good-bye, Piccadilly: British War Brides In America*. Urbana: University of Illinois

Polish Immigrants and Chicago's Progressive Parks: Creating Public Space in the City

Dominic A. Pacyga (Columbia College, Chicago)

Chicago's phenomenal growth in the nineteenth century was one of the wonders of the industrial world. The city epitomized American urban industrial society. Its streets were filled not only with the noise of commerce and industry, but also with the languages of all of Europe and most of the world beyond. In 1910 the foreign-born an their children made up roughly seventy-seven percent of the city's population.[1]

Chicago faced many problems. It simply had grown too quickly. In the traditions of laissez-faire, development occurred in a rather haphazard way. Very little formal planning took place, and, while businessmen generally shared cultural assumptions about how a city should look, market forces largely shaped its realities. The result was a city that served the rich and middle-classes well, but ignored the poor and working class. Chicago's rich enjoyed the beautiful boulevard and park systems, and the winds of off Lake Michigan freshened their neighborhoods. The poor lived largely in wooden slums far away from either the lake or the parks. Social and economic class divided Chicago. Ethnicity and race further divided the city. The various park systems reflected that reality.

Chicago's social problems attracted the attention of Progressive reformers who saw the squalor of the slum as a challenge to the American way of life. Jane Addams, Mary McDowell, Graham Taylor, and other settlement house pioneers tied the issues of disease, crime, and even machine politics to the living conditions of those who formed Chicago's industrial army. The playground and small parks movement provided one answer to the slum and its problems. Both of these fit nicely into the worldview of the Progressive Movement at the turn of the century. The idea of urban parks and playgrounds was at least in part the result of a belief that open spaces and fresh air were a necessary part of a child's upbringing. Many of the settlement house Progressives came from small town middle-class backgrounds and were raised as children far from the dirt and noise of the industrial city.[2]

In 1898 Charles Zeublin of the University of Chicago published an article in *The American Journal of Sociology* outlining Chicago's social problems and pre-

---

[1] For the growth of Chicago as "Shock City" see Harold L. Platt, *Shock Cities: The Environmental Transformation and Reform of Manchester and Chicago* (Chicago and London: University of Chicago Press, 2005). The best source for a look at ethnic development is Melvin J. Holli and Peter d'A Jones, eds., *Ethnic Chicago* (Grand Rapids, Michigan: Eerdmanns Publishing Company, 1980).

[2] For the ties between Progressivism and the Playground Movement see Benjamin McArthur, "The Chicago Playground Movement: A neglected Feature of Social Justice," *Social Service Review* (September 1975): 376-395. See also Allen F. Davis, *Spearheads of Reform: The Social Settlements and the Progressive Movement, 1890-1914.* (New York: Oxford University Press, 1967), p. 35.

senting the playgrounds movement as one possible solution. Zueblin pointed out that the boulevards and park systems in Chicago were inadequate for the industrial city that had developed since Frederick Law Olmsted had begun to plan the South Park System earlier in the nineteenth century. These parks and boulevards were largely inaccessible to the urban poor. Zueblin called for an intricate system of small parks and playgrounds in Chicago's industrial neighborhoods. He made the point that between 600,000 and 700,000 Chicagoans lived in areas not served by the existing parks. They also lived in some of the most crowded neighborhoods in America. A 1901 study by Northwestern University graduate student Alfred Tennyson Lloyd reiterated the problem and explained that the very young, the very old, and the very poor could not easily use the existing parks.[3] The need for neighborhood parks was a well-established fact by the turn of the century.

The question of whether the new parks should serve the ascetic or practical needs of industrial neighborhoods soon became an issue. The argument often divided along class lines. Middle-class reformers saw parks as a sylvan escape from the industrial city. Working-class communities demanded sports fields and gymnasiums for their children. Jane Addams was most determined about her vision of the small parks. Addams proposed a solution to the problem that combined both the concepts of the playground and that of a breathing space. She explained:

> "The most desirable thing is to reserve say a quarter of the space in a strip around the edge of the playground for trees and grass and for benches where the elders can sit. The London playgrounds reserve several rods around the edges in this way."[4]

Whatever the views concerning the nature of the new parks, observers generally agreed in general on where the parks should be located. Most targeted Chicago's crowded working-class wards.

Chicago's Back of the Yards was typical of the type of neighborhoods that Zueblin and Jane Addams had in mind when they called for a small parks program. Different industries dominated other neighborhoods such as steel in South Chicago or tanneries and other smaller businesses along the North Branch of the Chicago River. Often the housing and sanitary conditions in these other wards were comparable. The populations also had much in common. Though perhaps of different ethnicity or race, they were frequently new to Chicago and even to the industrial world. They also seemed to be isolated from the mainstream of American life in their ethnic enclaves. The districts frequently suffered from gang activities and high crime rates. Many middle-class Americans perceived the crowded industrial quarters not only as impoverished dis-

---

3   Charles Zueblin, "Municipal Playgrounds in Chicago," *The American Journal of Sociology* (September 1898): 146-148; Alfred Tennyson Lloyd, "The History and Administration of the Public Parks in Chicago with Suggestions for Making them More Useful," excerpted in uncited newspaper, Chicago Park District Clippings (CPDC), Vol. 1, p.46.
4   *Chicago Record-Herald*, June 1, 1902, CPDC, Vol. 2.

tricts, but also because of foreign cultures, labor strikes and occasional radical political activities, threats to the American way of life.[5]

Reformers aimed the legislation for small parks passed in 1901 at these neighborhoods. The parks that began to appear under the jurisdiction of the South Park Commission in 1905 can be classified, in the terms of historian Galen Cranz, as reform parks. They were part of a general movement to deal with the problems of the industrial immigrant city. Central to their design was a fieldhouse, which was intended for use by neighborhood residents.[6]

A good example of a South Park commission fieldhouse and small park was built near the Union Stock Yards. In February 1904 the *Chicago Tribune* printed an artist's rendition of Davis Square, one of the small parks to be opened in Back of the Yards the following summer. Designers laid out the ten-acre park much in the fashion that Jane Addams had proposed. Architects created large play areas surrounded by greenspaces for adults to sit and watch the activities in the center.[7] The fieldhouse provided the centerpiece of the park. It made Davis Square a year round neighborhood center. The building contained gymnasiums, showers, meeting rooms, a library, and even a cafeteria. An outdoor swimming pool lay behind the fieldhouse. It was designed to be a municipally maintained community center. Indeed the Chicago fieldhouse presented a model for parks all over the nation.[8]

On May 13, 1905 the South Park Commissioners opened Davis Square Park. A crowd of about 4,000 attended the opening ceremonies, which included a dedication speech by South Park Commissioner Henry G. Foreman. The entire ceremony had been orchestrated by Mary McDowell the head resident of the nearby University of Chicago Settlement House. Foreman proclaimed Davis Square to be the settlement ideal applied to parks. His speech further went on to outline the social theory behind Davis Square and all of the small parks of the period:

> "When you people who live in this part of Chicago
> come home tired at night, or when you have a holiday, or
> when you are tempted to do something wrong, come
> over here and listen to the music. Come and see your children
> work in the gymnasium; come and take a bath or swim, or see
> the trees and flowers.... If there is anything about this district
> you don't like, call a meeting in this room and talk it over. Use this
> assembly hall freely for any good purpose, except for
> religious or political meetings."

---

5 For a description of youth gangs and their locations in the working-class wards of Chicago during the 1920s see Frederic M. Thrasher, *The Gang: A Study of 1,313 Gangs in Chicago* (Chicago: University of Chicago Press, 1927).
6 Galen Cranz, *The Politics of Park Design: A History of Urban Parks in America* (Cambridge, Massachusetts, The MIT Press, 1984), p. 63.
7 *Chicago Tribune* 5 February 1904, CPD Clippings, Vol. 3.
8 Cranz, *Politics of Park Design*, p. 87,

Other notables also spoke to the group. John Smulski, the well-known Polish American banker and politician, addressed the heavily Slavic crowd. Later the Polish and Bohemian Sokols entertained the assembly with gymnastic feats.[9]

The intent of the reforms was symbolized in the organization of the parks. At first park personnel tightly regulated activities. They arranged gymnastics and various types of sports around strict rules of competition. Park supervisors established athletic leagues. The intent of both the recreational and hygiene facilities was to create a new kind of industrial resident. As one newspaper proclaimed, out of the slums would come "clean, healthy men and women." This was thought to be in sharp contrast with the realities of the industrial districts.[10]

The construction of the parks was not without controversy. The West Park District built two neighborhood parks in the heavily populated Polish neighborhood just to the northwest of the city's downtown, an area known as West Town, but to local Poles as Stanisławowo and Trojcowo. The first park, known simply as West Park No. 1 stood on land bordered by Chicago Avenue, Cornell, Nobel, and Chase Streets. The sight was directly across from St. Boniface Catholic Church, a parish founded by German Catholics in 1864. Parishioners had built a new church, which opened in 1903 to serve Germans and other Europeans in what was a neighborhood whose ethnic population was undergoing vast changes. By the early twentieth century Poles, Italians, Slovaks and others were making their way onto the streets leading to St. Boniface and Park No. 1. The pastor Father Albert Evers supported the small parks movement and agitated for the new park across from his church. Earlier in the nineteenth century there had been much hostility between the Poles and Germans in the neighborhood. Father Evers attempted to maintain the German character of the parish and neighborhood, but German parishioners kept moving out farther northwest. In regard to the new park Evans warned at the park's opening on August 1, 1908 about his Polish neighbors. The priest claimed the park had to be protected from the Polish taverns and dancehalls in the area. He mentioned drunken men and women cavorting in the establishments. The priest warned especially of Polish weddings stating, "The Polish wedding dance is the most vicious form of these entertainments. If the bridal party has money enough they dance continuously for three days." The priest warned that the scenes that attend these dances are at times disgraceful. He called for an end to this "nuisance."[11] Father Evers did not complain when hundreds of Poles were forced to move in order for the park to be built. The strain of maintaining the German culture of the neighborhood finally broke Father Evers and he resigned his position in 1916. Originally the Polish community had requested that Park No. 1 be named General Casimir Pulaski Park, but the petition was denied, perhaps taking Fr. Evers's biases into consideration, and the park was later named

---

9   *Chicago Tribune* 14 May 1905, CPD Clippings, Vol. 3.
10 No Date, No Citation, Page B, CPD Clippings, Vol. 3.
11 Rev. Msgr. Harry C. Koenig, S.T.D., ed. *A History of the Parishes of the Archdiocese of Chicago* (Chicago: The Archdiocese of Chicago, 1980) 2 Vols.. V1, pp: 136-137; *Chicago Tribune*, August 2, 1908.

after B.A. Eckhart the President of the West Chicago Park Commission at the time it was constructed.[12]

Gathering the land for what would become Eckhart Park proved to be a challenge. First the issue of issuing Small Park Bonds to pay for the land and construction presented itself. A long legal battle had to be fought to issue the bonds for the West Park District. In addition Mrs. Boal owned much of the land that had been chosen for the park and she originally said she did not want to sell the sight. In 1906 tenements covered the land designated for the park, many of whose owners simply rented the land for their buildings from Boal, the daughter of the original owner Enos Ayers. The West Park Commissioners Board then asked Boal to donate the land in honor of her father who had been one of the pioneers of Chicago. She refused, and then said she would consider a sale of the land. The Park Commissioners sent a police inspector to speak to the owners of the site. Meanwhile other West Side neighborhoods petitioned the West Park Board for a small park. In February 1906 the board agreed to pay Boal $158,997 as appraised by the Valuation Committee and to purchase improvements for $2,050. The owners wanted $400, 000. Finally Mrs. Boal accepted the offer. The West Park Commission now had to deal with the owners of the structures still on the land. Various offers were made. For example Stanley and Elizabeth Cichon accepted $2,236 for their structure on Lot 53. Joseph Kruszinski accepted $2,675. Other landowners also had to be compensated, but the land for the park was finally accumulated and construction could begin. By February 1908 a modern fieldhouse was erected at Park No. 1 site. It contained a large assembly hall, library and reading rooms, lunchrooms, an outdoor swimming pool along with dressing rooms and shower baths for both men and women together with an outdoor gymnasium, and a playfield, wading pool, and sand court for children. Plans called for the fieldhouse to be opened to the public in a few months.[13]

On Saturday August 1, 1908 the neighborhood gathered to celebrate the opening of the park. The Daily News Band as well as the Polish singing society, Chór Filaretów supplied the music. Both the Central Turnverein and the Norwegian Turners put on expositions. The Paderewski Club and the Moring Star Club sang Polish songs and performed traditional Polish dances in costume. In March 1909 the President of the West Park Commission, Jan Smulski, reported that Small Park No. 1 had been completed and was fully operating. When the natatorium opened in July, it became and instant success with an average daily attendance of over 2,200 men and boys and 245 women and girls. The wading pool saw over 470 children using it daily from September through November. Local residents also used the shower baths as the park served a neighborhood with few other such facilities either in homes or in public bathhouses. A kinder-

---

12   *Chicago Tribune*, January 29, 1913.
13   *Proceedings of the Board of the West Park Commissioners Official Record; February 13, 1906; February 27, 1906; June 26, 1906; February 6, 1907; February 14, 1907; May 28, 1907, February 25, 1908.*

garten soon opened as a continuation of the children's playground. Park district officials also promised concerts for the small parks as well.[14]

Six years later West Park Commissioners opened Pulaski Park about one half mile to the north of Eckhart Park (Park No. 1). The park occupied a space that had formerly held ninety buildings. It cleared the area directly in front of the Polish Catholic church of St. Stanislaus Kostka with its companion school. Originally the pastor of St. Stanislaus Kostka opposed the selection of the sight, which consisted of 8.68 acres, probably because he feared the removal of families and businesses that had supported his parish. The park would embrace some of the most densely occupied residential areas of the city. It was estimated in 1911 that roughly 20,000 people under the age of twenty-one lived within one-third of a mile of the proposed park.[15]

In many ways the small parks provided village squares for these densely populated immigrant neighborhood. In 1909 the Polish newspaper admonished the American Polonia for its high rate of juvenile delinquency and encouraged families to take advantage of the parks programs where youth could obtain healthful physical training.[16] From the beginning the Polish community saw the benefit of the parks and became active participants in park programs as well as agitating for the creation of more such public spaces in inner-city neighborhoods. Even before World War One the neighborhood parks saw Polish patriotic programs. In 1911 a commemoration of the November 1863 Polish Uprising against Czarist oppression was held in Bessemer Park in South Chicago near the Polish parishes of St. Bronisława, St. Mary Magdalene, and Immaculate Conception, B.V.M. the event began with a parade to Bessemer Park from Kosiba's Hall across the street from Immaculate Conception Church on 88th and Commercial Avenue.[17] The Polish community also used the park halls for educational purposes. The Association of Polish Physicians of Chicago gave a series of daily lectures to immigrant mothers on hygiene at Eckhart Park in 1917. In turn the Polish Singers Alliance and Promien Society gave concerts at the park. The, mostly Polish, Northwest Side Public Speaking Club met regularly at Eckhart Park and invited prominent Polish American politicians and public officials to address the group on civics. The Polish Esperanto Society even offered Esperanto language lectures in the fieldhouse. The Polish People's University gave free lectures on such topics as the "Evolution of the Earth" and "Geography," as well as "Technological Advances." Various Polish music schools presented concerts and lessons in Eckhart and Pulaski Park. The Polish National Alliance ran Saturday Polish language and culture schools in Davis Square and Sherman Park in

---

14 Proceedings of the Board of the West Park Commissioners Official Record; August 11, 1908; March 16, 1909.
15 Proceedings of the Board of the West Park Commissioners Official Record; February 7, 1911; The West Parks and Boulevards of Chicago (1913).
16 Dziennik Związkowy, June 21, 1909. (All non-English language newspaper notes from The Chicago Foreign Language Press Survey)
17 Dziennik Związkowy, February 4, 1911.

the Stock Yard District. In the spirit of Pan-Slavism and inter-ethnic competition Davis Square Park held an annual All Slavic Athletic Contest on its fields.[18]

The parks proved especially vital during World War One when immigrant communities felt concern for their homelands. As war clouds loomed over Europe the Polish community began first to organize for Polish war relief. In December 1916 various Polish societies marched from Pulaski Hall at 4831 S. Throop to Sherman Park to raise money to help starving Polish children. In August of 1917 after the United States had entered the fighting the Polish National Alliance held a huge rally of some 3,000 people in Pulaski Park to protest the arrest of General Józef Pilsudski and the disarming and internment of the Polish legions for refusing to swear allegiance to the German Kaiser and refusing to fight the Russians. Most importantly the parks witnessed efforts to raise a Polish Army to fight on the Western Front. Small parks in all Polish neighborhoods saw recruitment efforts and patriotic rallies. On the afternoon of May 5, 1918 Council III of the Polish National Alliance held a Polish Constitution Day celebration and Polish Army recruitment rally in Pulaski Park. Polish residents filled the park auditorium to capacity. Several weeks later a reception for the Polish Military Committee was held in South Chicago. A magnificent parade marched from Russell Square, across from the Polish church of St. Michael's in the Bush neighborhood, to Bessemer Park. The length of the parade was reported as twenty city blocks long. The Polish Military Band played the American, Polish, and French national anthems at Bessemer Park. Later that year Polish Army recruits were sent off from the Back of the Yards neighborhood. In October, Polish organizers again held a rally in the neighborhood and recruits gathered at Davis Square and marched to Słowacki Hall (Columbia Hall) on 48th Street.[19]

The parks indeed proved to be very lively village squares. Chicago's ethnic groups had long looked towards the larger and older parks as places in which to display their ethnic pride. The new small parks, however, really provided a public place to gather and celebrate or protest in one's own neighborhood. The new urban spaces provided a site for public recreation and entertainment.

The parks also provided spaces for attempts at assimilating the city's various ethnic groups. At first in a bid to attract immigrant groups to the parks, ethnic art, folk singing and dancing provided some of the entertainment. Polish ethnic organizations such as The Polish Singers Alliance in America organized lessons for a children's choir at Holstein Park on the city's Northwest Side. Children's choirs met at the Sherman Park fieldhouse in Back of the Yards, and the Polish director of Davis Square a couple of miles away, Thaddeus Sleszinek, arranged for Polish concerts in that park. The Towarzystwo Spiewów Imienia Paderewskiego and the organization Drużyna also were very active in the parks.[20]

---

18 *Dziennik Związkowy*, June 20, 1917, November 14, 1914, November 4, 1911, May 23, 1913, January 25, 1909, March 12, 1917, January 1, 1911, May 23, 1913.
19 *Dziennik Związkowy*, February 4, 1911, December 11, 1916, August 6, 1917, May 6, 1918, May 24, 1918, July 16, 1918, August 20, 1918, October 22, 1917.
20 *Dziennik Chicagoski*, January 25, 1922, *Dziennik Związkowy*, February 15, 1910, *Lietuva*, November 18, 1910.

American plays, dances, and movies aimed at the younger members of the ethnic communities made up many of the programs attached to the parks. Assimilation of the various ethnic groups was of course a goal of the park designers and reformers. During and after World War One this became very apparent. Park commissioners literally handed the parks over to the YMCA for Americanization classes. Davis Square, Dvorak Park, McKinley Park and Seward Park among others all provided Americanization courses. Over 1,000,000 Chicagoans attended these classes and lectures. To celebrate Washington's Birthday a concert was held at Pulaski Park. Three young Polish girls appeared in period costumes as Martha Washington and other grand dames of the Revolutionary War. The girls, Alice and Marie Moniuszko and Stella Chropliwy took part in singing American songs under the accompaniment of the Pulaski Park Band.[21] After the war the *Dziennik Zjednoczenia*, a newspaper sponsored by the Polish Roman Catholic Union, complained that over 125,000 of Chicago's Polish residents were not citizens and urged them to attend the citizenship classes at Pulaski Park.[22]

While Chicago park supervisors had specific plans for how the parks should be used, their location in the middle of working-class neighborhoods meant that they might also be used as center for various kinds of protests and gatherings. Davis Square situated just outside the gates of the city's major packinghouses, soon became a rallying point for union organizers. On March 31, 1918, Easter Sunday, a crowd of about 40,000 packinghouse workers and their families gathered in the park to hear the announcement of the arbitration award between the Amalgamated Meat Cutters and the packing companies granted by Judge Samuel Alschuler. John Kikulski, the Polish labor leader, and John Fitzpatrick of the Chicago Federation of Labor, addressed the multi-ethnic and inter-racial crowd.[23] Neighborhood residents obviously had taken the advice of Henry G. Foremen given in 1905 to use the park to discuss local problems. The South Park Commissioners, however, soon cut down on such activities. In 1919 they would not allow steel workers to hold a strike rally at Bessemer Park in South Chicago. The union simply moved the assembly to a nearby street corner and then to a hall donated by local merchants. Finally in 1921 Davis Square became the center of yet another labor struggle. Workers fought with police in the streets all around the park.[24]

The parks in the working-class districts continued to be the focal points of much community activity even after the labor struggles of the World War One period ended. In the 1930s Davis Square became the first headquarters of the Back of the Yards Neighborhood Council founded by Saul Alinsky and the then park supervisor Joseph Meegan. Russell Square near the gates of U.S. Steel's

---

21 Robert Henry Becker, "Teaching Good Citizenship in Chicago's Parks and Playgrounds," *Fort Dearborn Magazine* (September 1920): 19-20; *Chicago Tribune*, February 22, 1918.
22 *Dziennik Zjednoczenia*, March 11, 1922.
23 Mary E. McDowell, "Easter Day After the Decision," *The Survey* (13 April 1918): 38.
24 *New Majority* 4 October 1919; For a description of the Davis Square riot see Dominic A. Pacyga, *Polish Immigrants and Industrial Chicago: Workers on the South Side, 1880-1922* (Chicago: The University of Chicago Press, 2003), pp. 250-251.

South Works gave its name to the Russell Square Community Committee also organized in the 1930s.[25]

While the Chicago parks presented an assimilationist model to the ethnic communities, local residents often used them for ethnic purposes. Despite the fact that he parks were inclusive by their nature as public spaces, it is not surprising that certain ethnic and social class groups came to dominate them. The public parks were often better equipped because of public financing, and ethnic groups came to take advantage of these resources as they had of the resources of the earlier settlement house movement. Working-class children also showed their independence of the park programs. In a 1937 study of the recreation habits of working-class boys in the Back of the Yards showed that neighborhood children took part in various unorganized activities throughout the neighborhood. One favorite pastime was sneaking into the Union Stock Yards and playing amid the rail yards, livestock pens, and packinghouses that dominated that industrial neighborhood. The boys would sneak past the guards. There was always a great flow of people at the gates during the shift changes and the boys took advantage of it. A foot viaduct stood over the railroad tracks just inside the gates at Gross Ave. and 45th St., here the boys would wait until switch engines with their string of refrigerator cars moved along these tracks, and when the watchman became absorbed in supervising auto traffic in and out of the yards, the boys would slip into the industrial property. Other activities of boys in this industrial neighborhood included roaming around the local shopping district, looking for metal to sell to junkmen, and playing cards and dice. It is obvious that despite the efforts of reformers to create orderly recreation in playgrounds and parks, working-class youth often preferred the adventures afforded by living in a big industrial city.[26]

The small public parks provided much needed space in Chicago's working-class districts. Reformers saw them as a way of solving the problems of the inner city, and of assimilating and controlling the immigrant masses that filled Chicago's working-class districts. In reality the parks, with their well organized programs and good facilities, provided for a real need in the neighborhoods that grew near the mills, tanneries, and packinghouses. A need many of the ethnic communities could not provide for themselves in their private ethnic places. Residents used them in great numbers. The showers and swimming pools, the tennis and basketball courts, the meeting rooms and assembly halls all provided much needed public spaces in the crowded working-class neighborhoods. The residents made the small parks their own. The neighborhood spilled into them and the parks became a central part of it. Poles in Back of the Yards erected their magnificent church of St. John of God across from Sherman Park on 52nd

---

25 For an overview of the development of these two neighborhood organizations see Robert Slayton, *Back of the Yards: The Making of a Local Democracy* (Chicago: University of Chicago Press, 1987); and Dominic A. Pacyga, "The Russell Square Community Committee: An Ethnic Response to Urban Problems." *Journal of Urban History* (February 1989): 159-184.

26 E. Clinton Belknap, "Summer Activities of Boys Back of the Yards," (Master's Thesis, University of Chicago, 1937), p.67, 79, 97.

Street just west of Racine Avenue. Polish organizations met in the park's fieldhouse.[27] The South Park Commissioners named the park after John Sherman, the founder of the Union Stock Yard, but the park still belonged to the area's working-class residents. Public space was a precious commodity in the industrial city. The parks filled a void. They may not have played the role that their creators had originally hoped, but they acted as a dynamic force in the creation of a sense of community in the neighborhoods of Chicago. The parks, both public and private, provided a place for the urban working class to create a public sphere. This was crucial for the sense of community that emerged in these industrial communities, and I would argue for the creation of working-class solidarity during various union struggles. Eventually, as ethnic change and assimilation took place, particularly after the Second World War, the small public parks went through a transformation that saw them loose much of their central position in the life of Chicago's working-class neighborhoods.

References

Belknap, Clinton E. "Summer Activities of Boys Back of the Yards," Master's Thesis, University of Chicago, 1937.
Davis, Allen F. *Spearheads of Reform: The Social Settlements and the Progressive Movement, 1890-1914.* New York: Oxford University Press, 1967.
Galen, Cranz. *The Politics of Park Design: A History of Urban Parks in America.* Cambridge, Massachusetts: The MIT Press, 1984.
Holli, Melvin J., and Peter d'A. Jones, eds. *Ethnic Chicago.* Grand Rapids, Michigan: Eerdmanns Publishing Company, 1980.
Koenig, Harry C. S.T.D., ed. *A History of the Parishes of the Archdiocese of Chicago.* Chicago: The Archdiocese of Chicago, 1980.
McArthur, Benjamin. "The Chicago Playground Movement: A neglected Feature of Social Justice," *Social Service Review* (September 1975).
Pacyga, Dominic A. *Polish Immigrants and Industrial Chicago: Workers on the South Side, 1880-1922.* Chicago: The University of Chicago Press, 2003.
Pacyga, Dominic A., "The Russell Square Community Committee: An Ethnic Response to Urban Problems." *Journal of Urban History* (February 1989).
Platt, Harold L. *Shock Cities: The Environmental Transformation and Reform of Manchester and Chicago.* Chicago and London: University of Chicago Press, 2005.
Slayton, Robert, *Back of the Yards: The Making of a Local Democracy.* Chicago: University of Chicago Press, 1987.
Thrasher, Frederic M. *The Gang: A Study of 1,313 Gangs in Chicago.* Chicago: University of Chicago Press.
Zueblin, Charles. "Municipal Playgrounds in Chicago," *The American Journal of Sociology*, (September 1898).

---

27 *Dziennik Związkowy* (Chicago), 8 January 1918.

The Pitfalls of Macrohistory: the Case of Waterloo, Québec

Wolfgang Helbich (Ruhr Universität Bochum)

When, back in the 1990s, I started out on my Waterloo project, I committed no less than three mortal sins. I did not have a theory to guide me and justify what I was about to do. Nor did I have a preconceived methodology. And while I never doubted I was doing history, I had no idea which label for some subdiscipline or revisionism or especially "turn" of history I was supposed to paste on my work. But frankly, all that did not really worry me.

What I did know were my overriding questions behind the simple title, "Bicultural Cohabitation in Waterloo, Québec": How did Anglo and French Canadians get along in a face-to-face society with a sizeable representation of either group during a period for which sufficient source material is available, or what was their relationship? And how did they differ in their socio-economic data, their tastes and preferences, their local, provincial, and national politics? Finally, did living in a bicultural town result in attenuating conflicts that were acute elsewhere, and could living together even exert a mutual (or one-sided) influence sufficient to effect some change in behavior or values of one or the other group?

During the first stages of my project, when trying to explain my intentions to colleagues, I sometimes used the term "microhistory". For more than a decade, I had been researching biographical sketches for the writers of the letters we were editing,[1] on the basis of the U.S. Census, passenger lists, city directories, county histories and other sources, and all that of course for individuals. So quite apart from the content of the letters and their interpretation, I saw the major difference between our work and normal historiography in our "descending" to the individual level, and in our simultaneous "descending" to common rather than prominent people. So in my homespun definition I roughly equated individual level research with micro-history, and since in Waterloo I was also working with individuals, I felt justified in using "microhistory" as an explanatory device.

It was only later that I realized, to my great surprise, that in the elaborate discussions and literature about microhistory "research at the individual level" appeared nowhere as the key criterion constituting the difference between microhistory and the rest of history. There are indirect references, like opening

---

1   Wolfgang Helbich et al., eds., *Briefe aus Amerika* (München: Beck 1988); (translation:) Walter D. Kamphoefner et al., eds., *News From the Land of Freedom* (Ithaca: Cornell UP 1991). Helbich et al., eds., *Briefe von Front und Farm* (Paderborn: Schöningh 2002); Kamphoefner et al., eds. (translation:) *Germans in the Civil War* (Chapel Hill: University of NCP 2006).

history "to peoples who would be left out by other methods"² or "people who fall through the net of macro perspective".³

Of course, studies of one person, some of them belonging to the standard works of microhistory, are mentioned frequently, besides those of small places and events, whereas Wikipedia (French) says bluntly that microhistory studies "individuals instead of classes and masses." Admittedly, the latter definition is getting close, but does not quite make it, so that it seems that my decisive criterion of "individual level or not" also seems to fall through a net, this time that of microhistory.

A central concern of microhistorians is the relation of their discipline to conventional history, lumped together as macrohistory. Most representatives of microhistory are rather modest in their claims. For Wikipedia (German), the historical detail gained from analyzing small units is used to arrive at richer and better-substantiated results in larger contexts. As Carlo Ginsburg of Cheese and Worms fame has it, dealing with a small unit "constitutes the bases for a deeper generalization."⁴ Andrea Griesebner finds that "the observations made on a small scale are placed in a larger context and set in relation to macrohistorical questions.⁵

Otto Ulbricht, the most articulate German microhistorian, goes a significant step further. By asking big questions in small units, "the microhistorian can check if the conclusions of his colleagues are well-founded – or have to be corrected."⁶ Roughly the same sweeping claim was made by Georg Iggers when he wrote that "social scientists have made generalizations that do not hold up when tested against the concrete reality of the small-scale life they claim to explain."⁷ For this group of all-out microhistorians, their discipline cannot only enrich macrohistory, but also correct it. Predictably, the bitterest attacks against social history come from the same source, and in fact there is a tendency to define microhistory as the antithesis of *Annales* and of Bielefeld social history. Thus, macrohistory is reproached of "reducing life to the socio-economic dimension", or even worse, "degrading humans to bar codes".⁸

Matters might be clarified somewhat by mentioning some limits of microhistory. Landwehr believes that it is not useful for diachronic studies and

---

2   Edward Muir, "Introduction: Observing Trifles", in Muir and G. Ruggiero (eds.), *Microhistory and the Lost Peoples of Europe*, (Baltimore: Johns Hopkins UP 1991) xxi.
3   Proseminar History, Univeristy of Zürich, "Social Turn: Kritik der Alltags- und Mikrogeschichte", Winter term, 2004/2005, syllabus.
4   Quoted from Sibylle Salewski, "Carlo Ginsburg: Die Welt im Kleinen suchen, "*Tagesspiegel*, (Berlin), 17 Jul 2008.
5   Andrea Grieshaber, syllabus for seminar on microhistory, University of Vienna, Winter term, 2007/2008.
6   In an interview, *EPOC.DE: Magazin*, "Mikrogeschichte": Vergangenheit unter der Lupe", 6 Okt 2010.
7   Georg G. Iggers, *Historiography of the Twentieth Century*, (Hanover, NH: Wesleyan UP 1997), 108.
8   Note 5; Otto Ulbricht, *Mikrogeschichte. Menschen und Konflikte in der Frühen Neuzeit*, Frankfurt: Campus 2009, 10.

requires staying in one place and boring down deep, whereas Ginsburg emphasizes "one specific case, one person, one event" as appropriate subject-matter for microhistory.[9] There is an easily understood tendency to declare significant traits of landmark works constituents of microhistory, like the problem of how far common people are obedient to authorities.[10] Similarly, one can often read that the discipline deals mostly with people out of the ordinary rather than average individuals, or "they scrutinize those individuals who did not follow the paths of their average fellow countryman".[11]

However, Jürgen Schlumbohm, a renowned practitioner, contradicts in an article discussing his *Lebensläufe, Familie, Höfe*[12] It is true that he calls his work "a particular kind of microhistory," but microhistory nonetheless: instead of telling extraordinary histories about ordinary people based on exceptional documents, he reconstructs "the ordinary biographies of simple people"[13] Strangely, or because it is an obvious constituent element of microhistory, I have not encountered a single instance in which it was pointed out that virtually all the well-known microhistorical works deal with occurrences in early modern times in Europe and do not even reach into the 19th century.

So, passing these quotes and criteria muster, is what I am doing microhistory? In several ways, yes. I am dealing with a small unit, with people who remain invisible in macrohistory, and not with classes and masses. But there are also important conditions that my work does not meet. It is not early modern, but 19th and 20th century. Authorities do not figure in my research. Chronologically, it's not one point in time I am concerned with, but the development over 70 years. And I join Schlumbohm in certainly not dealing with extraordinary individuals, but very ordinary, mostly average people, and particularly in stating that if I am doing microhistory, it is "a very particular kind".

Much as one may be focussing on bicultural matters, the latter usually do not occur in isolation, but are deeply embedded in less specific situations, events, or developments. And unless one does one's research with blinders on, one cannot help noticing phenomena outside one's specific focus with some of them appearing to be in contradiction with what one knows of mainstream history. In the course of time, such issues may accumulate to the point that it seems worthwhile to put them in a paper. So the impression that this article does not present results of the main focus of my research, but of what one might disparagingly call a by-product, is largely justified.

One might begin with the obvious creed of conventional wisdom that French Catholics were held by their clergy to stay as far away from Protestants as possible so as to shield them from the temptations of liberalism and modern

---

9   Note 3, note 5.
10 Sigurdur Gylfi Magnusson, "What is Microhistory?" (5 Aug 2006), *George Mason University's History News Network*, http://hnn.us/articles/23720. html (7 Oct 2010); also note 2.
11 Note 7.
12 (Göttingen: Veröff. MPI Geschichte 110, 1994.)
13 "Quelques problèmes de micro-histoire d'une société locale ...", *Annales* 50 (1995). 775-802, qu. 775.

life, even loss of faith, and that Protestants considered Catholics not only obedient subjects of the Pope, but also backward and somehow inferior.

Yet what happened in 1862, just a year after Waterloo had obtained a direct railroad connection, which started the immigration of French-Canadian Catholics? The richest man in town, Anglican Asa B. Foster of railroad fame, donated a centrally located lot to Bishop Joseph LaRoque of Saint Hyacinthe for the construction of a church in Waterloo. Admittedly, this event becomes less spectacular if one realizes that he gave land to several Protestant denominations as well, and that as the owner of a huge tract of land in the village he had a not entirely spiritual interest in attracting people and businesses to Waterloo. The existence of a Catholic church would encourage Catholics to settle, and more inhabitants would increase the value of real estate. While this may weaken the significance of the gesture, it does show that a prominent Protestant had no qualms about attracting more Catholics to the village, and Bishop LaRoque saw no reason to refuse the gift.[14]

When on several occasions during the 1860s the building of the church came to a halt because the poor Catholic congregation could not provide the necessary funds in time, Foster repeatedly helped out with substantial cheap credits and outright gifts. And Selucia, widow of the wealthy trader Hezekiah Robinson, donated the building lot for a French school in 1883, even after the two school systems had been separated against the wishes of most Protestants.[15] Add to this that Foster apparently saw nothing wrong in writing a letter to Bishop LaRoque entreating him not to replace curé Gendreau and listing the reasons why he should not, while the bishop politely explained to the Protestant why it was necessary, and the pattern of the relationship between Catholics and Protestants in Waterloo seems somewhat at odds with the impression conveyed by one of the most reputable modern studies of Québec history: "deux mondes quasi imperméable l'un à l'autre".[16]

The second case to be presented here is even more striking, since it concerns not just accepting a gift or favorable credit conditions, but endangering the souls of Catholic children. Waterloo's school commission, nominally Protestant, had three Protestant and two Catholic commissioners with a revolving presidency, and managed all the local schools, both English and French. The school laws of the province of Québec permitted minority parents to opt out of the local school commission and have a dissident commission. The first such attempt was made in 1866, when several hundred French Catholics had moved in. The bishop and the signers of a petition desired dissidence, but most of the Protestants and an opposing Catholic petition, signed by Curé Gendreau and most Catholic notables defeated that initiative. In a letter to his bishop, the

---

14 Archives de l'Évêché de Saint Hyacinthe, Saint Hyacinthe, Québec, Correspondance des curés de Waterloo, 1862-1925, Deed of Donation, 9 May 1862.
15 Jahnke, Elke, *Migration und Identität in einer bikulturellen Gemeinde* (Frankfurt/New York: Campus 2002), 97-101, 129.
16 Paul-André Linteau et al., *Histoire du Québec contemporain*, vol. 2, (Montréal: Boréal ²1989), 257.

priest explained his position. For one thing, "nous avons eu pleine justice de la part des commissaires d'école" with a Protestant majority. But the main reason was that the Catholic congregation was too poor to afford decent schools of their own, and that the Catholic schools were heavily subsidized by the taxes of Protestant proprietors. All of 18 Dollars of school taxes had been collected from Catholic rate payers, whereas the cost of the French school in the village had been $150. Thus, "nous avons maintenant une école canadienne fréquenté par 50 enfants canadiens qui apprennent à lire et à écrire avec l'argent des américains".[17] Whereas a minority of Waterloo's Catholics set their faith and the religious control of their children's education above financial or educational concerns, the majority preferred a good education at the massive rebate provided by Protestant taxes.

For another 17 years, until 1883, when virtually all surrounding towns had long shifted to the two-commission model, both religious groups, or at least a majority of each, considered this arrangement advantageous. So in Waterloo, if there were walls between Catholics and Protestants, they were anything but impermeable for Protestant money, and even the lack of total clerical control over what was being taught and by whom in Waterloo's French-Canadian schools was accepted or rather suffered by the church. It is true that the bishops of Saint Hyacinthe, Moreau and from 1875 on Laroque found this situation disastrous and put increasing pressure on curé Phaneuf and he in turn on his congregation to change this unholy situation. However, there was stiff resistance against changing the status quo.

At long last, however, the constant warning by the clergy and some zealots in the congregation that accepting interference of outsiders in the education of Catholic children was sinful and betrayed a lack of loyalty to faith and (French-Canadian) nation, and perhaps growing confidence because of increased numbers and wealth finally caused a change of opinion. In 1883, the legal requirement for establishing a minority school commission was fulfilled by a petition signed by a sizeable number of Catholic ratepayers. Significantly, the true experts on the school situation, the Catholic commissioners in the mixed body, an entrepreneur and a physician, did their utmost to prevent such an outcome even at this late date, but in vain.[18]

The conventional wisdom claim that organized sports were largely segregated during the 19th century holds true up to a point in Waterloo. Certainly the Cricket Club and the Lawn Tennis Club were exclusively British, and although the militia had a sizeable minority of French-Canadian officers and men, the local Rifle Club, fully subsidized and armed by the militia and holding frequent shooting matches, had no francophone members. Even the (ice) hockey club started out as Royal Hockey Club and was very strongly English during the first

---

17 However "American" is to be explained, he meant of course English-speaking Waterloo residents. Correspondance, Gendreau to Bishop Moreau 13 juil 1866.
18 *Waterloo Advertiser* (WA) 23, 30 Mar 1883.

years. The others were small and rarely "bi-racial", as the contemporary designation went.[19]

The story was entirely different with base-ball, bal-au-but or bal-au-bat. It attracted both ethnicities equally and was an object of identification for both.[20] From the early 1880's on it was clearly the leading sport, fully integrated with regard to officers, players, and spectators, the most thoroughly covered in both papers. The *Journal de Waterloo*, otherwise wary of ethnic mixing and consistently reserving "notre club", "nos jeunes hommes" etc. for French-Canadians, here identified with "notre club local" or "le club de notre ville" and applauded a team that was as English as it was French. The Town Council during the first decade of the 20th century voted subsidies for only three institutions: the Public Library, the Brass Band, and the Baseball Club; it even tried to find a suitable baseball ground "for the young men of the town."[21]

A reorganization of the club to play in a formal league against neighboring towns and several Montréal teams took place in 1908. Of the 12 officers, four were French-Canadian. On two of the rare occasions when the names of the players were reported they were five English and four French players, and on the other occasion four and five.[22] Baseball was not only the one sport most clearly evoking citizen identification and pride and an arena where both ethnicities met in matches and in the board room, with roughly equal strength. This cooperation must have been extremely close, since success in a team sport depends on efficient management, intensive training and not least coherence of the team.[23]

Our micro approach not only contradicted, but more frequently confirmed macro impressions. There are even a few cases where the individual level yielded results than went beyond conventional wisdom, being more radical or extreme. The reluctance of Franco-Canadian young men in World War I to volunteer was bitterly attacked by contemporary Protestants, while later historians stated that their volunteering lagged behind that of Anglo-Canadians. Presently, it is perhaps politically inopportune to emphasize this point although, strangely, the fact that more than half of the total of English-language volunteers were born in Britain (though only 10 percent of Canada's population was British-born) is rarely used to at least partly "exculpate" the French.[24]

---

19 I owe much information on clubs and sports to the research of Axel Kircher, who was a research assistant with the Waterloo project 1997-2000.
20 *Journal de Waterloo* (JW) 16 juin 1904, 18 mai 1905, 16 mai 1907; Archives de la ville de W., *Council Minutes*, (Minutes) 24 Apr 1904.
21 JW 29 sep 1904, 18 mai 1905, Minutes 24 Apr 1904.
22 JW 30 avr 1908; JW 25 mai 1905, 27 mai 1909.
23 Despite its thoroughly mixed composition, the 1901 Census statistics for Waterloo with the very low rate of bilingualism for Anglo men reveal that English must have been the club's means of communication at every level.
24 Serge Durflinger, *French Canada and Recruitment During the First World War*, http://warmuseum.ca/cwm/explore/military-history/dispatches/French-canada-ar (12. Nov. 2010).

It is extremely difficult and a terribly frustrating endeavor to find out which young men from Waterloo served in the military.[25] Probably about 80 did. But the essential data for a full verification could be established for only 42. For 16 the information available was too incomplete to be counted in, and for the remaining 20 or so we have only vague hints of their existence. Of the 42, 29 were English and 13 French at a time when French-Canadians had reached a comfortable majority in Waterloo. Yet considering who volunteered and who was drafted, (the latter mainly during the last year of the war,) the French record is much worse (in the contemporary English-Canadian view): There were 26 English volunteers vs. 4 French, with the draftees tallying 3 to 9.

Several reasons may account for this extreme result. The local French newspaper, *Le Journal de Waterloo*, took a skeptical view of French-Canadian involvement in the War from the start. After all the oppression, violation and injustice the Canadiens had suffered from the British, they owed them no debt of gratitude. And whereas that was history, Ontario's Regulation 17, almost entirely banning French as language of instruction, stirred up bitter emotions. Why go abroad to fight the Prussians when Ontario's Prussians persecuting language and religion of French-Canadians were next door? The Canadiens should not pull Britain's chestnuts from the fire. And while the paper rejoiced about French victories during the first months of the war, the conflict soon receded from the headlines. Instead, the agitation against conscription became more and more radical. The *Journal*'s editor wrote in December of 1916, eight months before conscription came into effect:

> "Tous les Canadiens de 16 à 65 ans peuvent aller à l'abattoir impérialiste pour être livré ensuite comme pâture à l'ogre allemand afin d'apaiser le dieu couronné de la fière Albion qui ne peut compter sur ses propres fils pour la défendre."[26]

The jealousy and distrust between the two ethnicities as we know it from the textbooks seem to have been suspended in at least two spheres: politics and the intellectual intercourse between the educated of both groups. As early as 1867 a gentlemen's agreement was concluded that stipulated an English-language member of the House of Commons and a French one in the Québec Assembly. Until 1920, there were a couple of exceptions to that rule for specific reasons, but basically it was honored. When an election was approaching, the candidates wooed both constituencies, generally in both languages, and in case of serious differences regarding issues along ethnic lines tried to accommodate both sides.

---

25 In 2000, Dr. Elke Jahnke, at the time a DFG-sponsored researcher with the Waterloo project, went through Census and Tax lists, Waterloo militia and two Eastern Townships regiments' pay lists, the local newspapers, dozens of boxes in Archives Canada, RG 9 and laid the groundwork on which I could build. She compiled a list of 73 probable Waterloo soldiers, of which 32 could be verified. To the latter, I could add 10, thus getting the tally to 42. "Verification" means no contradiction in the other data and – sine qua non – presence of full Attestation Papers in *Library and Archives Canada* (www.collectionscanada.gc.ca, [2007-2008]), database "Soldiers of the First World War – CEF").

26 JW déc 14 1916.

At the Village and later Town Council level, there was occasional French grumbling about under-representation with (French:English councillors) 2:5, 3:6, 4:5, and from 1901 occasionally 5:4. In fact the adaptation to the growing numbers of French inhabitants usually lagged somewhat behind, but hardly so if one counted the relative numbers of property owners, who elected the Council. In most cases, members were elected mainly by their co-religionists, and they considered themselves spokesmen of their ethnicity, but generally also took their duty as representatives of the whole town quite seriously.[27] Their performance and cooperation was by and large quite respectable.

On the cultural side, the foundation of the Public Library shows a checkered picture, but certainly not one of strict cultural segregation. After some earlier starts, three men, perfectly balanced ethnically, lawyer Nutting, anglophone Protestant, notary de Varennes, francophone Catholic and anglophone Catholic Dr. Phelan, each possessing a sizeable library, founded the Waterloo Book Club in 1892.[28] Apparently Mrs. Henry Allen, wife of an affluent manufacturer, was the driving force behind this initiative and the following steps. They operated a lending library that gradually gained recognition and clients, until in 1900 the Waterloo Public Library Association was incorporated by the Town Council.[29]

Then there was the need for a building. The lot was donated by dentist Knowlton, the blueprints drawn up free of charge by architect Guidon. The money required, $2500, was to be raised by subscription and "entertainments" meant for, and attended by, members of both groups. Clearly, affluent francophones also donated their part. In 1902, construction could be started, the building committee being composed of a bank clerk and a manufacturer, both anglophones, and Dr. Pagé as chairman.[30] In 1903, the construction was finished. But that year the bicultural phase of the Library came to an end, or almost.

In early 1904, the "Section française de la bibliothèque publique" was formally inaugurated, with Madame Barry as guest of honor. She was founder and owner of *Le Journal de Françoise*, a bi-monthly magazine published in Montréal. In a short article, she had called for book donations for the planned French section, destined "au maintien et au développement de la langue française dans un milieu anglais", and obtained some 400 volumes." From now on, the building, the reading room and the annual subsidy from the town ($100; Brass Band and Baseball received $50 each) were shared[31], but everything else—solicited funds, administration, acquisition, the shelves, the opening hours were separate.[32] (By 2007, however, books were arranged by subject, no longer by language.)

---

27 Minutes 1867-1920, *passim*.
28 Mario Gendron, Richard Racine, *Waterloo: 125 ans d'histoire* (Granby: Société d'histoire de Shefford, 1992), 64.
29 Minutes 2 May 1900.
30 WA 3 May 1901, 9, 16 May, 10 Oct. 1902.
31 Minutes 24 Apr 1904, JW 6 avr, WA 14 Apr 1905.
32 Library and Archives Canada, *www.collectionscanada.ca/women/002026-281-f.html* (8 Sep. 2006); JW 31 déc 1903, 11 fév 1904; WA 5, 12 Feb 1904.

The story of the Library showed a friendly, almost eager cooperation of the educated village notables for a number of years. It came to an end without tension or strife when a larger public had to be considered and became involved. Before and after the division of the Library, there had been and followed a long sequence of bilingual efforts to exchange books, discuss controversial issues as well as literature and hear lectures, initiated mainly by the professionals of the town. The local and regional organisations of professionals comprised all practitioners regardless of ethnicity, and all physicians, notaries and lawyers in Waterloo had a clientele from both groups, and the mastery of both languages was a prerequisite of success in the professions, ambitious business enterprises and politics. With the village elite versed in the language and frequently in the novels and plays of the other culture, there was also a fair amount of purely social intercourse in those circles.

The conventional wisdom has it that in two of the great national crises – the execution of Louis Riel and the Manitoba school question – there was a clear-cut split between English and French Canada. In Waterloo, things were more complicated. In the first instance, the *Advertiser* did not join its fellow Liberals in Ontario and farther West demanding the death penalty, but remained fairly neutral. In the case of Manitoba, the paper softened its stand as time went by, but in 1891 made its siding with the French not only explicit, but also spelled out the reason: The Manitoba Catholics were in the same boat as the Québec Protestants. Taking away their schools even endangered the fair and just solution found in Eastern Canada. In both cases, the *Journal* supported the French and Catholic side without the slightest concession, while it is quite clear that the *Advertiser's* position was influenced by Waterloo's bicultural character and the Protestant minority's situation in Québec.[33]

Even long before the famous – and for French-Canadians infamous – Lord Durham in 1839 spelled it out in classical terms, and far into the 20th century, everyone knew that it was the British who stood for progress and modernity, ingenuity and enterprise, creating wealth and generally boosting the economy. The French, on the other hand, were known for their simplicity and traditionalism, agrarianism and submission to the clergy, inertia and lack of enterprise, blocking progress by their retrograde stubbornness. For Lord Durham and many before and after him, the only remedy would be anglifying the French, beginning with the language and the political system.

There were three major agents massively falsifying this rarely disputed dogma in Waterloo. They were, first and foremost, the two most active and most successful businessmen and manufacturers in town, Adolphe Savaria and Louis Bouchard. Secondly, the Conservative weekly *Journal de Waterloo*, constantly blaming Anglo councilmen of inertia and lack of initiative to attract industries and customers, warning of standstill while the surrounding towns were passing Waterloo in size and wealth. Beginning in the early 1890s, the paper incessantly called for financial enticement – easy credit, stock purchases, outright

---

33 WA 17 Apr 1891; WA and JW, 1885, passim, 1890-1897, passim.

bonus payments, land donation, tax exemption and several other devices to attract industries. And thirdly, the French councilmen who generally supported such demands, voted financial attractions and often persuaded their Anglo colleagues to go along.

As early as 1882, Bouchard and Savaria, who were the two French council members at the time, moved and seconded that R. Lefèbvre be given 10 years' tax exemption for his Star Manufacturing Co. and a bonus of $1000. The council voted accordingly.[34] It was the same two councilmen who in 1890 successfully moved for a bonus of $10 000 to one Mr. Cruikshank from Drummondville who proposed to produce knitted goods in Waterloo.[35] In 1892, Thomas Knowlton, a longtime Waterloo resident, asked for a bonus of $5000 and tax exemption for 5 years. A committee of two anglophones and two francophones was formed, submitted a positive report and the draft of by-law 3, which was passed after the rate-payers had approved.[36] Almost immediately afterwards an application was received from the Waterloo Wood Manufacturing Co. With the votes of all three French and three English councillors and one anglo 'nay', the acquisition of $5000's worth of the Company's stock was resolved.[37]

In all such decisions the ratepayers had to be consulted, in one vote per person and one for the amount of taxable property. In the three cases above, the results were 96:24, 76:36, and 83:44. With about 240 rate-payers in 1892, these figures show how many did not bother to vote. More interesting were the property vote results (like 138.483:82.991) in combination with the personal ones, for they allow to compute the average property holding of the voters. In all three votes, the 'aye' group was distinctly less affluent than the 'nay' side. Taking the three votes together, the average for the taxable property of those who wanted to attract industry was $1788 and for those who did not, $2647.[38]

During the following decade some smaller exemptions and bonuses were granted. But the battle royal was slowly and carefully being orchestrated. At a banquet for the newly elected mayor Éthier, Savaria, Bouchard, and councillor Hubert all agreed in their speeches that Waterloo stagnated because too little was being done to attract industry. Both Savaria and Bouchard claimed they

---

34   JW 27 mai 1882.
35   Minutes 6 May 1891.
36   Minutes 6,19, 20 Apr, 7 May, 25 Jun 1892.
37   Minutes 21 Jul 1890. The negative vote was councillor Spencer Shaw's. The well-to-do Methodist farmer stated that "he was opposed to the principle of granting bonuses and held that the towns indulging in that practice had made nothing by it in the end." WA 16 Dec 1892.
38   Considering that francophone owners were considerably less affluent than anglophone ones in 1892, that Bouchard and Savaria, the most outspoken champions of attracting industry, were repeatedly re-elected as municipal councillors mainly by francophone property owners, and that the *Journal* never stopped calling for bonuses, it is very likely that not only the leadership, but also the majority of the rank and file of the French community were more strongly inclined to provide incentives to manufacturing than the English constituents, several of whom had made no secret of their staunch opposition to bonuses. Statistics in Jahnke, 63, 193.

could manufacture far more and create far more employment if they could invest more. Only lawyer Nutting disagreed. According to the *Journal*'s report, he, too, wanted to attract people, but differently. Waterloo being the most beautiful town in the Eastern Townships, it should be further embellished in every possible way: "comme ça nous attirerons les gens riches, les capitalistes qui viendront se fixer au milieu de nous." The *Journal* stepped up its drumming for industry.[39]

In the fall of 1903, the *Journal* bitterly scolded the Council for having turned down the application of one James Aird, who would have created 100 jobs or more. (Instead, he established his shoe factory in Montréal.) Implicitly responding to lawyer Nutting's statement about capitalists, the weekly expressed the opposite position: The Council did effect occasional embellishments, but "c'est pour l'agrément de ceux qui ont de quoi vivre [...] la classe ouvrière, elle peut aller chercher sa vie ailleurs."[40]

Finally, in 1905, the cat jumped out of the bag. Adolphe Savaria asked for a shocking $30 000 bonus and a 20-year tax exemption for his Waterloo Knitting Co. Neighboring and much larger Granby had never granted such an amount. When the proposition came to a vote in the Town Council, it passed, but barely, 5:4, with three French and two English councillors for and three English and mayor Bouchard, who resigned a week later on the grounds of a technicality, against. With the proprietors' vote coming up, the *Journal* went into high gear in favor of the bonus, while the *Advertiser* made one of its rare statements on such matters, and that rather cryptic. One had to decide whether it was a good or a bad bargain. "If it is good, then those who have the best interests of the town at heart should support it." The editorial as a whole could be understood as a hesitant endorsement. The shrillest appeal against the bonus was supposed to have come from the pulpit of the Methodist church. The *Advertiser* reported as a rumor that the Rev. John Davidson had "advised all his people to vote against the by-law; that if they did not all the Protestant people would be driven out of the town in ten years";[41] When the taxpayers went to the polls, the endorsement of 124:101 was clear but no landslide; what is hard to interpret is the reversed picture of affluence. This time, the affirmative votes were close to previous results, $1811, but the negative ones were lower, and significantly so ($1570).[42]

The losing minority did not accept defeat. One group, of whom only four names are known, all anglophone, all of middling property value ($1825), three of them farmers, and three of them elderly, submitted a petition to annul the decision to the Circuit Court. The decision being contested, the Council had to vote again, on whether to oppose the petition. More clearly than before, Mayor Call and all four francophone councillors voted 'aye', all four of the anglophone ones 'nay', i.e. demanding in fact to revoke the by-law. To everybody's surprise,

---

39 JW 8 jan, 29 jan, WA 30 Jan 1903.
40 JW 24 sep, (WA 2 Oct) 1903.
41 WA 1 Sep 1905.
42 WA 8 Sep 1905.

the Court obliged on the grounds that Waterloo's tax burden was thereby pushed over the legal limit.[43]

But mayor Éthier did not let go. He re-submitted the identical bonus bill, and this time the Court let it pass, the tax limit having changed. The votes had to be repeated, and the results were virtually identical. Reporting this, the *Journal* sounded a vague, but serious warning. The opponents of the bonus should desist from further obstruction "s'ils veulent conserver, parmi notre population cette paix et cette entente qui a régné jusqu'ici". This was as clear a statement of an ethnic cleavage in the bonus affair as the Rev Davidson's rumored remarks had been.[44]

The end of this story is anticlimactic. After all those efforts and excitements, the bitterness and strife, Savaria did not receive the bonus, because he moved his establishment to Carleton Place, Ontario, which apparently offered him even more. So the French-Canadian Catholic (and Conservative politician) displayed another trait the conventional wisdom had reserved for the English: mobility.

Quite clearly, in the economic sphere the French-Canadians in Waterloo played precisely the role mainstream history had attributed to the English. Waterloo's major entrepreneurs were French, the important initiatives for attracting industry came from French-Canadians, and so was most of the pressure exerted to realize such ventures. It was a (Conservative) French-Canadian newspaper that stridently called for industry, while the (Liberal) English weekly was indifferent and hesitant at best, and it seems certain that a solid majority of the French-Canadians was ready to pay higher taxes in the interest of expanding manufacturing, whereas the only visible opposition was English.

So there is a considerable array of fields in which Waterloo contradicted macrohistorical findings: the churches, the schools, sports, World War volunteers, politics, cultural collaboration, Riel hanging and Manitoba schools, and weightiest of all, the economy. Many but not all of these divergences can be largely attributed to the bicultural or mixed composition of Waterloo's population. I do not conclude that our findings prove the results of mainstream historians wrong or in need of correction, but at most that their generalizations do not necessarily apply to the communities in some ethnically mixed areas of Québec, like the Ouatouais, the Gaspé, the Eastern Townships, or of Eastern Ontario. One step further might be to hypothesize that the situation in Waterloo was not untypical for the towns and villages in those areas. As in so many other instances, parallel case studies would be very helpful. A promising early start was made by Chad Gaffield,[45] whereas Pierre Louis Lapointe's study,[46] though topically closer, is too idiosyncratic to be of much use here.

With the Waterloo project, it has never been my intention to generalize my findings. I am quite satisfied reconstructing the situation in this place and at that time, as far as the available sources permit. The same applies to the "by-

---

43   Minutes 29 Sep 1905; JW 30 nov 1905.
44   JW 10 mai, also WA 11 May 1906.
45   *Language, Schooling and Cultural Conflict* (Kingston: McGill-Queens UP 1987).
46   *Les Québecois de la bonne entente* (Sillery, Qu:Septentrion 1998).

product" I am presenting here. It has been quite rewarding to trace the instances in which Waterloo did not fit into the macrohistoric framework. But I do not draw conclusions with regard to the works of mainstream historians – except for pointing out that in this one instance things were different. Going further would be perhaps exciting speculation, but not history. Not even "a particular kind of microhistory."

References

Gaffield, Chad. *Language, Schooling and Cultural Conflict*. Kingston: McGill-Queens UP 1987.
Gendron, Mario, and Richard Racine. *Waterloo: 125 ans d'histoire*. Granby: Société d'histoire de Shefford, 1992.
Helbich, Wolfgang, et al., eds. *Briefe aus Amerika*. München: Beck 1988.
Helbich, Wolfgang, et al., eds. *Briefe von Front und Farm*. Paderborn: Schöningh 2002.
Iggers, Georg G. *Historiography of the Twentieth Century*. Hanover, NH: Wesleyan UP 1997.
Jahnke, Elke. *Migration und Identität in einer bikulturellen Gemeinde*. Frankfurt/New York: Campus 2002.
Kamphoefner, Walter D., and Wolfgang Helbich, eds. *Germans in the Civil War*. Chapel Hill: University of NCP 2006.
Lapointe, Pierre Louis. *Les Québécois de la bonne entente*. Sillery, Qu:Septentrion 1998.
Muir, Edward. "Introduction: Observing Trifles," in *Microhistory and the Lost Peoples of Europe*. Ed. Edward Muir and Guido Ruggiero. Baltimore: Johns Hopkins UP 1991.
Linteau, Paul-André, et al. *Histoire du Québec contemporain*, vol. 2, Montréal: Boréal 1989.
"Quelques problèmes de micro-histoire d'une société locale ...," *Annales* 50, 1995.
Ulbricht, Otto. *Mikrogeschichte. Menschen und Konflikte in der Frühen Neuzeit*. Frankfurt: Campus 2009.

Different.
Polish and Post-Soviet Jewish Immigrants in New York City
Anna Sosnowska (University of Warsaw)

This paper argues that Polish immigrants' and post-Soviet Jewish immigrants', the two largest post-communist immigrant groups, position on the New York City job market is very different and quite closely, although not entirely, correspond, respectively, with the Alba and Nee's (2005) concepts of immigrant-laborer and high cultural capital immigrant-professional. I argue that the effect of the common post-communist legacy is weak. The traditional difference in cultural capital between Polish and Jewish immigrants during the great wave of immigration to the industrial United States at the turn of the 19th and 20th century has been reinforced in the late 20th century by the difference in legal status, and position of ethnic groups that were formed by the descendants of immigrants 100 year ago.

My argument refers to several sources of evidence: the U.S. census statistics, the existing qualitative research on post-Soviet Jewish community in New York City and my own research including interviews with the Polish immigrant community leaders in Greenpoint, Brooklyn, the largest Polish neighborhood in the city.

Jews have had a long tradition of immigration in New York City (Diner 2006). The mass inflow of Eastern European Jews at the turn of the 19th and 20th century changed not only the Jewish American community but also the city itself. Seven out of 10 Jewish immigrants from Eastern Europe chose the city as a place of settlement so that by the 1920s Jews made the largest ethnic group in the city and a quarter of its population (Daniels 1990). New York City history as a center of such a variety of activities as garment industry and fashion business, labor unionism and musical theater has been connected with the presence of Eastern European Jewish immigrants and their descendants.

Poles have never made a comparable imprint on the city's demography, economy and culture. Although a similar number of about 2,5 million of Polish immigrants came to the United States between 1880 and 1920, they formed in New York City a community of 150,000 in 1905 (Daniels 1990). Most of them headed for the heavy industry centers in the mid-Atlantic and mid-Western states. The largest among the old Polish parishes are located in parts of the city with – as for the city specialization in light-industry small shops – high concentration of heavy industry and male working class population: Greenpoint and northern Williamsburg (Freeman 2000, Piątkowska 2003, Bukowczyk 1987, Reiss 2001). They joined a uniquely American group of 'Catholic working class' (Greene 1980: 796) whose political culture and lifestyles in New York City were dominated by more numerous groups of the Irish and Italians (Glazer and Moynihan 1970).

Even what they had in common, that is an Eastern European background, equipped them rather with the potential for difference than similarity in the new country. Jewish and Polish immigrants 100 years ago shared the experience of life in a multiethnic empire that, for Western standards, was economically miserable and politically oppressive. As the research by Witold Kula et al. and Ewa Morawska shows, migrants sometimes shared memories of the very same rural landscape and a small town where they met on a market day. However, the two groups created in Eastern Europe separate social networks as intermarriage rate was close to zero, and religious institutions encouraged rather mutual suspicion than cooperation (Morawska 1985, 1996, Kula 1973). Therefore, they traveled to and lived their new lives in America separately.

The two groups even differently interpreted their situation as international migrants. Jewish migrants usually treated their migration as an act of permanent and family resettlement, and thought of a new country as a homeland. Polish peasants, on the other hand, more often aimed at maximal saving and returning home, and treated America as a place of fast earned money. As Hasia Diner demonstrates in her analysis of the role of the Lower East Side of the Jewish American collective memory, interpretation of immigrants' trip from Russia to the United States as a passage from biblical Egypt-like land of slavery to a promised land stimulated second generation's enthusiastic Americanization. It integrated the Eastern European Jewish myth into an older and hegemonic American of departure from morally corrupted Europe to the New World where religious communities could exercise their life ideals, free from political repression (Diner 2000).

This attitude substantially differed from the dominant Polish, and other non-Jewish, for that matter, memory of migration as an act of painful uprooting and transformation from a peasant surrounded by nature into a worker trapped in the industrial hell.[1] Old country, although poor, was more often an object of nostalgia and return (Kula 1973, Gabaccia 1984).

Now, like a century ago, Jews and Poles are among the most numerous immigrant groups coming to the United States from Europe. In the era when Central America, Asia and the Caribbean dominate as sources of the U.S. immigration, post-Soviet Jews and Poles were the only Europeans among the top 20 immigrant groups that arrived in the city in the 1990s, the last decade for which the census data is at the moment available. Like 100 years ago, New York City was a favorite destination for Russian speaking Jews in the 1990s and about 50% of them decided to settle there (Orleck 2000). Postindustrial economy has changed Polish, like many other job-hungry immigrant groups, preferences for settlement and a larger share of them became New Yorkers upon their arrival in the U.S. in the 1990s (The Newest New Yorkers: 13, 17).

Unlike then, however, when Europeans dominated among immigrants, and Jews and Poles accompanied Italians among the largest groups, now they are

---

1 Although the Oscar Handlin paradigm has been doomed inapproapriate, the historical evidence supports its claims although does not undermine the John Bodnar's 'transplanted' paradigm.

just two largest groups of European numerical minority. Unlike other European immigrants among the 20 most numerous groups in the city, such as Italians and Greeks, whose immigration slowed down in the 1980s, Poles and post-Soviet Jews still migrated intensively well into the 1990s. What is more, it was the late 20th century fall of communism that encouraged new wave of mass emigration from Poland and newly created post-Soviet countries once the post-communist countries' borders opened. Italy and Greece by that time had passed the peak point of emigration to the US and other more industrialized countries while they themselves became the countries attractive to immigrants from poorer areas of Europe, North Africa and Middle East.

The dramatic changes that Eastern Europe experienced in the 20th century: communism, Holocaust, several changes of international borders, emergence and collapse of the entire countries, and post-communist transformation seem to have conserved the role of international migration as an important life option in the region. The communist modernization, did not use the export of surplus labor into the more developed areas, as capitalist one did in peripheral European countries, and blocked such migrations for political reasons.

Now they share not only Eastern European background like 100 years ago but also memory of Holocaust, communist and postcommunist experience and Europeaness – whiteness that became a differentiating element only in the era of global migrations.

Poor professionals and top rank laborers. Post-Soviet Jewish and Polish immigrants on a NYC job market.

According to the U.S. 2000 census data, Russian and Ukrainian immigrants' position on the New York City job market is different than that of the Polish immigrants. Among those who participate in the labor market, post-Soviet and Polish immigrants are located on extreme positions. Adjusting the categories of immigrants developed by Alba and Nee (2005) to Eastern Europeans in New York City, the former could be classified as a poor professional while the latter – as a top rank laborer.

Alba and Nee argued convincingly that the new wave of mass immigration to the U.S. in the late 20th century brought about new types of immigrants that did not exist 100 years ago during the previous wave of immigration. Unlike the industrial economy based on Fordist way of manufacturing that needed immigrants to provide simple and routinized tasks, the U.S. postindustrial economy, still hungry for the unskilled service laborers, provide a space for the high human capital immigrants – professionals and entrepreneurs. Professionals are immigrants who enter the U.S. already with sophisticated skills acquired in the higher education institutions, often are English proficient and able to join American middle or upper middle class right at the entrance of the job market. This type of immigrant is associated with Asian groups but post-Soviet European immigrants fit the pattern as well. Especially the Russian and Ukrainian male's human capital measured by education and occupation is high.

Immigrants from Russia and Ukraine are better educated than most of the other immigrant groups in New York City (Table 2). Only among Filipino and Indian immigrants, classical professional groups, the share of college graduates is higher.

Amongst the immigrant groups, the Filipinos and the Russians most often occupy the prestigious positions of managers and specialists – even more often than the native New Yorkers. Amongst the male immigrants, the highest level of employment on highest occupational positions has been reached by the Ukrainians and the Indians.

Post-Soviet model of an immigrant-professional diverge from the classical one, as Alba and Nee constructed it, that best reflects in New York City the standing of Filipinos and Indians. The high level of education in this group is not accompanied by post-Soviet immigrants' high English proficiency and does not translate into high income (Table 3). By measures of average household income, percent of persons in poverty and percent of households with public assistance income, the post-Soviet immigrants belong to the poorest ones, along with those from the least educated Latin American groups from Dominican Republic, Honduras and Mexico.

Polish immigrants' educational and occupational profile resembles the traditional type of an immigrant-laborer. The share of college graduates among them is higher than among the classical laborer groups from Latin American countries, but only slightly higher than among Italians and Greeks, the older European immigrants from traditionally peripheral countries with uninterrupted history of labor migrations in the 19th and 20th centuries, and much lower than among the top groups. Polish immigrants' household income are relatively low, only slightly better than the classical laborer groups and lag behind those of the wealthiest Indians and Filipinos as well as older and less educated European groups. While among the male immigrants, the highest income groups' – Italians and Greeks' – employment structure shows only slight overrepresentation in construction and building maintenance, Polish male immigrants' position in this sector stands far apart from the rest of immigrant groups. Almost 40% of employed Polish male immigrants worked in this one sector alone.

The construction business is, as Roger Waldinger's (1996) research shows, one of the most appreciated sector by the male working class – immigrant and native born. It provides the best paid jobs among those available to men without much professional credentials. Polish male immigrants' outstandingly strong position in this sector, combined with relatively low level of education, sets the group among laborers (rather then professionals or entrepreneurs) but the top rank ones. Another feature that sets Poles apart from the rest of laborer type of immigrant groups, is a relatively low percent of persons in poverty and of households whose income includes public assistance (Table 3). It is lower than the one among post-Soviets and most of Latin American groups and on a similar level to West Indian groups. Paradoxically, in this respect Polish immigrants are much more similar to the wealthiest Filipino and Indian professionals than post-Soviet immigrants are.

What sets Polish immigrants from the prototypical Latin American laborers from Dominican Republic, Honduras and Mexico but also the old European groups and make them closer to better doing West Indian ones is that a relatively low percent of college graduates is accompanied by a relatively low share of the least educated, those with less than high school completed. But Polish men's income is on average higher than for the whole group and gives way only to the incomes of the professionals (Indians, Filipinos, Russians, Ukrainians) and the oldest European groups of Italians and Greeks.

On the other hand, Polish female income level and occupational profile is similar to the one of West Indians: from Jamaica, Guyana, Haiti and Trinidad & Tobago. About 40% of them work in service sector, although the share of those working in managerial and professional posts is higher among the West Indians. All enjoy relatively high incomes. Although in all these groups, male earnings exceed, on average, female ones. The difference between male and female earnings is, however, much higher in Polish case, over $7,000, while for West Indian groups it is about $3,000. West Indian strong position among immigrants-laborers is importantly a result of female immigrants' occupational success in curving a niche in public health care sector. In Polish case this is the male burden to a greater degree (The Newest New Yorkers: 160-172).

The two post-communist groups share some characteristics but I see no reasonable explanation that would connect these features with communist or post-communist legacy.

Poles, Russians and Ukrainians share also a middle level of self-employment and relatively low level of government sector employment among the top 20 immigrant groups in the city. Poles and Russians have the highest percent of non-family households, 39.5% and 34.2% respectively, but Ukrainians are close to immigrant average with 28.9% of their households being a non-family ones. The two common post-communist groups, both male and female, have the lowest labor force participation rate. This makes them similar to the other European groups who, however, are on average 10 years older than them. Although Europeans make the oldest immigrant group in the city, there are more children among the post-communist groups than among the Italians and Greeks.

Although the Europeans are the oldest among the top 20 immigrant groups in the city, only in case of Italians, Greeks and Poles it is connected with the long tradition of immigration and comparative advantage on the *immigrant* job market. Although a large share of legal immigrants from Eastern Europe came to the U.S. in the 1990s, it is only in case of Ukrainians and Russians that the figure is a majority – about 70%. Polish immigrant population, on the other hand, is more divided in terms of decade of entry – more than 1/3 of them came before 1980, about 1/5 in the 1980s and more than 2/5 in the 1990s (Table 1). On the other hand, in the post-1980 period, Italian and Greek immigration dramatically dropped. This situates Polish immigrants in-between older immigrants from European peripheral countries with long – uninterrupted by communism – tradition of labor migrations and newer immigrants from European post-communist countries, rather than clearly on the side of post-communist one.

Affinity to old European immigrant groups could serve as an explanatory factor of occupational position only in case of Poles. Polish males much more often than other groups work in construction and maintenance of buildings, two old sectors that successfully made it through the post-industrial transformation in New York City economy. Since the 19th century, this sector has been dominated by the white immigrants: Irishmen and the Italians (Binder & Rimers 1990). My survey of the job announcements in *Nowy Dziennik*, the most popular Polish daily in New York indicate that the Poles entered this sector in the 1980's, at the eve of mass immigration from the non-European countries, when they were still one of the largest immigrant groups in the city.

Strong position of the Polish immigrant men in construction and building maintenance sector points to the continuity of Polish labor migration and, what is more, to white ethnic solidarity and succession. It should be seen, I think, as a testimony to the fact that this was Polish immigrants' membership in the white ethnic groups that facilitated the ethnic succession from the wealthier Irish and Italian men to the newer immigrants from Poland.

As the most desired sector among laborers, it has been an object of fierce competition in the course of impressive history of construction in New York City. As Waldinger shows, the system of recruiting by recommendation Irish and Italian family members and friends as well as segregated labor unions, did not allow African Americans to enter the sector until the 1960s. Even later, despite the affirmative action policies, construction has remained dominated in New York City by white ethnics and their immigrant cousins. "Construction became an ethnic niche for successive waves of white immigrants and their descendants, who, once entrenched in the industry, succeeded in using both informal and formal means to exclude blacks" (Waldinger 1996: 205).

As I indicated above, official statistics, in which authorized immigrants are most probably overrepresented[2], indicate that they share with old European groups indicators of stability and 'in-rootness' and a low poverty and welfare enrolment level accompanied by low level of living in overcrowded environment (The Newest: 153). The succession in construction business and the above indicators, could suggest that Polish immigrants, and especially male ones, although less often than old Europeans are self-employed or work in governmental sector

---

2   Several Greenpoint community leaders that I interviewed complained that Polish immigrants do not register with the census and therefore Polish community is underrepresented in the official statistics. They explained this reluctance with the communist legacy and suspicion toward governmental enterprises. The leaders were also convinced that illegal immigrants who were concerned with the possibility of deportation were less willing to report to the census takers. Therefore, the official statistics most probably give a picture of rather legal immigrants than those who overstayed their tourist visas or were smuggled through the border and those who have stayed longer and had a chance to get familiar with the American institutions and regulations. That the census data on Polish immigrants is not completely correct is visible in the case of Polish arrivals in New York City in the 1980s.

(The Newest: 165) once in New York City, are ready to join and inherit from the white ethnics.

Finally, the difference between the two groups that is probably responsible for the difference in professional standing of the immigrants of comparable education and English proficiency is their legal status. Overwhelming majority of post-Soviet immigrants entered the New York City as refugees. The figure for the period of most intensive migration period in the 1990s is 85.8%. Taking into account only those Polish migrants who decided to report to the U.S. census, that are most probably rather legal immigrants, in the 1980s decade that started with Solidarity movement and the martial law of 1981, refugees made about 40% of all admitted while family reunification was a basis of admission of 30% of immigrants. In the post-communist 1990s these were diversity visa holders who made the largest group, almost 47%. (The Newest, 28-29)

Table 1. Decade of entry of the largest European immigrant groups in New York City in 2000

	Rank	Number	Percent arriving in 1990-2000	Percent arriving in 1980-1990	Percent arriving before 1980
Russia	10	81.408	66,9	17,0	16,1
Italy	11	72.481	9,6	6,8	83,7
Ukraine	13	69.727	71,3	15,4	13,4
Poland	15	65.999	43,4	20,9	35,7
Greece	20	29.805	11,2	13,2	75,6

Source: Newest New Yorkers 2000: 13

Table 2. Human capital of the top 20 source of the foreign born in New York City in 2000. Population 25 and over

Rank	Country	Percent not English proficient	Percent college graduates or more	Percent less than high school graduates
1	Dominican Republic	70	7,7	56,2
2	China	74,6	24,4	45,4
3	Jamaica	1,7	15,9	31,3
4	Guyana	3,1	12,8	34,6
5	Mexico	76,2	5,0	65,3
6	Ecuador	71,2	8,7	47,2
7	Haiti	49,9	16,1	31,2
8	Trinidad & Tobago	1,5	13,0	27,0
9	Columbia	69,1	14,8	35,5
10	Russia	58	45,6	14,6
11	Italy	50,8	12,6	53,3
12	Korea	69,8	40,9	16,6
13	Ukraine	70,6	42,8	15,2
14	India	36,7	49,9	20,1
15	Poland	56,9	20,7	30,7
16	Philippines	24,9	65,3	6,6
17	Bangladesh	58,6	39,2	25,5
18	Pakistan	51,8	30,8	32,4
19	Honduras	64,5	6,3	57,7
20	Greece	56,5	15,3	49,1

Source: The Newest New Yorkers 2000: 154

Table 3. Socio-economic situation of the top 20 source of the foreign born in New York City in 2000. Source countries are ranked according to median household income

	Median household income	Ratio: sub-group to total	Average workers per household	Percent of persons in poverty	Percent of households with public assistance income
Total, New York City	37.700	1,00		21,1	7,5
Native-born	39.900	1,06		21,5	7,8
Foreign-born	35.000	0,93		20,4	7,0
Philippines	70.500	1,87	1,6	5,3	2,0
India	50.000	1,33	1,5	14,4	2,7
Greece	43.930	1,17	1,2	13,4	1,8
Guyana	41.960	1,11	1,5	13,4	5,5
Italy	39.500	1,05	1,00	10,4	2,2
Jamaica	38.500	1,02	1,3	14,6	6,0
Pakistan	36.500	0,97	1,4	26,1	3,1
Trinidad & Tobago	36.300	0,96	1,3	16,5	4,9
Ecuador	36.000	0,95	1,5	21,9	8,0
Haiti	36.000	0,95	1,3	19,1	5,9
Korea	35.200	0,93	1,3	17,7	2,9
Columbia	35.000	0,93	1,3	20,2	6,2
China	33.320	0,88	1,5	21,7	4,5
Bangladesh	33.300	0,88	1,5	31	5,1
Poland	33.100	0,88	0,9	14,1	2,9
Mexico	32.000	0,85	1,8	32	12,5
Russia	28.000	0,74	1,0	22,2	8,3
Honduras	27.000	0,72	1,1	27,7	13,1
Dominican Republic	25.300	0,67	1,1	30,9	18,6
Ukraine	23.100	0,61	0,9	20,8	9,5

Source: The Newest New Yorkers 2000: 159

Economic culture

The fieldwork research in the New York City largest Polish immigrant community in Brooklyn's northern neighborhood of Greenpoint convinced me that the profile of the Polish immigrant labor force, with its male specialization in construction, could be even closer to the top rank laborer one than the census data can recognize as many of them are believed to be unauthorized. Even if a similar tendency of ignoring the U.S. census call in 2000 was true for illegal Russian and Ukrainian immigrants, the share of the refugee population among the latter's largest 1990 cohort decides that the general poor professional profile would not be questioned.

My own qualitative research including 54 interviews with community leaders and 27 – with domestic workers conducted in 2006 and 2010, and the somewhat older research on post-Soviet immigrants in New York City including its summary prepared by Annelise Orleck (Orleck 2000) confirm the census based picture of a post-Soviet poor professional and Polish top rank laborer.

About the research

As it should, it introduces human touch and bring more details on the Polish and post-Soviet immigrant experience on the city job market. What is more, this research provides explanations (independent variables) of the fundamental difference between the two groups that goes beyond the census data. In Polish immigrant case, it also gives an insight into the work experience of the unauthorized immigrants who, according to the leaders, make a significant share of the Polish community but would hesitate reporting to the U.S. census.

The most important discovery beyond census that my own research brought is that the leaders were almost unanimously convinced that the domestic and office cleaning had become a Polish female immigrant specialization on the city job market as much as the construction and renovation jobs had for Polish men, that the census data identified. Several male leaders were also convinced that Polish men did better than women, exactly because of their access to and talent for the construction and building maintenance crafts.

> Typical jobs for the [Polish] immigrants – cleaning, elderly care, and for the men – construction (L1).
> Women are one thing, men are another. Women (...) mostly work somewhere with a broom and a mop at least in the beginning until they learn the language (...) but men have got it much better I guess, because Polish men have a good flair for construction and all those construction related professions [...] and principally everybody coming with papers or not, with the language or not can get into a construction firm, unless he is completely unfit (L3).

On the other hand, the research on post-Soviet immigrants brings the picture of them as New York City's newest professionals. Younger of them "by the early 1980s had begun to make their presence felt throughout New York as physicians, entrepreneurs, stock analysts, industrial researchers, accountants, and computer specialists" (Orleck 2000: 120). Clerical and service jobs that the older professionals had to take were signs of terrible downward mobility. The qualitative research results brought a deeper sense of the importance of difference in formal education that the census data analysis identified. It allowed me to locate the other three factors of difference: one from the human capital department: **economic culture** related to the formal education but also steaming also from the city/countryside experience and social class background, one the **social capital** type: assistance provided by the American ethnic groups and immigrant oriented organizations, and third: **legal status**.

Although some leaders talked with irony about the Polish Greenpoint immigrants as *the top of their dreams is to work in a building [maintenance] (L15)*, others, including those with experience in such jobs themselves appreciated the job of office buildings cleaners. This work, as some of my interlocutors claimed, corresponds with the Polish economic culture – hard, systematic, predictable work and scrimp. Contrary to the cleaning of private apartments, whose owners could be poor and stingy, cleaning of the office buildings is not only well paid, but also connected with the protection by the labor union, health insurance and pension plan. Additionally, the evening job in an office building can be combined with jobs performed during the day time. This sector, traditionally immigrant and black, has become an object of desire and competition in times of new mass immigration of laborers since the 1980s (Waldinger 1996). Additional difficulty to get the job is that the access is limited to authorized immigrants. The office buildings cleaners constitute an aristocracy on the huge and diversified New York cleaning market.

As one of the community leaders with Ph.D. in humanities, now retired but with experience in variety of jobs, including office cleaning gives the rationale of this job desirability to immigrants: it's stable, well-paid and not exhaustive in comparison to other jobs available to English improficient immigrants. It fits the best the life strategy based on long hour work, saving for a house (or several of them).

> One of the most cherished jobs here is the job in the building (...) cleaning those huge skyscrapers in Manhattan. Now, how does it work? The job starts after the office is closed, that is after five (...) if they start the work at 6 pm, they are back around 1, 2 am. (...) It was well paid, (...) the union controlled it and it was difficult to get there (...) It was relatively easy (...) job, 'cause one can swing/wave with a duster... Lot of men also worked in buildings as let's say janitors (...) doormen, cleaning those hallways etc. And I know several men who bought two or three houses thanks to that job. Having the insurance and putting aside, let's say, some money every week, they could accumulate it and then invest, so until now there has still been a great demand for that job. (...) They are hard workers, scrimp that money, put it in the bank, but don't know what to do with it next, so they count on some small interest, but they want to sleep calmly" (L17)

Being accustomed to modest or even humiliating life conditions that results in minimal consumption and high savings is another important characteristic of the Polish immigrants' economic culture, indicated by a small ethnic business owner with the university degree who originated from other area that the migrants she thought made the majority in Greenpoint:

> Well yes, most of the people coming here from the Białystok, Kielce, Rzeszów areas, lived in Poland on a farm and tried to survive on four chickens and one cow. And coming here, they've got a job that's less exhaustive [lżejsza] than what they did back in Poland, and they can support themselves, their families, send money to Poland and build a house (L31)

Second aspect of Polish immigrants' economic culture that my respondents underlined is that the jobs in which the Poles have specialized in New York City are based on skills acquired in their households and farms back in Poland. New York City became a place that these skills could be for the first time commercialized, become a commodity that can be sold. In case of women, female leaders and especially domestic workers themselves often stated with pride that they were clean and diligent (meaning 'cleaner and more diligent than other immigrant women') which gave them comparative advantage on the domestic cleaning market.

> We are simply clean in general as women, we like everything to be sorted out. An acquaintance of mine, who is a curator in one of the five museums here, those big ones in New York City, who's got a beautiful house (...), told me 'no one would iron my

beddings, because they don't do it here, but I've got a Polish lady who irons my beddings' (L1)
Polish women are highly appreciated as nannies and are cheaper than...they are more appreciated than the Russian ones, from what I've heard, they are diligent (L2)

The apartment cleaning job, despised by the leaders, is considered attractive by the female workers themselves as they compare it with their situation back at home in the old country. It is a sort of discovery for them that the ordinary skills acquired by managing their own household can have a commercial value and could lead to personal emancipation as well as financial independence. They discover that their domestic work as cleaners, baby sitters and elderly care providers could have a market value and not the lowest one. If that is not a live-in job, their working hours are clearly separated from the free time – an unknown phenomenon both in the village households and in the homes with children, as was underlined by one of an elderly female immigrant, who used to work as a domestic worker in New York City:

And so we were talking, talking about America, and 'so, would you like to come [to America]?' (...) I say I would like to, and he says: but you know that you would have to be a servant there, and I say look, I am a servant here, standing behind the counter, I go home where I've got five children and I'm again a servant, doing everything by myself (R8)

The men for their part, especially those from the countryside, are able to renovate, and even build a house single handedly. Immigrants associated their capability to perform hard manual labor with the kind of training they underwent in their families' rural households:
That I endured it physically... (...) I was not afraid of tough manual labor as we, as villagers, had a piece of farm land, 60 acres so we grew potatoes there and cereals, and we had a cow, and pigs too, right, so one had to take care of all that (L34), recalled one of the middle aged leaders, a teacher and a musician, English improficient whose initially worked in New York City in a feather-processing plant and in an envelope factory. Similar opinions were expressed by another leader, Ph.D. in history, English improficient, employed now in one of the Polish immigrant organizations, who worked in building demolitions and later in construction for several years:

I was simply not afraid of physical labor, for I was brought up in a village, exhausting, manual labor all the time. I was not afraid of physical labor. And the work was hard! Awful. For that was hammering a concrete on a garage to re-made a roof (L22).

Thirdly, the community leaders, often commented on Polish attitude toward self-employment. Among the leaders I interviewed, all of 24 owners of businesses – usually small and ethnic – in Greenpoint, emphasized that these were the immigrants of the 1980s who more often than earlier ones turned to self-employment, including contracting companies in construction. Their intuition (confirmed by Erdmans, Jałowiecki in Okólski Grabowska 2009) was that there in this cohort there were more urbanities and university degree holders than among earlier ones. Only one of them, an owner of a tourist agency in Greenpoint, however, argued that the stereotype of Polish immigrants "with a broom and a hammer' was unfair and false.

> More and more people have the imaginativeness and the courage to open up their own business, really, I see that in my own backyard, in apartment house we live in. My husband [who was a building maintenance supervisor] has been renting a piece of cubbyhole to a Pole, who was illegal here and who opened up his own business. (...) He was sanding floors for some years, he even paid taxes [...] and later at some point when he started missing Poland and said he was leaving and 'What are you going to do with the firm? It's a prosperous one!' and he was making a very good money and had lots of commissions (...) Anyway he sold his firm and even sold it quite good, it appears that he sold it for about $ 100.000 to someone, can you imagine ... (...) I think that now, at the moment, there are about 20 firms that have sprung from that first one, people simply mustered and now they're owning their own vans, their own machines, their own employees and all this has expanded so that each one of them now is employing 5 to 10 people ... all this out of one small firm (L31).

Finally, my interviews show that unauthorized status of an immigrant limits the immigrant's occupational options in many ways.

Post-Soviet Jewish economic culture

As Orleck shows, post-Soviet Jewish immigrants also experience professional degradation, difficulties connected with the nostrification of diplomas and working bellow the qualifications is frequent, especially amongst the female-migrants from the Soviet Union. These are, however, problems characteristic for professionals with a refugee status. "Many adult women have gone through periods of profound depression, mourning the loss of respect, professional identity, and careers that they will probably never have again (...) Such dramatic loss of professional status, coupled with frustration over the inability to speak English and initial incompetence at such basic tasks as job hunting, shopping and reading official mail, has caused severe emotional and psychological problems for many older working-age immigrants" (Orleck 2000: 121-122).

The research shows that Post-Soviet Jewish immigrants-professional differ in their attitude toward occupational prestige. The difference was noticed by my respondents, both leaders and non-leaders, with a mixture of resentment and admiration. A middle age, English proficient, a Polish engineer, with years of experience as domestic cleaner, baby sitter, building supervisor and home attendant in New York City metropolitan area recalled: *When I said to a Russian granny [for whom she worked as a home attendant – AS] once that (...:) 'maybe granny has got such a person who could help'.[She replied to that:] What? My grand daughter to clean? Only Poles could work like that* (R3).

While it was quite appreciated job among Polish immigrants-laborers, for the elderly post-Soviet professionals "a minimum-wage job as a companion and chore worker for an elderly woman" (Orleck 2000: 121) brought a frustrating sense of degradation and often became source of clinical depression.

The Jewish migrants are not only better educated than Polish ones but probably more often stem from big urban agglomerations than the Poles. During the first – the most elite, as Orleck thinks - wave of Soviet migrations at the beginning of 1970's, not less than 85% of the newcomers "originated from Russia and Ukraine's biggest cities – Odessa, Moscow, Leningrad and Kiyov. [This group consisted of] assimilated urban professionals who were doing rather well. For them the departure was a way to escape the anti-Semitism in the USSR, the limitations they were facing to their professional development and to the education of their children as well as all the more severe lacks of food supplies affecting all inhabitants of the USSR" (2001: 115). There is no estimation of the proportion of the urbanities among Polish immigrants. The community leaders, including those who work with or for New York City Poles beyond Greenpoint, however, were clear about the Polish New Yorkers' predominantly rural and least developed regions origins in Eastern Poland. Probability of it is high as rural population from these regions have long been overrepresented among international migrants to the U.S. and Germany and now to open job markets of European Union countries (Okólski, Grabowska-Lusińska 2009).

Finally, my research shows that the respondents with the experience in domestic or office cleaning, both authorized and unauthorized immigrants, appreciated these jobs by comparing them the with alternative jobs available to immigrants-laborers in the U.S., newcomers with much English proficiency and other marketable skills: in factories and plants, e.g. sweatshops of garment industry that again became an important immigrant sector in New York City in the 1980s, or at the back of stores and restaurants. (Smith 2005; Grasmuck i Pessar 1991; Waldinger 1986, 1996). Immigrants compared them also with the dead end jobs and poverty in communist Poland or prospects of unemployment in post-communist Poland. They value cleaning jobs for higher wage, variety of tasks and places, more autonomy and less supervision, and control over the work pace.[3] Unlike the community leaders who lament Polish specialization in cleaning, the workers themselves, unconcerned with the very low prestige of the job (Gilbert 2007 after GSS 2000). It could be seen as an element of the working class attitude toward job, as Mary Erdmans (2003) convincingly argued following the classics of the research in social class. It is also a consequence of transnational character of immigrants' social class as Michał Garapich did (2006). In a figure of immigrant-laborer the two meet. As a working class member, a cleaner or construction worker without much of formal education treats her or his job as a source of income and survival rather than prestige. To associate one's job with prestige and treat it as a source of identity is characteristic of the educated middle and upper middle class. Also, the existential situation of a migrant, especially temporary and unauthorized one such as many of the Polish ones, is to take the prestige and broader social recognition into brackets, suspend it, treat it as non-existent. Additionally, as Morawska's research on Poles in Philadelphia shows, Polish immigrants engaged in transnational activities, and this is true for some of my respondents, compensate for the low occupational prestige in the

---

3   I write more about Polish Greenpoint immigrants' experience as cleaners in New York City in: Sosnowska, Cleaning and the City. Polish Female Immigrants on a New York City Job Market (manuscript)

U.S. with their high status in Poland where they are treated with admiration and respect as successful individuals or remittance providers (Morawska 2004).

Post-Soviet Jewish immigrants-professionals, if experience downward social mobility and suffer from the loss of prestige, do not compensate with transnational connections but with the quality of education and occupational position of their children. Since their migrations more often than Polish ones had resettlement character and almost always legal character, sacrifice for children means bringing them to the U.S. to provide them with better life opportunities in a safer, more just and richer country. For a Polish immigrant-laborer, especially unauthorized one who migrated without a family and with intention to save, send money and return, sacrifice for children means sending remittances, similarly to other laborers from Latin America and West Indies (e.g. Smith 2005).

Social capital. Ethnic NGO assistance

The Jewish immigrants from the former Soviet Union have not only a higher cultural capital, but also a higher social one. The researchers unanimously underline the key role played by the Jewish-American organizations in the refugees' political and professional adjustment in and the United States (por. Markowitz 1993; Orleck 2001; Zeltzer-Zubida 2004). They also underline the legal and practical help provided in the U.S. by the Hebrew Immigrant Aid Society and New York Association for New Americans (NYANA). The latter has been especially important to those who settled in New York City. The resettlement was organized carefully, to provide smooth acculturation and professional adaptation of the newcomers, "in historically Jewish neighborhoods, where (...) the local populations would be most welcoming and where a social service system was already in place to care for the Jewish elderly. (...) NYANA assigned vocational counselors to each working-age adult, tested them for English proficiency, and enrolled them in English as a Second Language courses. (...) The agency then offered vocational training In business and accounting, industrial trades, carpentry, building maintenance, and food service. It also provided retraining and licensing courses for engineers, computer scientists, and health care professionals" (Orleck 2001: 119).

The level of the Polish social capital is substantially lower. The leaders of the Polish Greenpoint community with whom I spoke in 2006, unanimously complained about the weakness of the Polish-American organizations, comparing them with envy with the Jewish ones. It seems that the ethnic Catholic churches with services in Polish language are – just like 100 years ago – the main place of Polish gathering and a source of the Polish social capital (Babiński 2006, Chałasiński 1935). According to the head of one of the two Polish churches in Greenpoint, *this* [Polish – A.S.] *culture does not have such cultural means like the ones that the Jews have got, their own centers, halls.... It is all going on around the church, (...) they can come [to the church], get together in the church, [after the service] talk to one another, have a look at one another, be a part of the crowd,* feel that Polishness, (...) because there is no other Polish organization. (L24) Both the NGO activists that were disappointed with low donation from the migrants and the migrants who expected more generous assistance from the organizations complained just the same about the weakness of the Polish organizations. The most important ethnic organization providing assistance to the needy and immigrants in New York City is the Polish-Slavic Center (PSC) with headquarter in Greenpoint. It was founded in 1973 by a priest Leon Tołczyk. It has been financed by the contributions of the members of the Polish-Slavic Federal Credit Union as well as by the city subsidies. At present, its programs include a senior program, English as a Second Language courses and legal advice, almost all covered by the municipal budget. My fieldwork indicate that the PSC serves mostly to long term immigrants and has never undertaken resettlement actions on a scale comparable to that of NYANA.[4]

Finally, the fieldwork research indicates that the difference between of the two groups in professional performance steaming from the difference in cultural and social capital, is reinforced by the legal status that American immigration policies offered to the two groups.

Legal immigrant and refugee regulations since 1970s

The mass Eastern European migrations to the U.S. at the turn of the 19th and 20th century slowed down by the I World War and were almost completely blocked by the immigration laws introduced in the 1920's. The American quota system and the passport restrictions introduced by the communist regimes in Eastern Europe successfully diminished the immigration flow up until the 1970's.[5]

"Wakacjusze", refugees and the diversity immigrants

In the post-quota era, the new categories of immigrants have become important for the understanding of the Eastern Europeans' situation in the U.S.: 'wakacjusze' – unauthorized immigrants (who entered the U.S. on a tourist visa and overstayed it or crossed the border illegally), political refugees and diversity immigrants.

Since the 1970's the 'wakacjusze' have become a Polish specialty in the U.S. (Erdmans 1998; Iglicka 2007; Babiński 2006).

---

[4] Several leaders were convinced that in these respects it is much better in Chicago. However, the research conducted by Erdmans (1998) in the 1980s and 1990s shows that the animosities amongst the various organizations, and especially the prejudices between the immigrants and the Polish-American ethnic group in the States are the dominant type of relation also in Chicago. The lack of well structured life has also been confirmed by Barbara Sakson's (2005) Chicago respondents.

[5] Jewish and Polish 'displaced persons' were accepted in the 1930's and 1940's within the quotas, amounting to more than 100.000 people.

Erdmans estimates that about 1/3 of those coming with the tourist visa prolonged their stay, which gives the number of around 250.000 'wakacjusze' from Poland in the U.S. in 1991, on the eve of the post-communist era. The number of earning-oriented departures for the U.S. increased right after 1989.[6] Taken all together, the decisive majority of the immigrants between 1960 and 1993 (about one million) arrived as tourists, while a smaller group came as legal immigrants, majority of whom came in under family preferences rather than occupation preferences offered by the 1965 immigration act (Erdmans 1998: 58, 65). Krystyna Iglicka's research on the participants of the summer Work and Travel programs shows how much Polish students associate their compatriots' position in the United States with 'being illegal' and the discomfort of being 'wakacjusz' (Iglicka 2007).

In 1980 the American policy towards refugees was systematized. A United Nations definition of a refugee as a person who has justified fear of persecution in the country of origin was accepted. On the basis of the Refugee Law from 1980, they acquired the right not only to legal stay and work, but also to a periodical federal financial aid. So after 1980, the U.S. refugee policies became one more tool of the Cold War struggle and privileged those fleeing the communist countries. This opportunity was seized by refugees from Cuba, Vietnam, Laos and Cambodia as well as from Eastern Europe.

The 30,000 refugees in the U.S., just like in other Western countries, were only a part, although probably the most characteristic one, of the overall 2-milion migration from Poland in the 1980's (Kaczmarczyk 2005: 125). Erdmans argues, and this was confirmed by my own interviews, that those who were granted the refugee status differed from the 'wakacjusze' not that much in regard to their political activity as in the knowledge how to acquire the refugee status. This went hand in hand with better education, urban origin, determination to resettle permanently, lack of family ties abroad and the readiness to pass through refugee camps in one of the European countries (Erdmans 1998).

Erdmans is convinced that in case of all immigrants of the communist period, economic motivations were mixed with political and existential ones. A key motivation of the migrants was the fantastic conversion rate of the dollar into zloty. In the 1960's and 1970's the "minimal weekly wage in the USA more or less equaled the annual salary in Poland" (Erdmans 1998: 61). In the 1980's, and especially in the 1900's, the dollar rate was not that high but it was still very attractive.

The currency rate, the difficulties with obtaining the visa and the high travel costs created some sort of a mythology out of the American New York City expeditions: heroism of the step into the unknown, shock of the first days, life in crowded cellar-apartments, run down neighborhoods, cleaning or renovation

---

6   Legal immigrants arrived on the basis of immigration act of 1990 that increased the number of immigrants admitted under numerical limitations and provided for "diversity immigrants', defined as aliens form countries that were adversely affected by the 1965 Immigration Act", that is primarily for Europeans. In result, between 1990 and 1993 more than 90.000 of legal immigrants from Poland were admitted "while in the three previous decades combined only 201.606" (Erdmans 1998: 65).

jobs in humiliating conditions, fear of deportation, 'hunting cockroaches', sexual and alcoholic excesses, obsessive saving was reflected in the literary and film imagery: *Dolorado* and *Szczuropolacy* by Edward Redliński, or *Szczęśliwego Nowego Jorku* by Sylwester Chęciński, a film made on the basis of the later novel, *Hunting Cockroaches* or a play *Antigone in New York* by Janusz Głowacki. Similar experiences of the *wakacjusze* are depicted in the research conducted by the team from the Centre for Migration Studies (University of Warsaw) in the municipalities of Perlejewo and Mońki at the end of the 1990's. "The job was treated as an ultimate value, and together with the growing problems of obtaining it the phenomenon of 'buying the job' appeared. (...) The work was for the most part difficult, the harsh treatment by the employers was a norm, but the awareness of the value of the work had a decisive importance". (...) A couple of years stays were the dominant model ('once you undertake something you have to stick to it'), some of which eventually led to resettlement and starting a new family which obviously meant a tragedy for the members of the family remaining in the country" (Hirszfeld and Kaczmarczyk 1999: 11).

The refugee migrations played a definitely key role in the history of foreign migrations from the Soviet Union and the successor countries. Vast majority of those to whom the Soviet government allowed departure at the beginning of the 1970's, as well as those who arrived after 1991, were given the refugee status in the United States. The special legal status of that group enjoyed to that extent only Cubans. The refugee status is very friendly to the potential workers, who receive "federal subsidies for their accommodation, education and professional training" (Orleck 2001: 113). It also encourages the migration of elderly and children by granting them public assistance.

Conclusions

The very different position of the two immigrant groups from the post-communist countries on the New York City job market: post-Soviet Jewish average standing as a poor professional and Polish average standing as a top rank professional should be explained primarily by the huge difference in human capital measured by the level of formal education. However, the more detailed analysis shows that this initial difference has been reinforced by the economic culture and acceptable job image as well as support from ethnic organizations and American immigration policies. On the whole, the post-Soviet Jews rely on their high human and social capital and a refugee status, while Poles take advantage of their ethnic group's affinity to New York City white ethnics and skills acquired in their households.

The difference between Polish and post-Soviet immigrants in NYC does not reflect the difference between Poland and Soviet Union, as Polish immigrants often think, or the difference between Poles and Soviet Jews, as educated New Yorkers think sometimes. American immigration laws made a selection of different groups of immigrants out of these two societies plus, once in the country, provided them with different opportunities.

References

Alba, Richard, and Victor Nee. *Remaking the American Mainstream: Assimilation and Contemporary Immigration*. Cambridge, Massachusetts: Harvard University Press 2005.
Babiński, Grzegorz, and Henryk Chałupczak, ed. *Diaspora polska w procesach globalizacji. Stan i perspektywy badań*. Kraków: Grell, 2006.
Bodnar, John, et al. *Lives of Their Own: Blacks, Italians, and Poles in Pittsburgh, 1900-1960*. Urbana: University of Illinois Press, 1982.
Bukowczyk, John. *And My Children Did Not Know Me. A History of the Polish-Americans*. Bloomington and Indianapolis: Indiana University Press, 1987.
Daniels, Roger. *Coming to America. A History of Immigration and Ethnicity in American Life*. New York: HarperCollins, 1990.
Diner, Hasia. *Lower East Side Memories. A Jewish place in America*. Princeton: Princeton University Press, 2000.
Diner, Hasia. *The Jews of the United States, 1654-2000*. Berkeley: University of California Press, 2006.
Erdmans, Mary. "Pozarynkowe warunki osiągania satysfakcji z pracy." *Przegląd Polonijny* no 2 (1996).
Erdmans, Mary. *Opposite Poles. Immigrants and ethnics in Polish Chicago, 1976-1990*. University Park: Pennsylvania State University Press, 1998.
Golab, Caroline. *Immigrant Destinations*. Philadelphia: Temple University Press, 1977.
Grasmuck, Sherri and Patricia Pessar. *Between Two Islands. Dominican International Migration*. Berkeley, Los Angeles, Oxford: University of California Press, 1991.
Hirszfeld, Ziemowit, and Paweł Kaczmarczyk. "Ekonomiczne i społeczne skutki migracji na poziomie mikrospołecznym. Wnioski z badania terenowego w gminie Perlejewo." *CMR Working Papers*, Nr 21, Warszawa (1999).
Iglicka, Krystyna. "Badanie nad migracjami zarobkowymi z Polski po 1 maja 2004 roku do USA." *Biuletyn Migracyjny- Dodatek*, no 15 (Listopad 2007).
Jaroszyńska-Kirchmann, Anna. *The Exile Mission. The Polish Political Diaspora and Polish Americans, 1939-1956*. Athens: Ohio University Press, 2004.
Kaczmarczyk, Paweł. *Migracje zarobkowe Polaków w dobie przemian*. Warszawa: Wydawnictwo Uniwersytetu Warszawskiego, 2005.
Lipset, Seymour. *American Exceptionalism. A Double-edged Sword*. New York: W.W. Norton, 1996.
Markowitz, Fran. *A Community in Spite of Itself; Soviet Jewish Emigres in New York*. Washington: Smithsonian Institution Press, 1993.
Mierzyńska, Zofia. *Wakacjuszka*. Warszawa: Polonia, 1990.
Morawska, Ewa. "Exploring Diversity in Immigrant Assimilation and Transnationalism: Poles and Russian Jews in Philadelphia." *The International Migration Review*, vol. 38, Issue 4 (2004).
Morawska, Ewa. *For bread with butter: the life-worlds of East Central Europeans in Johnstown, Pennsylvania, 1890-1940*. Cambridge and New York: Cambridge University Press, 1985.
Morawska, Ewa. *Insecure Prosperity. Small-town Jews in industrial America, 1890-1940*. Princeton: Princeton University Press, 1996.
Mostwin, Danuta. *Ameryko! Ameryko!*. Toruń: Oficyna Wydawnicza Kucharski, 2004.
Mostwin, Danuta. *Polscy emigranci w USA*. Lublin: KUL, 1991.
Orleck, Annelise. "Soviet Jews: The City's Newest Immigrants Transform New York Jewish Life," in *New Immigrants in New York*. Ed. Nancy Foner. New York: Columbia University Press, 2001.
Pacyga, Dominic A. *Polish Immigrants and Industrial Chicago. Workers on the South Side, 1880-1922*. Columbus : Ohio State University Press, 1991.

Portes, Alejandro and Ruben Rumbaut. *Immigrant America. A Portrait*. Berkeley: University of California Press, 2006.
Redliński, Edward. *Dolorado*. Nowy Jork: Contemporary Images INT'L, 1984.
Redliński, Edward. *Szczuropolacy*. Warszawa: BGW, 1994.
Sakson, Barbara. "Po drugiej stronie Oceanu. Nowi emigranci z Polski w metropolii Chicagowskiej." *CMR Working Papers*, no 5/(63), Warszawa (2005).
Smith, Robert. *Mexican New York. Transnational Lives of New Immigrants*. Berkeley: University of California Press, 2005.
Stola, Dariusz. "Migracje w okresie PRL-u," in *Ludzie na huśtawce. Migracje między peryferiami Polski i Zachodu*. Ed. Ewa Jaźwinska and Marek Okólski. Warszawa: Scholar, 2001.
The Newest New Yorkers. Immigrant New York in the New Millennium. New York: New York City Department of City Planning Population Division, 2004.
Waldinger, Roger. *Through the Eye of the Needle: Immigrants and Enterprise in New York's Garment Trades*. New York: New York University Press, 1986.
Waldinger, Roger. *Still the Promised City? African-Americans and New Immigrants in Postindustrial New York*. Cambridge, Massachusetts: Harvard University Press, 1996.
Zeltzer-Zubida, Aviva. "Affinities and Affiliations: The Many Ways of Being a Russian Jewish American," in *Becoming New Yorkers. Ethnographies of the New Second Generation*. Ed. John Mollenkopf, Mary Waters and Philip Kasinitz. New York: Russell Sage Foundation, 2004.

From Oświęcim to Ellis Island: Jewish and Other Transmigrants and the Evolution of Border Controls Along Germany's Eastern Border, 1885-1914

Tobias Brinkmann (Penn State University)

Since the establishment of migration studies as a (loosely organized) field in the 1960s historians and social scientists covering the period after 1800 have predominantly concentrated on processes of immigration or emigration. In the United States and to a lesser extent in Britain, Australia, France and other countries, which experienced significant immigration in the last two hundred years, scholars examine primarily arrival, community building, and adaptation processes, frequently of a specific group at a specific place. Another closely studied subject is the immigration policy of a specific state. The concentration on arrival and immigration policy is hardly surprising. After 1800 the emerging nation state defined the terms of inclusion and exclusion, of belonging, and access – for its citizens and non-citizens. Immigration has an obvious relevance because of the impact new arrivals made (or are making) on host societies, and the sources are concentrated at the point of arrival and thus relatively easy to retrieve. In contrast, retracing the routes taken by migrants through several countries and determining the causes of migration for larger groups can be challenging. Not all states have kept records on emigrants, let alone transmigrants. In fact, many subjects of the Russian Empire left illegally because it was often difficult and costly to obtain the officially required paperwork.[1]

In the American context, authors tend to concentrate on specific immigrant groups defined by a common ethnicity, frequently their own. Only few studies compare different immigrant groups at the same place or members of one group at different places. Since millions of Irish, Germans, Scandinavians, and Poles left for greener pastures during the long nineteenth century, many for the United States, migration historians in the respective countries of origin concentrated on emigration and its causes. This constellation has led to a fruitful collaboration between scholars working on specific immigrant and ethnic groups in the United States, and their counterparts in Europe who followed "their" people across the Atlantic. Yet for many sending countries, especially in Asia, the research on out-migration has not reached a comparable level.[2]

Representatives of transnational and global history often point to migration as a key field of study. Yet only few migration historians have risen to the challenge. Most are reluctant to venture beyond the boundaries of a specific nation-state or the ethnic paradigm. Apart from comparative research a closer exami-

---

1 Hans Rogger, "Tsarist Policy on Jewish Emigration," *Soviet Jewish Affairs* 3 (1973): 26-36.
2 See for instance: *People in Transit: German Migrations in Comparative Perspective, 1820–1920*, ed. Dirk Hoerder (Cambridge: Cambridge University Press, 1995); on China see: Philip A. Kuhn, *Chinese Among Others: Emigration in Modern Times* (Lanham, MD: Rowman & Littlefield, 2009).

nation of the actual process of migration offers the possibility to broaden the perspective. Immigration and emigration are rather fluid and imprecise terms describing two aspects of the same process. Where one stage ends and the other begins, or if they overlap remains open to discussion. Sojourners and return migrants do not fit into this simplistic framework, not to mention permanent migrants, nomads but also displaced people who cannot not return home or move to a destination of their choice. Illegal migrants and stateless people often cannot officially become immigrants because they do not exist in a legal sense. The terms immigration and emigration betray political and legal origins and do not necessarily reflect the social reality on the ground.[3]

Following migrants around the globe after 1800 on the journey to, within, through, out of, and back to (emerging) states and Empires shines new light on the redefinition of political borders and the emergence of an internationally recognized system of cross border movement. Such an analysis also highlights the obvious but little studied correlation between the (im-)migration policies of different states. In the following paragraphs I will trace the transmigration of Jews and other migrants from Eastern Europe by looking at two crucial "points of passage," the port of Hamburg and two adjacent train stations along the border of Upper Silesia and West Galicia. Until 1918, the former region belonged to Germany's largest state Prussia, and the latter to the Austrian part of the Habsburg monarchy. The train station in the Upper Silesian mining town Myslowitz (Myslowice) was situated only a short walk from the so-called "Dreikaisereck" (Three Emperor's Corner), the spot where the borders of the German, Russian, and Austro-Hungarian Empires met until 1918. Myslowitz was the first German stop for trains originating in Oswiecim or Krakow. Trains from nearby Sosnowiec in the Russian Empire did not touch Myslowitz but went to Kattowitz (Katowice). Until the recent erection of a small monument only a few pre-1914 postcards recalled the history of the "Dreikaisereck." This site was, after all, a powerful symbol of the division of Poland. Fifteen miles further south, the situation could not be more different. Around 1900, Oswiecim was a West Galician border town with a small garrison of Austrian troops. However, it was also an important railroad hub at the center of a circle formed by Central Europe's main cities at the time: Warsaw, Berlin, Vienna, Prague, and Budapest. While few readers of this essay will have even heard of Myslowitz/Myslowice, most will recognize some of the place names associated with Oswiecim, today the site of the Auschwitz-Birkenau Memorial and State Museum. The decision to expand the concentration camp at Oswiecim into a giant extermination facility was in no small part related to the town's location at the center of the European rail network.[4]

---

3   Annemarie Steidl, "Introduction," *European Mobility: Internal, International, and Transatlantic Moves in the 19th and 20th Centuries*, eds. Annemarie Steidl/Josef Ehmer/ Stan Nadel/Hermann Zeitlhofer (eds.), (Göttingen: V&R Unipress, 2009), 7.
4   Deborah Dwork and Robert Jan van Pelt, *Auschwitz: 1270 to the Present* (New York: Norton, 1996), 284–299.

Kiliszewski's Journey

In the summer of 1891 a police official from the German city-state of Hamburg embarked on an inspection tour of the eastern border of Imperial Germany.[5] In the spring of the same year the migration from Eastern Europe to the United States had dramatically increased. Many migrants were Jews from Russia. Since Hamburg was a port preferred by Russian migrants en route to Britain and the United States, Hamburg's government, the Senate, was alarmed. As migrants were arriving in large groups, more than ever before were stranded in Hamburg. Most were destitute and did not even have a ticket for the overseas journey. Others clearly did not meet American entry requirements, for instance, if they were suffering from the eye disease trachoma. Thus Hamburg faced a financial and administrative burden of unknown proportions. The Senate reasoned that everything had to be done to prevent migrants who would require public support from even reaching Hamburg. The police official whose name was Kiliszewski was dispatched to collect information about the handling of controls along the main rail routes from the border to Hamburg and especially at key border crossings.

In 1891, Hamburg was a rapidly expanding city within Imperial Germany. The small city-state was surrounded on all sides by Prussia. This vast state covered the eastern and northern part of Imperial Germany. Prussia controlled the German land border with the Russian Empire, a long stretch of the border with the Austro-Hungarian Empire, and Germany's western border with Belgium and the Netherlands. Therefore Prussian officials – usually one or two local policemen – were in charge of most major border checkpoints for migrants from Eastern Europe crossing into Germany en route to Hamburg, Bremen, and ports in Western Europe. In 1891 the Hamburg Senate wondered whether the Prussian authorities would be able to deal with the transmigrant masses. Prussia, of course, was even more affected by migrants who required support, especially in cities along the main transit routes, such as Königsberg, Posen, Danzig, Breslau, and, above all, Berlin.[6]

On his way east, Kiliszewski briefly stopped in Prussian and German capital. He did not meet with government officials but with the leaders of the impromptu Jewish Central Committee for Russian Jews that worked closely with branch committees on the main border crossings.[7] During the meeting Kiliszewski received information about the work of the committee and about the background of most migrants. According to the Central Committee, Jewish "border committees" had been instructed to support only migrants who had enough money, a

---

[5] For references in the following paragraphs on Kiliszewski's journey in July and August 1891 please refer to: Hamburg State Archive, Auswanderungsamt I, 373-7 I, II E I 1b Beiheft 1, Registrier- und Kontrollstationen- Dienstreisen, Reiseberichte, July 18–August 7, 1891 (letters by Kiliszewski to Senator Dr. Sthamer).

[6] For background see: Tobias Brinkmann, "Why Paul Nathan Attacked Albert Ballin: The Transatlantic Mass Migration and the Privatization of Prussia's Eastern Border Inspection, 1886–1914," *Central European History* 43 (2010): 47–83.

[7] *Erster Bericht des Deutschen Central-Komitee für die Russischen Juden* (Berlin, 1891).

ship ticket, and met American admission criteria. All others would be held back and persuaded to return home. Across Western and Central Europe Jewish communities had established an informal support infrastructure for Jewish migrants from Eastern Europe since the late 1860s. The origins of this transnational network are quite complex. An obvious reason was to lend a helping hand to Jewish communities near the border crossings because these were occasionally overwhelmed by transmigrants seeking support. But established Jews especially in Germany also worried about their recently gained status as full-fledged citizens, reasoning they had to solve the problem of destitute Jewish strangers on their own. The rise of organized anti-Semitism in Germany and France during the 1880s only reconfirmed such worries. Yet, leading Jews in the West also realized that the long-term prospects for Jewish life in Eastern Europe were not good. Initially some had argued for developing the infrastructure of Jewish life in Eastern Europe to prevent mass migration to the West. But during the 1890s even Jewish leaders in the United States considered migration as the preferred solution. In 1891, after responding successfully to the migration crises of the late 1860s and the early 1880s, Jewish aid organizations knew how to manage even a large increase in the migration. More important, since they funded the journey of migrants to their destination, or back home, the Prussian state and the Hamburg government accepted Jewish organizations and communities as legitimate partners. Jewish leaders openly talked with officials like Kiliszewski because this cooperation gave them some leverage to lobby on behalf of Jewish migrants who had been arrested and faced deportation.[8]

As he left Berlin, Kiliszewski observed that the Berlin police did not check a single transmigrant, not even suspicious looking persons. In the following days he toured the land border from the northernmost point near Memel on the Baltic Sea, along the eastern border of the province of Posen, to Upper Silesia. At towns near the main crossings, he met with members of Jewish border committees, mostly small businessmen and rabbis. In his eyes these men were decent and responsible, but far too compassionate and thus not effective as gatekeepers. But at least they did interact with the migrants, even sending some back home, in contrast to Prussian state officials who were either invisible or overstretched. Almost everywhere Kiliszewski witnessed unchecked mass migration across an unguarded border. Many of the migrants were Jews who ostensibly were fleeing violent persecution in Russia. A few miles north of the Baltic port city Memel Kiliszewski even walked across the border in both directions without encountering Prussian officials. The local Russian border troops apparently had been bribed, and remained passive as large groups crossed the border, most in carriages steered by local smugglers. Only in the city of Thorn (Torun) on the

---

8   Tobias Brinkmann, "Managing mass migration. Jewish philanthropic organizations and Jewish mass migration from Eastern Europe, 1868/69–1914," *Leidschrift, Historisch Tijdschrift* 22 (2007), 71–90; Rainer Liedtke, *Jewish Welfare in Hamburg and Manchester, c. 1850–1914* (Oxford: Oxford University Press, 1998); David Vital, *A People Apart: The Jews in Europe, 1789-1939* (Oxford: Oxford University Press, 1999), 324–334.

Vistula the local Prussian *Landrat* (head of the county administration) had ordered the police to treat suspicious migrants "with unremitting sternness."

If hundreds crossed the border into East Prussia and the Prussian province of Posen every day, these numbers paled in comparison to the Myslowitz-Oswiecim crossing. In fact, Oswiecim had already a notorious reputation among German officials. Three years previously, a massive illegal smuggling operation had been uncovered here. Several ticket agents had cheated hundreds, if not thousands of migrants from Galicia and Slovakia. Transmigrants arriving at Oswiecim were forced to buy vastly overpriced steamship tickets that sometimes were forgeries. Others were led across the border and were overcharged or robbed. Most local officials, ranging from policemen to the local Austrian governor for West Galicia, had been bribed. In 1888 the Austrian police uncovered the operation after receiving information from migrants. The main organizers were put on trial in nearby Wadowice but received light sentences. The Hamburg Senate closely followed the trial as an extensive file with newspaper clippings illustrates. Several of the main accused were Jewish. The difference in the reporting of the Vienna based *Deutsches Volksblatt*, a German-nationalist and anti-Semitic paper, and the liberal *Neue Freie Presse*, is striking. The former blamed "the" Jews for exploiting the migrants and buying the services of local peasants and Austrian officials. The *Neue Freie Presse*, in contrast, covered the proceedings objectively. The trial illustrates how private entrepreneurs, some without doubt swindlers, filled a crucial void, mediating between migrants' concrete needs and the still undeveloped marketing and distribution ticket selling network of the steamship lines, and circumventing the rigid policies of imperial governments in St. Petersburg, Vienna, and Berlin.[9]

Further research needs to clarify how many of the small entrepreneurs, smugglers, and ticket agents at the border were actually Jewish. It is certainly too shortsighted to describe these men and women as crooks whose only interest was to take advantage of the migrants. A recently published popular account on emigration from Galicia highlights the pitfalls of an uninformed analysis that makes use of problematic stereotypes. The author Martin Pollock draws general conclusions from the trial, ignoring the context. Most migrants were hardly ignorant but belonged to networks. They had relatively precise information about travel routes, trustworthy men like local rabbis, and meeting points near the border. Indeed, most smugglers were facilitators who provided a necessary service, since the governments of Russia, Prussia, and Austria-Hungary proved incapable to regulate the mass migration sufficiently.[10]

As he arrived in Oswiecim in early August 1891, Kiliszewski encountered chaotic conditions. The available waiting facilities and hostels could not accommodate the migrant masses. Most of the migrants Kiliszewski met were not Ruthenians, Poles, and Jews from Galicia and Slovaks who usually crossed into

---

9 "Betr. das Treiben der oesterreichischen Agenten in Oswiecim, Strafprozess im Landgericht in Wadowice," in State Archive Hamburg, Auswanderungsamt, II A III 1 b.
10 Martin Pollack, *Kaiser von Amerika: Die große Flucht aus Galizien* (Wien: Zsolnay, 2010). Pollack does not provide specific references to his sources.

Germany via Oswiecim but Russian subjects. From Southern Russia the Galician transit was the shortest route to the North Sea ports. Some, however, reasoned (correctly) that the controls at the German-Austrian border would be more lax and easier to circumvent than at the German-Russian border. In early August 1891, hundreds of migrants were camping in the open fields between the small hamlet Brzezinka and the Oswiecim train station. Admittedly during the warmest month of the year the conditions, if not ideal, were relatively benign. Some were waiting for connecting trains. Others had to arrange their transatlantic journey and the transit through Germany at one of the ticket agencies near the Oswiecim train station. Kiliszewski praised the tireless efforts of Oswiecim rabbi Abraham Schnur who worked "day and night" to support distressed migrants. Every day he accompanied large groups to the Prussian border post at the Myslowitz train station. However, hundreds simply crossed the border illegally, usually with the help of innkeepers and smugglers who, as Kiliszewski emphasized, were all Jewish. The smugglers circumvented the Prussian checkpoint in Myslowitz, by taking migrants with carriages to the Kattowitz train station. Prussian police intercepted some trains further west in Oppeln (Opole) but these controls were not systematic. Kiliszewski summed up the situation in Upper Silesia as extremely unsatisfactory. A serious problem for the authorities, he conceded, was that most transmigrants were hardly distinguishable from the local population.

The Beginnings of "Remote Control"

The sudden increase of the Eastern European migration in the spring of 1891 was highly ambivalent for Hamburg. On the one hand, the Senate worried about social disorder and destitute migrants who could not afford to return home on their own. On the other hand, Hamburg's economy benefited enormously from the rising migration from Eastern Europe across the Atlantic. During the 1880s the rapidly expanding Hamburg-America Line (HAPAG), already one of the world's largest steamship lines, successfully embraced the Eastern European migration to compensate for the declining America-migration from Imperial Germany. HAPAG and its Bremen-based competitor, the North German Lloyd, established a network of ticket selling agents across Eastern Europe. By the early 1890s most migrants from the Russian Empire traveled via Hamburg to America, overwhelmingly on HAPAG ships. The Lloyd concentrated on the passenger market in the Austro-Hungarian Empire.[11]

The two German lines owed their strong position largely to the favorable location of Germany. The train line through Germany was the shortest route from the Russian Empire to the North Sea ports. The direct journey from a Russian port to Britain or America was frequently cheaper, but only an option for few Russian subjects because it was almost impossible to leave the Russian Empire legally. Service from the Imperial ports was limited and unreliable, and migrants had to pass an inspection by Russian state officials. Russia's long land border

---

11   For background see: Brinkmann, "Why Paul Nathan Attacked Albert Ballin," 47–83.

was relatively easy to cross with the help of smugglers. The authorities in the Austro-Hungarian Empire did allow emigration but young males intending to evade military service were well advised to avoid official border crossings and ports on the Adriatic Sea. Thus geography and political circumstances favored Germany, turning it into a key transit country for Eastern European migrants bound for Western Europe and overseas, and providing the two established German steamship lines with a unique advantage over their foreign competitors.[12]

Immigrating to Germany, rather than to the United States and other overseas countries, was not a feasible option for most Eastern Europeans. The German industrial sector expanded rapidly during the 1870s and Germany attracted rising numbers of labor migrants. Especially at the large agricultural estates in the eastern Prussian provinces laborers from the Russian and Austro-Hungarian Empires were in much demand. But in the 1880s Prussia turned against immigration from Eastern Europe, by instrumentalizing widespread xenophobic and anti-Semitic fears of an "invasion" from the east. Between 1885 and 1888 the Berlin government deported more than 30,000 foreign Poles and Jews. In addition, many transmigrants en route to the United States were prevented from crossing the border, or turned back while in transit. As of 1885 only transmigrants, who could prove they carried sufficient funds for an eventual return journey (400 Marks per adult and 100 Marks per child), were allowed to cross through Germany. This sum was beyond the means of almost all transmigrants. It simply gave state officials the legal cover to deport transmigrants at any time. The Prussian policy against transmigrants was a response to the decision by the United States to return "undesirable" immigrants to the European port of embarkation. Hamburg and Prussia had to fund the bulk of the costs associated with the repatriation of involuntary return migrants, who often had not means. Involuntary Jewish return migrants were usually cared for by the transnational network of Jewish aid associations.

The Prussian mass deportations soon triggered protests from the big landowners who depended on cheap Polish labor migrants from the Russian and Austro-Hungarian Empires to compensate for German laborers (many Polish-speakers) who had moved to industrial centers in America, Berlin, and on the Ruhr after 1870. The German steamship lines also lobbied against the deportations in Berlin because the protectionist Prussian policy threatened their lucrative Eastern Europe business. In 1888 the deportations were stopped, and a so-

---

12 Bernhard Karlsberg, *History and Importance of the German Control of Emigrants in Transit* (Hamburg and Leipzig: Gebrüder Enoch, 1922); Erich Murken, *Die großen transatlantischen Linienreederei-Verbände, Pools und Interessengemeinschaften bis zum Ausbruch des Weltkrieges: Ihre Entstehung, Organisation und Wirksamkeit* (Jena: G. Fischer, 1922); Rogger, "Tsarist Policy on Jewish Emigration;" on migration from Galicia see: Annemarie Steidl, Engelbert Stockhammer and Hermann Zeitlhofer, "Relations among Internal, Continental, and Transatlantic Migration in Late Imperial Austria," *Social Science History* 31 (2007): 61-92; Leopold Caro, *Auswanderung und Auswanderungspolitik in Österreich* (Leipzig: Duncker & Humblot, 1909); Hans Weichmann, *Die Auswanderung aus Österreich und Rußland über die Deutschen Häfen* (Berlin: Frensdorf, 1913).

phisticated control system was put in place that allowed foreigners to come to Germany legally as seasonal workers. Since the border could not be controlled systematically all seasonal workers had to carry state-issued identification cards. Prussia also addressed the concerns of the steamship lines. The cash-requirement for transmigrants was waived for all migrants in possession of a ticket issued by the Lloyd or HAPAG. In return, the steamship lines promised to cover all costs their passengers might cause for the Prussian state.[13]

The dramatic increase of the migration during the first half of 1891 appeared to overwhelm the existing transit system. Yet the rising migration was not the only motivation behind Kiliszewski's journey. In spring 1891, unrelated to the Russian expulsions and the rising migration, the United States Congress imposed additional restrictions on immigration. One of the most important innovations was the reform of the immigrant inspection. The inadequate reception facility at Castle Garden on the southern tip of Manhattan had closed in 1890. In January 1892, a new immigration station went into operation at Ellis Island in New York harbor. At other ports such as Baltimore, Boston, and Philadelphia smaller immigration stations were erected. All arriving immigrants traveling in third class or steerage were taken to Ellis Island and other stations for a thorough examination. German officials expected that after the opening of Ellis Island, many more "undesirables" would be returned. Leading American lawmakers, like Senator William E. Chandler, chairman of the immigration committee, did little to dispel such concerns. Chandler hinted openly at even tighter restrictions.[14]

Migration scholar Aristide Zolberg has described the rejection of migrants bound for the United States, before they even reached America's shores, as a policy "remote control." Since Europeans and Asians could reach the western hemisphere only by ship it was relatively easy for the United States to keep unwanted persons out. Some, of course, began to circumvent ports in the United States by migrating through Canada and Mexico. But after the United States began to step up controls on the northern border and at Canadian ports, and to a lesser extent, along the border with Mexico, these detours carried increasing risks. "Remote control" presented a challenge for the transit countries, especially if they had long land borders that could not be policed. To get a better understanding of "remote control" scholars need to look beyond the state. To increase the impact of "remote control" the United States also began to put pressure on the steamship lines not to take "problematic" passengers on board. This back-

---

13 Prussian Minister of the Interior and Prussian Minster of Trade and Commerce to Count Bismarck, July 21, 1885, in Geheimes Staatsarchiv Berlin, Preußisches Ministerium für Handel und Gewerbe, Bestimmungen zum Schutze und zur Fürsorge für die Auswanderung und Kolonisation, XIII, 20, 1 (abbreviated hereafter as Auswanderung und Kolonisation), vol. 13; Ballin to Hamburg Emigration Authority, 29 April 1887; Report, Hanseatic Legation at Berlin [Hanseatische Gesandschaft zu Berlin], Berlin, 6 July 1887, in State Archive Hamburg, Auswanderungsamt I, 373-7 I [abbreviated as *Auswanderungsamt*], II E I 1; Karlsberg, *History and Importance of the German Control of Emigrants in Transit*, 10–44.
14 *New York Times*, April 17, 1891.

ground helps to explain why the German steamship lines rather than the Prussian state took the initiative soon after 1891.[15]

Privatizing Transmigration

Almost fifteen years later, in November 1905, Kiliszewski returned to Oswiecim for another inspection tour. Much had changed in the meantime. Soon after 1900 the migration from Eastern Europe had increased to even higher levels than in the early 1890s. However, the haphazard transmigration infrastructure that almost collapsed in the summer of 1891 had been replaced by an efficient system that was privately managed and funded.

Kiliszewski had made a career move. He was in charge of the police post at the Hamburg *Auswandererhallen*. This state-of-the-art facility for transmigrants traveling with HAPAG had opened its doors in 1902. The isolated compound, situated several miles from the city center, on the southern edge of the huge port, could accommodate more than one thousand people. All incoming migrants were disinfected and housed in modern dormitories instead of having to rely on often overpriced and unclean hostels in central Hamburg. Jewish passengers received Kosher meals, and HAPAG had erected a synagogue and an interdenominational church. The facilities in Bremen and Bremerhaven were also modernized around 1900.[16]

The takeover of the German transit system by HAPAG and Lloyd was a consequence of the rising migration but also of the inability of the Prussian state to control its eastern border, as observed by Kiliszewski. The new system was based on a simple logic. The Prussian state was not able to organize the transmigration efficiently. Apart from providing the necessary infrastructure for the transport of huge numbers of people, the state had to guarantee social order on the border and near the transit routes. Prussia could not prevent migrants from crossing into Germany, who would not be admitted in the United States. Therefore, the mass transmigration posed an incalculable financial and administrative burden. For the steamship lines the same migrants represented a lucrative market. Indeed, the profits were so high, that HAPAG and Lloyd could easily shoulder the costs associated with problematic migrants. And the steamship lines

---

15   Aristide R. Zolberg, *A Nation by Design: Immigration Policy in the Fashioning of America* (Cambridge: Harvard University Press, 2006), 264–267; Erika Lee, "Enforcing the Borders: Chinese Exclusion along the U.S. Borders with Canada and Mexico, 1882–1924," in *Journal of American History* 89 (2002), 54–86; Dorothee Schneider, "The United States Government and the Investigation of European Emigration in the Open Door Era," in *Citizenship and Those Who Leave: The Politics of Emigration and Expatriation*, eds. Nancy Green and François Weil (Urbana: University of Illinois Press, 2007), 195–210.

16   Walter Sthamer, *Die Auswandererhallen in Hamburg* (Hamburg: Hamburg-Amerika Linie, 1904); Auswandererüberwachung/Auswandererunterbringung, 4,21-507, Bd. 1; Bremer Auswandererhallen (F. Mißler) und Logierhaus Stadt Warschau, 4,21-509, State Archive Bremen.

could (and had to) respond much more quickly to American policy changes than the Prussian state.[17]

The final trigger behind the privatization and reorganization of the German transit migration was the 1892 Cholera epidemic in Hamburg. For months the Hamburg Senate struggled to contain the disease, which was blamed widely (albeit wrongly) on Russian transmigrants. The transatlantic and European passenger service from Hamburg was interrupted for months. A simultaneous Cholera outbreak in central Russia explains why Prussia immediately closed its border with Russia but not with Austria-Hungary. A second inspection journey by Kiliszewski in the summer of 1892, in the wake of the Cholera epidemic, revealed that Prussia's borders were actually wide open. Many Russian migrants were continuing to cross, in violation of the official ban. Since no ships departed from Hamburg, they traveled via Bremen and Western European ports. It was hardly a surprise that the United States immigration authorities were alarmed when they learned of the Cholera outbreak in one of Europe's main ports of embarkation. Earlier in 1892 New York had been affected by a small Typhus epidemic, which was blamed on European immigrants. For several months in the fall of 1892 the transatlantic migration from most European ports, not just Hamburg, was effectively closed down. Only when the epidemic had been contained in January 1893, did Washington lift the ban. After March 1893, all migrants from the Russian Empire had to undergo a disinfection procedure before embarkation and remain in quarantine for several days.[18]

Following this crisis, the leading managers of the two German steamship lines opened negotiations with the Prussian government, convincing the Prussian prime minister Count Botho zu Eulenburg that the state would not be able to police the borders by conventional means. They proposed a system that would at once satisfy the concerns by the United States and the German authorities, without threatening their business interests. The centerpiece of this proposal was the so-called control station, a facility where transmigrants were screened for communicable diseases, thoroughly disinfected, and had to prove they were not paupers. The model for the control station was not Ellis Island but a facility that had gone into operation in November 1891 in Ruhleben, a suburb of Berlin, a few weeks before Ellis Island opened its doors. The initial purpose of the Ruhleben station was to remove transmigrants from the busy Berlin train stations, to contain suspicious persons, and deport them if necessary. The decision by the Prussian government to open Ruhleben was clearly influenced by the United States 1891 immigration act. Sometime in 1893, soon after the Hamburg Cholera, Ruhleben was equipped with disinfection facilities. Mary Antin, a Jewish girl from Polotzk on the way to Boston, recorded her rather up-

---

17 Brinkmann, "Why Paul Nathan Attacked Albert Ballin."
18 Richard Evans, *Death in Hamburg: Society and Politics in the Cholera Years 1830–1910* (Oxford: Oxford University Press, 1987), 279–284; Howard Markel, *Quarantine! East European Jewish Immigrants and the New York City Epidemics of 1892* (Baltimore: Johns Hopkins University Press, 1997).

setting impressions of the screening and disinfection procedures at Ruhleben in the spring of 1894.[19]

By transplanting the Ruhleben model to other points along the main transit routes it became possible to effectively police the open border. Migrants had to enter the control stations near the main border crossings voluntarily. After the screening the admitted migrants received a transit passport that was valid for a few days and required to board the ships in Hamburg or Bremen. The others were deported across the nearby border. The control stations were managed and funded by HAPAG and Lloyd. The decision about admission and rejection was not made by a Prussian or American official but by employees of the steamship lines. At the control stations many migrants boarded sealed trains that took them directly to Hamburg or Bremen, and sometimes to the Dutch, Belgian, or French border and from there to the ports Rotterdam, Antwerp, Le Havre, or Cherbourg.

Migrants who crossed the border in some distance from a control station were usually screened at control stations at the railway hubs Leipzig or Berlin, and in more than a few cases at Bremen or Hamburg itself. However, migrants who had intentionally bypassed a control station and encountered state officials during the transit journey were often deported. In the late summer of 1905, for instance, small groups of destitute Russian Jews arrived daily at the small railway hub Bebra in Hesse. Although they had valid train tickets for Antwerp and steamship tickets for New York, the police arrested them because they had circumvented the control stations in Leipzig and at Myslowitz. Most migrants were deported to Oswiecim. It is not known what the Austrian authorities did with these men. But it is likely that they were deported back to Russia. The main culprits were apparently "ruthless agents" who had given these migrants wrong advice or cheated them. The U.S. immigration commissioner praised the control station system even before it went into operation in 1894. Suffice to say, the low rejection rate at Ellis Island between 1892 and 1914 was in part due to the effectiveness of the privately managed German "remote control" system.[20]

Of course, HAPAG and Lloyd were not the only steamship lines providing transatlantic service. Indeed, British and other Western European lines offered cheaper tickets than HAPAG and Lloyd. Yet in order to reach ports in Western Europe, migrants had to cross through Germany – and through the control stations that were managed by HAPAG and Lloyd. The domination of the Eastern European passenger market gave the German lines enough leverage to cooperate with their Western European and American competitors in the early 1890s. A leading HAPAG manager, Albert Ballin, was the main architect of the so-

---

19 Mary Antin, *From Plotzk to Boston*. With a Foreword by Israel Zangwill (Boston: W. B. Clarke, 1899), 41–43.
20 *Israelitisches Familienblatt* (Hamburg), 22 September 1905; *Annual Report of the Commissioner General of Immigration for the Fiscal Year Ended June 30th 1894* (Washington, D.C.: Government Printing Office, 1894), 16; *Emigrant Conditions in Europe, in 61st Congress, 3rd Session, Senate, Reports of the Immigrant Commission*, presented by Mr. Dillingham (Washington, D.C.: Government Printing Office, 1911), 93–97.

called North Atlantic Steamship Conference. The members of this price-fixing cartel negotiated their respective shares of different markets, such as Scandinavia, Eastern Europe, Britain, and the Mediterranean. This system prevented tariff wars and kept the passage prices at a relatively high level. While some Eastern Europeans could travel via Western European ports, the majority went through Hamburg and Bremen. Migrants, notably from South Eastern Europe, could have used ports such as Fiume, Naples, or Athens. But many opted for Bremen. Ironically, the good reputation of the German screening system gave them a better chance to be admitted at Ellis Island.[21]

But the system had a number of loopholes. At the Myslowitz train station the control station was actually designated as a "registration station," just like at other Prussian-Austrian border crossings and at Leipzig, the main railway hub for migrants originating in the Austro-Hungarian Empire. Registration stations lacked the disinfection facilities of the control stations, although usually a physician was present who did inspect suspicious migrants. The United States was primarily concerned about Russian disease carriers. And in contrast to the St. Petersburg government its counterpart in Vienna repeatedly intervened on behalf of its citizens in Berlin, usually after Austrians had been deported on flimsy grounds or were abused by Prussian officials. However, even before 1891 the relatively lax controls at Myslowitz had attracted many Russian transmigrants to this crossing. Therefore it was hardly surprising that the Oswiecim-Myslowitz crossing became even more important after the implementation of the control-station system. Since only few migrants carried passports, Prussian officials and the employees of the steamship lines at the registration stations frequently were not certain whether a migrant was from Galicia or the Russian Empire. To avoid further protests by the Austrian government only migrants who clearly did not meet American access criteria were rejected.[22]

And indeed, Kiliszewski's November 1905 visit of Oswiecim seems to prove this assumption. In Myslowitz he arrived shortly after 9,000 (!) migrants apparently had tried to storm across the border from nearby Sosnowiec, which belonged to the Russian Empire. Prussian border guards and policemen, however, had been warned and had foiled this "attack." It is not possible to ascertain whether this was simply a rumor; the number was probably exaggerated. In Oswiecim itself, little had changed. The town was "overflowing" with migrants. "Every inhabitant of Oswiecim," so Kilisewski's assessment, "participates in the smuggling and exploiting of emigrants." While some emigrants crossed the border legally, he observed "Jewish carriage drivers" who took many others illegally across the border. Indeed, Oswiecim was the preferred crossing point for Russian migrants with dodgy credentials who risked being rejected at the control stations. During the remainder of the journey, which took him along the Silesian-Bohemian border to Leipzig, Kiliszewski noted more illegal activities. However, in Leipzig and Berlin, the two leading railway hubs in Central Europe, mi-

---

21 Schneider, "The United States Government and the Investigation of European Emigration in the Open Door Era," 203–204.
22 Karlsberg, *History and Importance of the German Control of Emigrants in Transit*.

grants faced two inland control stations they could not easily evade. By chance, Kiliszewski watched how a group of Russian Jews successfully circumvented the controls at Leipzig. Yet the systematic screening at the *Auswandererhallen* and in Bremen usually caught up with Russian migrants who had evaded the control (or registration) stations at the border and in Berlin and Leipzig. And as the above-mentioned arrests at Bebra prove, Russian migrants who avoided the control- or registration-stations risked immediate deportation.[23]

In 1907, Anna Herkner, an immigration inspector disguised as migrant inspected Myslowitz on behalf of the United States Congress Immigration Commission. She arrived at the Myslowitz train station with a group of Galician migrants traveling via Krakow. Upon arrival Russian and Austrian passengers were divided into different groups. The former had to submit their clothing and baggage for disinfection. A doctor inspected all migrants. Even though Herkner noted some hygienic problems at the Myslowitz train station and overpriced food (sold by an "intoxicated" innkeeper), she and her fellow passengers had no possibility to avoid the inspection or leave the station, other than by train. After waiting for more than twenty-four hours for the inspection the admitted migrants boarded sealed carriages attached to a regular train, continuing their journey to an unnamed North Sea port.[24]

Conclusion

Two recently published histories of Ellis Island and Angel Island highlight the possibilities and limitations in recent American immigration historiography. The authors provide a thorough overview of the history of the two famous immigrant reception centers. The study on Angel Island reveals a little known story of the transpacific migration and much stricter policies against unwanted migrants than at Ellis Island before 1914. Both authors transcend the long-dominant ethnic paradigm, adding a social dimension to the history of American immigration policy. Yet they focus solely on the respective institution and arriving immigrants (as well as detainees and deportees). Migrants who did not reach the reception centers are not part of their story.[25]

This article has revealed a more complex history of Ellis Island in its first twenty years that reaches far beyond America's shores – to ports such as Hamburg and border crossings as the one between Myslowitz and Oswiecim. The successful implementation of "remote control" measures prevented many Eastern Europeans from getting even close to the United States. Many failed to pass

---

23 Hamburg State Archive, Auswanderungsamt I, 373-7 I, II E I 1b Beiheft 2, Registrier- und Kontrollstationen- Dienstreisen, Reiseberichte, November 1–18, 1905 (letters by Kiliszewski to Senator Dr. Sthamer).
24 Steerage Conditions: Partial Report, on Behalf of the Immigration Commission, on Steerage Conditions. (Washington, D.C.: Government Printing Office, 1909), 27–28.
25 Vincent J. Cannato, *American Passage: The History of Ellis Island* (New York: HarperCollins, 2009); Erika Lee, Judy Yung, *Angel Island: Immigrant Gateway to America* (Oxford: Oxford University Press, 2010).

screenings at checkpoints resembling Ellis Island at Germany's border with the Russian and Austro-Hungarian Empires, along the transit routes, and at the ports of Hamburg and Bremen. Indeed, a look at "points of passage" highlights the merits of analyzing migration not from the vantage point of immigration or emigration but in a broader transnational setting.

As this essay has shown, the Prussian, Russian, Austro-Hungarian, and Hamburg government struggled to control the mass (trans-) migration. Responding to the growing crisis, the two German steamship lines took over the control of Germany's eastern border in 1894. For HAPAG and Lloyd the Eastern European mass migration represented a lucrative market, and they could easily shoulder the costs associated with "problematic" migrants. The steamship lines also reacted much more flexibly to changes in migration policies than state governments, because their business depended on adhering to the respective rules. The privatization of the German transit migration system deprived migrants of agency. But during the 1880s and early 1890s, transmigrants were hardly in a better situation, often facing harsh treatment by Prussian officials. And transmigrants could do little, if they were arrested and deported. Moreover, the state archive in Hamburg contains files proving that complaints by migrants about abuse at the control stations were followed up and investigated by Hamburg police officials such as Kiliszewski.[26] More important, as I have shown elsewhere, Jewish aid association – important forerunners of contemporary transnational humanitarian NGO's – acted as watchdogs, so did the German press, especially the leftwing daily *Vorwärts*, which repeatedly sent investigative reporters through the transit system. In 1904, the public protest of the German-Jewish *Hilfsverein der Deutschen Juden* (Aid Association of the German Jews) forced HAPAG and Lloyd to improve the treatment of transmigrants and allow for more competition with other steamship lines.[27] Today, airlines continue to act as remote control agents for governments in frequently distant destination countries. Only passengers with valid papers and a legitimate cause for travel are allowed to board planes. Problematic passengers are blacklisted and sometimes arbitrarily prevented from boarding. Just like steamship lines then airlines today have to operate within the tightly set parameters set different state governments, yet they also have a genuine interest to transport as many passengers as possible.

References

Antin, Mary. *From Plotzk to Boston*. With a Foreword by Israel Zangwill. Boston, Massachusetts: W. B. Clarke, 1899.
Brinkmann, Tobias. "Why Paul Nathan Attacked Albert Ballin: The Transatlantic Mass Migration and the Privatization of Prussia's Eastern Border Inspection, 1886–1914." *Central European History* 43 (2010).

---

26 Report by Kiliszewki, 28 November 1907, in State Archive Hamburg, Auswanderungsamt I, 373-7 I, II E I 1b Beiheft 2.
27 Brinkmann, "Why Paul Nathan Attacked Albert Ballin."

Brinkmann, Tobias. "Managing mass migration. Jewish philanthropic organizations and Jewish mass migration from Eastern Europe, 1868/69–1914." *Leidschrift, Historisch Tijdschrift* 22 (2007).

Cannato, Vincent J. *American Passage: The History of Ellis Island*. New York: HarperCollins, 2009.

Caro, Leopold. *Auswanderung und Auswanderungspolitik in Österreich*. Leipzig: Duncker & Humblot, 1909.

Dwork, Deborah, and Robert Jan van Pelt. *Auschwitz: 1270 to the Present*. New York: Norton, 1996.

Erster Bericht des Deutschen Central-Komitee für die Russischen Juden. Berlin, 1891.

Evans, Richard. *Death in Hamburg: Society and Politics in the Cholera Years 1830–1910*. Oxford: Oxford University Press, 1987.

Hans, Weichmann. *Die Auswanderung aus Österreich und Rußland über die Deutschen Häfen*. Berlin: Frensdorf, 1913.

Hoerder, Dirk, ed. *People in Transit: German Migrations in Comparative Perspective, 1820–1920*. Cambridge: Cambridge University Press, 1995.

Karlsberg, Bernhard. *History and Importance of the German Control of Emigrants in Transit*. Hamburg and Leipzig: Gebrüder Enoch, 1922.

Kuhn, Philip A. *Chinese Among Others: Emigration in Modern Times*. Lanham, MD: Rowman & Littlefield, 2009.

Lee, Erika. "Enforcing the Borders: Chinese Exclusion along the U.S. Borders with Canada and Mexico, 1882–1924." *Journal of American History* 89 (2002).

Lee, Erika and Judy Yung, *Angel Island: Immigrant Gateway to America*. Oxford: Oxford University Press, 2010.

Liedtke, Rainer. *Jewish Welfare in Hamburg and Manchester, c. 1850–1914*. Oxford: Oxford University Press, 1998.

Markel, Howard. *Quarantine! East European Jewish Immigrants and the New York City Epidemics of 1892*. Baltimore: Johns Hopkins University Press, 1997.

Murken, Erich. *Die großen transatlantischen Linienreederei-Verbände, Pools und Interessengemeinschaften bis zum Ausbruch des Weltkrieges: Ihre Entstehung, Organisation und Wirksamkeit*. Jena: G. Fischer, 1922.

Pollack, Martin. *Kaiser von Amerika: Die große Flucht aus Galizien*. Wien: Zsolnay, 2010.

Rogger, Hans. "Tsarist Policy on Jewish Emigration." *Soviet Jewish Affairs* 3 (1973).

Schneider, Dorothee. "The United States Government and the Investigation of European Emigration in the Open Door Era," in *Citizenship and Those Who Leave: The Politics of Emigration and Expatriation*. Ed. Nancy Green and François Weil. Urbana: University of Illinois Press, 2007.

Steidl, Annemarie. "Introduction," in *European Mobility: Internal, International, and Transatlantic Moves in the 19th and 20th Centuries*. Ed. Annemarie Steidl, Josef Ehmer, Stan Nadel, Hermann Zeitlhofer. Göttingen: V&R Unipress, 2009.

Steidl, Annemarie, Engelbert Stockhammer, and Hermann Zeitlhofer. "Relations among Internal, Continental, and Transatlantic Migration in Late Imperial Austria." *Social Science History* 31 (2007).

Vital, David. *A People Apart: The Jews in Europe, 1789-1939*. Oxford: Oxford University Press, 1999.

Walter, Sthamer. *Die Auswandererhallen in Hamburg*. Hamburg: Hamburg-Amerika Linie, 1904.

Zolberg, Aristide R. *A Nation by Design: Immigration Policy in the Fashioning of America*. Cambridge, Massachusetts: Harvard University Press, 2006.

Before "The Holocaust": American Jews Confront Catastrophe, 1945-1962
Hasia Diner (New York University)

In the decade and a half following the end of World War II, that global conflagration which brought about the deaths of one-third of the Jewish people and the destruction of much of European Jewish communal life at the hands of the Germans and their collaborators, American Jewry found many times, places, and modes of expression to articulate its intense reactions to that calamity. While historians may find it difficult, if not nearly impossible, to recreate the ways in which individual Jews in their homes talked about this catastrophic event or how they incorporated direct references and analogies to it into the discourse of their private spheres of everyday life, Jewish institutions including a range of organizations, synagogues, schools, summer camps, publishing houses, magazines and newspapers left an easily recoverable paper trail which revealed a community that felt itself obliged to remember and commemorate. These formal institutions of American Jewish life, spanning a spectrum of ideologies and political positions vis-à-vis the concerns of the day, wove the details of the catastrophe into their rhetorical repertoires and used references to it to shape their political projects.

The ways in which they "used" the calamity of European Jewry, referred to consistently in the copious material produced in Yiddish as the *"hurban,"* or destruction, reflected the concerns and sensibilities of their times. From the perspective of the early twenty-first century with its ubiquitous invocations of the Holocaust and the widespread highly public impress of that European event on to the American landscape, the post-war references and performances of American Jews may seem oblique and wan. Such comparisons however should be seen as ahistorical and lacking any kind of sensitivity to the project which confronted American Jewry in the years after the war.

At the most simple level of analysis, the post-war memorial texts reflected the concerns, language, and sensibilities of the post-war period, while the memorial activities that predominated a half century later took on the vocabulary and values of a very different time. The two Jewries differed in so many other ways that looking for consistency in Holocaust memorial practice would be akin to looking for consistency in how they dealt with issues of gender, as one of many examples which could be summoned to show how much American Jewry had changed in the intervening years.

The Jews of the United States emerged in 1945 from the trauma of World War II confronting a new reality. The United States had become *the* only large, organized, and functioning center of Jewish life as a result of the brutal liquidation of 6,000,000 Jews in Europe. The memorial texts and performances which American Jews created for their schools, synagogues, and community centers, as well as those which they crafted to share with their non-Jewish neighbors represented experiments in expression.

These post-war American Jews had to create a culture of commemoration from scratch in the context of a global Jewish world which through the early 1960's lived with the aftershocks of the catastrophe. They had no precedent or example to follow as they took the first steps towards creating ceremonies and words, graphic images and music to remember what had just transpired. In the inner discussions of boards of organizations, school committees, and American Jews struggled amongst themselves as to the best, most appropriate and most effective means by which to remember the victims, confront the perpetrators, and salvage the lives of the survivors. They made direct linkages between the memorial objects and practices that they fashioned with some of the political events which continued to rattle world Jewry as a result of the Nazi brutality. As such comparisons, positive or negative between the Holocaust projects of the early twenty-first century with those of the mid-twentieth century do little to further historical understanding of how a group of people –American Jews—at a particular moment—the years 1945 through 1962—went about the process of expressing their reaction to an event –the mass murder of 6,000,000 European Jews—which involved them deeply but which few of them had lived through.

In the years from the cessation of hostilities and the defeat of Nazi Germany in 1945 until 1962 when the capture, trial, and execution of Adolph Eichmann, chief of the operations which had enabled the mass murder of millions of European Jews to take place, made the Holocaust a matter of broad political commentary beyond the confines of the Jewish community, the Jews of the United States created works of liturgy, pageantry, drama, imaginative literature, sermons, pedagogical material, graphic arts, and scholarship to describe the catastrophe that had so recently engulfed their people. The testimonies of those who had endured the Nazi onslaught found their way into the pages of Jewish publications, onto the airwaves of Jewish radio programs, and into books, including those designed to memorialize the towns and regions of Europe, where once Jews lived but did so no longer. In newspapers, magazines, newsletters, books, articles, press releases, and the publications of Jewish organizations, written in English, Yiddish, and Hebrew, American Jews from across the political, denominational, class, and geographic spectrum wrote about the tragedy of European Jewry and its implications for the Jews of the United States. They used the mass media, radio and television, to broadcast to themselves and to their American neighbors, aspects of their recent tragic history.

In the process of creating a series of texts in print and on the air by which they described themselves to other Americans, they felt called up to invoke the mass murder of the Jews of Europe. Although they themselves had lived so far from the scenes of suffering, they used the details of those horrific years to narrate their own American story. They also used imagery of the Nazi horrors as perpetrated upon the Jews to make a number of political points about themselves in America, about the Jews as a global people, and about America as a civilization which they, at one and the same time, embraced but sought to change. Their uses of the details of the slaughter, as specific fact and as analogy, went beyond the boundaries of the Jewish community. Their rhetorical repertoire of these years as they addressed the larger American public, including, those who held the reins of power as well as the public at large, included references direct and indirect to the Nazi era and its brutalities as visited upon the Jews

Americans, Jews and non-Jews of the latter part of the twentieth century, have become familiar with and accustomed to films, books, plays, museums, memorial markers, and other kinds of cultural works dealing with the Holocaust. The terminology of the Holocaust has entered into the contemporary lexicon and it has come to be used by advocates of many causes for a multitude of political and cultural purposes. Within the ranks of American Jewry the Holocaust serves as a powerful icon representing group membership and leaders of nearly all of its many segments have marshaled it in hopes of achieving some particular end. What has come to be referred to as "Holocaust-consciousness" continues in the opening years of the twenty-first century to function as a key element in the culture of American Jews, intended for general consumption as much as for identity building enterprises within.

The emergence of an American Jewish culture shaped, in part, by the images of this Jewish tragedy and the reality that it might serve political functions, broadly defined, took shape in the immediate years after the end of World War II, the post-war period, with the 1950s as the epicenter of that era. Post-war American Jews, in the realms of politics, religion, the arts, philanthropy, and pedagogy, set the terms for the contemporary memorial culture. In those years of the late 1940s through the early 1960s when the term "Holocaust" had not yet been universalized as the way to name this tragedy and when American Jews did not see it as history but as the past present, they began the process of creating a culture of memory which has grown with time but which has not changed substantially.

Yet according to the regnant scholarship and indeed to a broadly believed American Jewish community consensus none of this happened. Historians and other commentators, from within the Jewish world and from without, have with near unanimity agreed that American Jews, in the aftermath of the World War with its revelations of mass murder, did not articulate any deep sense of anguish nor did they engage in acts of public mourning. They did not, according to this unquestioned assumption about the past, use the Holocaust in the pursuit of their political and social agenda of the 1950's in particular, except in as much as post-war Jews, according to one group of historians, they invoked the horrors of Nazism in order to fit into the culture of American anti-communism as it developed during the Cold War. American Jews, the leaders of the defense organizations specifically, twinned the evils of Nazism and those of Communism, and created, historians have asserted, a rhetorical trope that depicted a generalized kind of totalitarianism without specifically Jewish victims, and which allowed American Jews to participate in the anti-communist frenzy of the post-war period.[1]

---

1 Michael Staub, *Torn at the Roots: The Crisis of Jewish Liberalism in Postwar America* (New York: Columbia University Press, 2002).

The silence of American Jews, their unwillingness, disinterest, or inability to talk about the Nazi catastrophe in their communal institutions and in the rhetoric they crafted for the broader American public, functions as one of the key "truths" of the overall narrative of American Jewish history. Scholars have invested much analytic significance in the fact that post-war American Jews did not include the Holocaust in their communal culture. That silence, they claim, revealed much about the particular political position and cultural project of American Jewry.

Few have found this silence particularly impressive. Statements claiming the truth of American Jews' refusal to memorialize the European catastrophe or their embarrassment about invoking it in public have been cast in decidedly negative terms, laden with direct or implied condemnations of those went about their lives in the emerging affluence of 1950s America without any nod whatsoever to the horrors so recently concluded. The assertion that post-war Jews kept silent, speaking only in privately and furtively about the tragedy, exists as not just a scholarly paradigm but also as a broadly accepted communal belief which spans otherwise intense political divides within the American Jewish world.[2]

Had it in fact been true that American Jews of the postwar period failed to remember, recall, and invoke the European tragedy of their people they would indeed merit the opprobrium of later generations. Had they actually not fused the legacy of that event with a series of political actions later generations, both historians and the broad Jewish public, would be justified in investing much analytic significance to the behavior of their forbears of a half century earlier.

But the widely accepted emphatic assertions that a culture of memorialization did not develop in the postwar period and the sweeping interpretations based upon them have been built on near nothingness. The works of history as well as the deeply held communal truth have behind them little evidence and stand in stark contrast to the troves of empirical data which exist in archives, newspapers, and the other primary sources which historians, at least, must consult before offering their interpretations of what happened and how.

American Jews, in fact, individuals as creators of texts and formally organized institutions, produced a large corpus of projects in nearly every media available in these years which referred to, represented, and lamented the horrors of the Nazi era. In these works in words and images, in artistic endeavors and political projects they made amply clear that Jews had been the victims, that the Germans had perpetrated a crime upon the Jewish people who had been the chief victims, alt-

---

2   One of the few commentators to describe American Jewish interactions with the memory of the Holocaust in decidedly positive terms was Jacob Neusner, not a scholar of American Jewish history, but of Talmud. Neusner commenting on the 1950's, he wrote that it was not that people failed to "notice the absence of more than five million European Jews...." Rather they did not manifest the obsession with it that came to characterize, he asserted, later American Jewish cultural tendencies. In the 1950's, Neusner, assessed, much of what was performed vis-à-vis the European tragedy was imbued with an aura of "refinement, restraint, and dignity." See, Jacob Neusner, "How the Extermination of European Jewry Became 'The Holocaust,'" in, *Stranger at Home: "The Holocaust," Zionism, and American Judaism* (Chicago: University of Chicago Press, 1981), pp. 82-91.

hough millions of others had suffered as well, and that the implications of the slaughter had left an indelible mark on world Jewry. Each swathe of Jewish opinion or ideology, each language group—Anglophones, Yiddish-speakers, and committed Hebraists—used its tongue of choice to articulate its anguish and its sense of the obligation to remember. While each group expressed its feelings differently and derived particular lessons from the horrors, they agreed on what had happened –the Germans and their allies had slaughtered millions of Jews, about one-third of the Jewish people—and that that wholesale liquidation destroyed full communities, cultures, and brought violently into being a new era in Jewish history.

How can we account for the vast chasm which divides the reality that American Jews created a staggeringly large repertoire of works for distribution in print, on the air, on the stage and from the pulpit that invoked the catastrophe and the overwhelming thrust of the scholarship and commentary which has determinedly asserted that such acts of memorialization never took place? What forces have been in operations which have blinded historians to the existence of such material, available in plain sight for them to have seen and analyzed?

The fullest explanation of the disjunction between the easily retrievable evidence and the prevailing orthodoxy which takes for granted that such sources do not exist requires two scholarly projects. One, the larger, must uncover, array, and analyze the broad range Jewish texts created in the period 1945 to 1962 that fully or partially dealt with the European catastrophe. These texts include those constructed of words to be read or heard in American Jewry's three languages, English, Yiddish, and Hebrew, directed at adults and at children. Some texts that depicted the concentration camps and ghettoes, the victims and the villains, used graphic images, ink on paper, paint on canvas, black-and-white photographs, stained glass, marble and granite, while yet others relied upon music, composed for use in synagogues, community centers, schools and concert halls. All these must be displayed and analyzed as evidence to demonstrate that America's Jews in the post-war era did not feel obliged or able to refrain from paying respect to their recent calamity. The second aspect of the project asks why this body of material disappeared. Why did historians from within and without the Jewish world, from the left and from the right, as well as communal activists, and the general American Jewish public as a whole construct the truth of American Jewish post-war "Holocaust-avoidance"? This second focus then must probe the historiography and the evolution of the communal commentary and explain how and why a particular rendition of the past—one that in fact deviated radically from the empirically evidence—triumphed in airbrushing out of existence the cultural works of American Jewry in the crucial years between the end of World War II with its ghastly revelations and the execution of Adolph Eichmann in 1962.

EXPERIMENTS IN EXPRESSION

American Jews in these years produced a mountain of texts which highlighted the European Jewish calamity. Some of these circulated exclusively, or nearly so, within the confines of the Jewish world. While they would have eluded the eyes of non-Jews, they infused American Jewish life. Because writers, journalists, radio program producers and performers created a good deal of this material in Yiddish, the memorial culture served a distinctly inner Jewish purpose. These years saw a massive journalistic outpouring in the Yiddish press, in Yiddish publications of memoir, fiction, essays, and books of essays, all consumed by a Yiddish-reading public. The late 1940s saw the first publication of *yizkor bikher*—memorial books—compiled by both the survivors of the calamity and their compatriots who had left their towns and cites before the storm destroyed their "old homes." Published by committees made up of those who had experienced the *hurban* themselves and those who had sat out those grim years in the United States, Canada, South America, South Africa, and Palestine, the memorial books of the post-war period included vignettes of life before the catastrophe, black-bordered pages listing the names of the murdered, as well as photographs of the notable places which had been leveled and of the men and women who had lived there and then went to their deaths at the hands of the Nazis. These volumes circulated almost exclusively among those Jews with ties to the particular place being memorialized. But nationally circulating Jewish books like the *American Jewish Yearbook*, published by the American Jewish Committee and the *Jewish Book Annual* yearly listed the names of the published *yizker bikher*, and as such disseminated information about the memorial projects to American Jews who might otherwise not even have known the names of these towns being mourned.

Some holocaust texts functioned exclusively within the boundaries of the American Jewish world, although written in English. Starting immediately at the end of the war, holocaust material found its way into prayer books and material fashioned for synagogues, Jewish community centers, Jewish youth organizations, and religious schools. A good deal of this material served a memorial purpose. As liturgy or pageantry, as physical marker or printed memorial book, these documents recalled the memories of the Jewish people slaughtered by the Germans and their allies. They resembled Jewish memorial materials created out of other earlier catastrophes in Jewish history, the Crusades and the pogroms, to name but two, and invoked images and metaphors of the Jewish past of suffering and bravery.[3]

At the same time though American Jews created texts for the consumption of a broad public which included non-Jews as well as Jews as the intended audience. Books of fiction and non-fiction, which bore the imprimatur of mainstream publishing houses, and which those companies marketed and distributed as they did other books which did not focus on the extermination of the Jews

---

3 See David Roskies, *Against the Apocalypse: Responses to Catastrophe in Modern Jewish Culture* (Cambridge: Harvard University Press, 1984).

under Hitler, made it possible for the idiom of the destruction to filter into the larger American world. A few examples of this will have to suffice. Viking, one of the country's largest and most prestigious publishers, brought out in 1954 Irving Howe and Eliezer Greenberg's, *A Treasury of Yiddish Stories*, an anthology which bore the "Dedication: To the Six Million." To Greenberg and Howe the history of Yiddish literature as represented by these stories could not be disassociated from the fact that "no one could know until the world of the East European Jews came to its end in the ashes of Maidenek and Auschwitz—at the time and place, that is, when Western civilization collapsed," nor, they declared, could the stories be read without an awareness that "Zionism and Socialism came to attract the best young minds; and then came the century of Maidenek and Auschwitz." For each short story written by a victim of the Nazi horror, Howe and Greenberg duly noted the horrific fate of the author. story written by a survivor, the editors likewise told the tale of miraculous redemption.[4]

Philip Bernstein, like many rabbis of the postwar period wrote brief books intended for lay audiences, Jews and non-Jews, intended to lay out the essence of Judaism, as they saw it. He peppered his 1951 *What the Jews Believe*, published by Farrar, Straus and Young with dozens of references to holocaust. In describing the fall holiday of Sukkot, for example, he noted that "the Nazis, according to the survivors of the concentration camps, derived exquisite joy from cruelty." Yet, according to Bernstein and as told by survivors he encountered at a Displaced Persons Camps, Babehausen, they found ways to celebrate. Bernstein described a memorial service at Feldafing, yet another DP camp, where "nearly every worshipper grieved for the loss of most of his family. The rabbi, himself a mourner, offered no easy consolation." And in praise of American Jewry and its response to the catastrophe, the rabbi, detailed their vast financial outpouring of assistance, one that in 1948 saw the United Jewish Appeal raise more money than the Red Cross. The purpose of the money—"to save the survivors of the Nazi onslaught"— made it clear that in Bernstein's mind, the events of the Nazi era had become inextricably bound up with the project of explaining "what the Jews believe."[5]

More dramatically and reaching a far larger public, Leon Uris's 1958 block buster novel, *Exodus*, dominated best seller lists for weeks. While the book took as its dramatic setting the struggle of the Jews in Palestine for a state of their own, it devoted pages on end to the experiences of the survivors of the death camps, whose blistering encounters with "the memories [that] would never leave," transformed them into recruits for the nationalist enterprise. Much of the *Exodus* narrative emerged from the memories of Dov Landau, who sitting in a Displaced Persons camp in Cyprus asked himself, "When had he been outside of barbed wire? It was so very long ago it was hard to remember. Barbed wire-guns-soldiers-Was there a real life beyond them?" From this point onward the

---

4   Irving Howe and Eliezer Greenberg, *A Treasury of Yiddish Stories* (New York: Viking, 1954), particularly pp. 12, 19, 67, 70, 72.

5   Philip S. Bernstein, *What the Jews Believe* (New York: Farrar, Straus, and Young, 1951), pp.40, 22, 31.

novel needed Dov's evolving story told through the chronology of the dehumanization of the Jews in the ghetto in Warsaw, of the pits of Babi Yar, Treblinka, Auschwitz, Birkenau, and other sites of Nazi brutality, in order to tell that of the heroic battle for the Jewish State. As Uris told his millions of readers about Dov, "As he looked at his arm with the blue tattooed number he relived the grotesque second when the doors of the gas chamber were flung open. Time and time and time again he saw his mother and his sister Ruth being removed from such a chamber at Treblinka. Time and time again he held that flickering candle close to the smothering bodies in the bunker in the Warsaw ghetto.... Over and over again he saw the skulls the Germans used as paperweights as his mother and his sister."[6]

Texts like these, one a wildly successful mass market novel, operated in a two-faced manner, addressing both Jews and non-Jews in the same document and linked private Jewish mourning with the larger reading public. They demonstrated that Jews, creating cultural works in the post-war period did not necessarily shy away from invoking the European calamity, even when those books came out of general publishing houses.

While much of the material produced in the decade and a half after the end of World War II functioned as means by which to recall and to remember, other texts that focused attention on the Holocaust served more complicated and political purposes, made necessary by the exigencies of the post-war moment. American Jews produced vast amount of Holocaust related material intended to help raise money for refugees and assist in their resettlement, to pressure the governments of the United States, the Federal Republic of Germany, and of other European nations to provide financial restitution and reparations to the Jewish victims of the Nazi crimes, to monitor the resurgence of Nazism in Germany and elsewhere in the world, to ensure that Nazi perpetrators be brought to justice, to help in facilitating family reunification, particularly in the cases of Jewish children who had been placed by their parents in Christian institutions to save them and who well into the middle of the 1950's had not been restored to their families, and finally to lend support for the creation and sustenance of a Jewish homeland, Israel. American Jews through their organizations and as reported in their press spent the decade and a half following the end of World War II picking up the pieces left in the wake of the cataclysm of the Holocaust. In their efforts to do just that they continuously told and retold the details of what happened, who did it, and how devastating it had been for those who went through this ordeal. They did not fail to note how much this event represented a tectonic shift in Jewish history. Every single volume, for example, of the *American Jewish Yearbook*, published in these years told in minute details about the projects and programs of American and world Jewry vis-à-vis the political aftershocks of the Holocaust. The annual reference books which the American Jewish Committee, the sponsoring body sent gratis to public officials around the country, described

---

6   Leon Uris, *Exodus* (Garden City, N.Y.: Doubleday and Company, 1958). Much of Dov's confrontation with the memories of the Nazis and the death camps can be found in Chapters 22-26, pp. 117-154.

pointedly how the destruction of European Jewry had created a set of political crises –in the United States, western Europe, eastern Europe, South America, and Israel—and the reference books, dry as they might seem from their covers, made it abundantly clear to anyone who read the material on its pages, that into the early 1960's the Holocaust continued to reverberate in the lives of the Jewish people.[7]

Additionally, as American Jews participated in some of the momentous events of the late 1940s, 1950s, and early 1960s most notably the flowering of the American civil rights movement and the frightening unfolding of the Cold War, they produced and used texts which put the cruelties of the Nazis and their systematic slaughter of the Jews of Europe into the foreground. As they confronted a series of political events in the United States, for example, the battle over prayer in public schools and the nagging issue of the need to reform immigration policy, American Jewish organizations and publications invoked the events of Europe of the 1930s and 1940s as metaphor and analogy which they believed should shape their behaviors.

The assembling this material has proven for me an exhilarating detective process and one far from completed. Seeking the ways American Jews made use of the Holocaust in these years and invoked it for one purpose or another has taken me into the source material of nearly every possible corner of the American Jewish world of the middle of the twentieth century. It has allowed me to look into the texts and practices of Orthodox, Conservative, Reform, and Reconstructionist Judaism. It has brought me into Hebrew, Yiddish, and English materials created by secular as well as religious groups, intellectuals and communal workers, pedagogs and youth group leaders. I have looked at material from the American Jewish left and Zionist material, as well as that produced by the more staid and establishment groups like the American Jewish Committee. I have looked to national bodies and to the local, to individuals acting on their own and those who represented formal organizations and institutions. Here let me offer just a few examples of the places where American Jews talked about, performed, and used the Holocaust in these years.

American Judaism of the late 1940s, 1950s and early 1960s, functioned as a complex of denominations, synagogues, and seminaries. This era in fact represented the high point of synagogue affiliation and although many rabbis and intellectuals decried what they considered the shallowness of the "religious revival" of these years, much of organized American Jewish life pivoted around the congregations. These years saw the creation of new institutions and texts which linked the practice of the Jewish religion to the horrors of Nazi Germany. In 1948 the Reconstructionist movement published its first high holiday prayer book while the Conservative movement issued its in 1951. Both *mahzorim* used

---

[7] It would be impossible to list every reference to the Holocaust that appeared in the various volumes of the *American Jewish Yearbook*. Literally hundreds of references appeared in each volume and well into the 1960s the writers and editors of the *Yearbook* demonstrated how much the event loomed in their consciousness as well as in that of the women and men who were involved in the various projects around the world.

the Yom Kippur "martyrology" liturgy to memorialize the Jews who perished in Europe. In the Reconstructionist *mahzor* the editors, who considered themselves free to tamper with traditional texts, replaced the conventional Hebrew words of the "Eleh Ezkerah" –these I shall remember, a lengthy paean to ten rabbis who had been tortured and executed by the Romans for their refusal to obey a ban on the teaching of Torah an the ordaining of disciples—with a poem by Hannah Sennesh, a young Hungarian Jewish woman who had moved to Palestine but then parachuted back into Hungary as a soldier. Captured by the Nazis who proceeded to kill her, Senesh's poetry lived on in this prayer book. Additionally a "Tribute to the Martyrs of the Bialystok Ghetto" became part of the Yom Kippur day's prayer cycle in the Reconstructionist text.[8] The Conservative *mahzor*, typical of the movement's attitude toward liturgical innovation, kept the *"Eleh Ezkerah"* but in English appended a poetic reading, "To Our Six Million"[9]

In the fall of 1958 proponents of modern Orthodoxy, associated particularly with Yeshiva University launched a new publication, *Tradition: A Journal of Orthodox Jewish Thought*, edited by Norman Lamm. Lamm introduced and justified the enterprise "The Need for Tradition," with its double meaning in terms of "changes on the world scene that have caused, particularly in America, a perceptible reorientation vis-à-vis Orthodoxy in the total Jewish community. The horrors of the Hitler era have profoundly shaken man's confidence in the beneficent use of the power he has gotten. The creation of the State of Israel has done more than give all Jews a collective pride in their people. It has also given them a sense of rootedness in the long history which gave birth to the little bit of Middle Eastern geography." Not only did Tradition present itself to its audience as growing out of a new Jewish world shaped by the Holocaust, but it filled its pages with articles, book reviews, and references to the Nazi horrors. As befitted an Orthodox journal which took Jewish law as fundamental and serious, it notified its readers of rabbinic rulings on a variety of matters, numerous of which reflected Jewry's on going engagements with the Holocaust. In a 1960 issue, for example, it reported on a *halakhic* ruling involving, "Human Skin." The problem discussed in *Tradition* told of "A *Kohen* [a member of the priestly class] who has received books from Germany which are bound in the skin of concentration camp victims." The ruling on this matter, delivered by Rabbi Mosheh Feinstein and discussed in the journal, stated emphatically that the recipient "may not bring them into his home because he is not permitted to defile himself by contact with any part of a corpse. He is also not permitted to sell them to anyone. He must bury the binding because it is part of a human body."[10]

---

8 *High Holiday Prayer Book* (New York: Reconstructionist Foundation, 1948), pp. 387-396
9 United Synagogue of America, *High Holiday Prayer Book* (Hartford, Connecticut: Prayerbook Press, 1951), p. 386.
10 Norman Lamm, "The Need for Tradition: The Editor's Introduction to a New Journal," *Tradition: A Journal of Orthodox Jewish Thought*, 1, 1 (Fall, 1958), p. 10; *Tradition* 3,1 (Fall, 1960), p. 80.

Within the world of Orthodox Judaism, the sermon represented a relatively recent innovation of the middle of the twentieth century. Historically the absence of English language sermons functioned as one of the hallmarks of traditional congregations. By the 1940s American Orthodox congregations began to incorporate what had previously been viewed as a modernist deviation, and in the middle of World War II the Orthodoxy body, the Rabbinical Council of America began to publish every year exemplary holiday and Sabbath sermons delivered by its members. Distributed presumably so other rabbis could draw upon this material for the orations which they now felt they had to give to their congregants, the details of the recent calamity emerged repeatedly in the sermon anthologies. Rabbi Solomon Roodman used it for his Purim *drash*—homily—of 1957, "Why the Jew Laughs," noting that "the most trenchant example of the true spirit of Jewish humor and unyielding faith which it motivates was confirmed by the many discoveries made in the ghettoes and extermination centers of Nazi Europe. Search teams which had visited those areas after the Nazis were brought to their knees discovered thousands of capsules containing manuscripts left by the victims of Nazidom." In a 1952 sermon, "Here the Child Asks," by Rabbi Moses Mescheloff, imparted words of wisdom for services on the first day of Passover. "The ancient Talmud legend of the salvation of the Jewish children is more than a hoary episode out of the past of our people. We, we in our own time have witnessed its repetition. Is it not the identical act that the Nazis committed against our youth? Did not the Nazis pursue our youth bereft of parental protection throughout Europe seeking their extermination? Did not our children hide in forests and caverns to escape their brutal persecutors?....With my own eyes have I seen such children. There are tens of thousands of them in Israel this very day. There are those with blue tattoo marks, mementos of the concentration camp, and those who escaped even this stamp of modern Egypt. They have been gathered together out of the impossible, impassable wastelands in Europe...brought back to Israel."[11]

The Reform movement did not issue any new prayer books in these years but in 1948 when the Hebrew Union College opened its School for Sacred Music, the first school founded in the United States to train cantors, it declared in its press release that the reason for creating such an academy grew out of the movement's awareness that "the disappearance of the great centers of Jewish culture and learning in Europe during the occupation by the Nazi horde has posed many serious problems for world Jewry....Among other things, the inspiration for Jewish sacred music has dried up in Europe, and we must look to other centers of Jewish life to fill the void."[12] This creative use of the destruction reverberated in Reform congregations through the 1950's. In 1957 Rabbi Louis I.

---

11 Rabbinical Council, *Manual of Holiday and Sabbath Sermons* (New York: Rabbinical Council Press, 1957), 137-138; Rabbinical Council, *Manual of Holiday and Sabbath Sermons* (New York: Rabbinical Council Press, 1952), 143-144 are two of hundreds of possible examples.

12 "Hebrew Union College-Jewish Institute of Religion." Nearprint Collection. Document Group 20. American Jewish Archives.

Newman of New York's Reform congregation Rodeph Shalom published a book of plays and cantatas which he had written and which had been staged in his congregation, performed by school children and adult members. "Pangs of the Messiah: A Play of World War II" won second place in a national play contest sponsored by AZA (Aleph Zadik Aleph), the B'nai B'rith Youth Organization. It explored the reactions of a group of Jews on the "Eastern War Zone" as the Nazis entered their town. The trapped Jews debated among themselves what to do –to fight, to submit, to pray—in the face of the Nazi menace and the play came to a close with an impassioned oration of the Rabbi, who linked the particular Jewish crisis faced by his townspeople with some universal human dilemmas:

> Every people, all humanity must learn to be its own
> Messiah...And we...are the people who must labor
> also for the coming of the Messianic days. The torments
> and horrors we are enduring—these may truly be the
> pangs of the Messiah.

Another play in the Newman anthology, *"Ein Breirah: No Alternative,"* declaimed that "out of the camps of desolation, the flaming Ghettos of the cities, was born the saga of fortitude unto death." Newman's member chorus then sang the "Song of the Partisans" a "Vilna Ghetto song."[3]

The linking of the *hurban* with the practice of Jewish ritual took place outside of strictly denominational projects. In 1957, for example, three authors Meyer Waxman, Sulamith Ish-Kishor and Jacob Sloan got together to compile a gift book especially designed to be given to girls on the occasion their bat mitzvah, a relatively recent American innovation to mark a girl's 13th birthday. Not sponsored by any one of the "branches" of American Judaism, the book graced the shelves of Jewish bookstores and was advertised in Jewish magazines. In *Blessed is the Daughter* the authors depicted for the teenage girls, the intended recipients of the book, the cycle of the Jewish year. They included "The Day of Carnage," that is the tenth day of the month of Tevet, a day which linked, "the begging of the siege of Jerusalem by the Babylonians in 588 B.C.E. through the slaughter of six million Jews by the Nazis during the second World War." That long history which involved "series of holocausts" had been "designated by world Jewry to commemorate the slaughter of the last war. The destruction of the great Eastern and Central European Jewish civilizations was the culminating tragedy of the process begun by the Babylonians 2,600 years ago." The text describing "Assarah be'Teveth" included a photograph of "Chief Rabbi of Israel, Dr. Isaac Herzog, Planting the First Tree in the Forest of the Six Million Martyrs, Israel." For Simhat Torah, the fall holiday marking the end of the liturgical year and the beginning of a new cycle of the reading of the Torah, Waxman and the other writers offered a story "The Last Dance" depicting the last Simhat Torah in Warsaw, a reading taken from an already published Holocaust memoir, the diary of a young boy, Hillel Seidman. In this gift book geared for adolescent girls

---

13 Louis I. Newman, *Pangs of the Messiah and Other Plays, Pageants and Cantatas* (New York: Bloch Publishing Company, 1957) pp. 3, 27, 222.

the authors included as well a special reading about two girls, Chajke and Frumke, who served as couriers for the Jewish underground, their life stories drawn from Emmanuel Ringelblum's "monumental contemporary record" of the Warsaw ghetto, published by McGraw Hill, as well as a portrait of Hannah Szenes and an historical account of the "Catastrophe in Europe" when "six million Jews of Europe –more than one-third of all the Jews in the world—had been slaughtered by the Germans under Hitler." Finally, despite the brevity of the volume and the festive occasion for which the authors intended it, they also provided a poem by Marie Syrkin, an American Zionist leader, "The Silent Army" focusing on the newly created State of Israel, which exhorted:

> Do not believe that we are few
> Though few the figures on the hill;
> A host ascends the mountain-side
> Whose solemn ranks are marching still?
> Among the waste six million trudge
> Up to the Negev's burning rim;
> The bodies seared at Maidanek
> Can bear the flame at Nitzanim.[14]

A few more random bits and pieces of Holocaust memorialization from the enormous corpus will have to suffice here, perhaps as tantalizing foretastes of the fuller corpus of material that will be part of a book-length study. Song books, designed for community sings in youth groups and at Jewish centers all included a number of songs like "Ani Ma'amin," and "The Song of the Partisans," pieces of music associated with the ghettoes and concentration camps. All of the songsters stated directly in their introductions and on the pages where the songs appeared that the words and music had been drawn from the Jewish repertoire of the Nazi era. Ruth Rubin's, *A Treasury of Jewish Folksongs* of 1950 included these same songs of the partisans and she described them in detail and placed them in their Holocaust-era context. In her introduction she told her readers –and singers—that, "in the dark yeas of the Nazi domination of Europe, a host of songs arose that record the heroic struggle of the Jewish people against the German overlord."[15]

In 1954 a number of popular books of American Jewish history appeared in library and book store shelves and they connected the history of American Jews with the recent calamity. Elma Ehrlich Levinger's, *Jewish Adventures in America: The Story of 300 Years of Jewish Life in the United States*, for example, found multiple ways to link the story of the catastrophe with her larger, celebratory narrative. In a biographical treatment of the philanthropist Nathan Straus, for example, she noted that "He gave large sums for the relief of those who suffered from the First World War. His death spared him the knowledge of the horrors of the Hitler persecution and of another conflict even more terrible than the last." She devoted a lengthy section to the efforts of American Jews to rescue the

---

14   Meyer Waxman, Sulamith Ish-Kishor, and Jacob Sloan, *Blessed is the Daughter* (New York: Shengold Publishers, 1957), n.p., 86-87, 134-135, 136, 137, 151-152.
15   Ruth Rubin, *A Treasury of Jewish Folksong* (New York: Schocken, 1950, pp. 12, 175.

Jews of Europe as the shadow of Nazism fell over them—"American Jews to the Rescue"—and an equally full one which treated the post-war philanthropic juggernaut of American Jews "to aid many of Hitler's victims....There had never been such an appeal before." Likewise, she described Rabbi Stephen Wise as someone "who lived to see the persecution of Hitler which doomed six million Jews to death." Her popular historical account of American Jewry made it clear that from the perspective of the middle of the 1950's, in a book published by a Jewish publishing house, intended probably for a primarily Jewish readership, American Jewish history, however upbeat and positive, could not be disassociated from the history of an era in which "six million Jews, not only those of German birth but....from German-conquered territory, perished in cattle cars, in concentration camps and crematoria."[16]

1954, the year of American Jewry's 300th anniversary festivities saw numerous efforts to commemorate the holocaust. In that year a committee formed in New York to create a Passover reading, entitled "A Seder of Remembrance." Originally formed under the auspices of the American Jewish Congress, the committee, lead by writer and communal activist Rufus Learsi, became independent, and over the course of the next years annually distributed thousands of copies of the English and Hebrew text through Jewish community councils, synagogues, and other organizations. The Seder committee also placed full-page copies of the bi-lingual text in dozens of American Jewish newspapers around the country every spring in anticipation of Passover. Dedicated to the memory of "the six million of our brothers of the European exile," who had been slaughtered "by a tyrant, more wicked than the Pharaoh who enslaved our forefathers in the land of Egypt" the short piece described the Nazis as "the evil ones" whose brutality "defamed the image of God in which man was created." The seder night had particular resonance for creators of this and other Holocaust texts. On the first night of Passover 1943 the "remnants of the Warsaw Ghetto" had risen up "to slay their oppressors as they were about to be slain." The reading that in fact got much usage as evidenced by the large number of letters sent to the committee in praise of the power of its words and images, depicted the survivors of the concentration camps and ghettos as people who emerged from their trauma still able to envision a day "when justice and brotherhood would reign among men."[17]

In a not dissimilar vein, Louis Ruchames, a Reform rabbi, Hillel director for the colleges of western Massachusetts, including Smith, Mount Holyoke, and Amherst, and an historian who specialized in African-American history addressed the Grand Street Boy's Club during Negro History Week in February of 1955. The Grand Street Boy's Club consisted of men who had grown up on New York's Lower East Side, had moved away, done quite well economically, and maintained a lively interest in the "old neighborhood." Ruchames spoke to them in part to mark the three-hundredth anniversary of Jewish settlement in Ameri-

---

16 Elma Ehrlich Levinger, *Jewish Adventures in America: The Story of 300 Years of Jewish Life in the United States* (New York: Bloch, 1954), pp. 233-235, 238-240, 277.
17 "Seder Ritual," I-50, American Jewish Historical Society.

ca, and he chose as his topic the "Parallels of Jewish and Negro History." His speech, later republished in the *Bulletin of Negro History* commented on the imperative that, "We Jews" must understand the "problems which have confronted the Negro." To Ruchames the parallel of suffering which linked the two peoples had very immediate resonance, since, "in our day, the lesson that men have had to relearn in every generation, that the rights of all men are interrelated, that no minority group is safe while others are the victims of persecution has been seared into our minds and hearts through the burning flesh of six million of our brethren in Europe."[18]

Ruchames words notably straddled the Jewish and the non-Jewish world. Delivered to a Jewish audience to mark Negro History Week and the festivities of the Tercentenary of Jewish settlement of North America, the speech then became an article for consumption by an audience composed primarily of African American readers. He, like the creators of the seder reading, effortlessly linked the utterly Jewish with the universal in the same text and evinced no embarrassment in making the Nazi holocaust a central element in Jewish self-consciousness.

In the middle of the 1950s when Ruchames served as the Hillel rabbi at Smith College, the young Jewish women of the elite school which had a quite small Jewish student body, took a radio play, "The Ballad of the Warsaw Ghetto" originally broadcast as part of the "Eternal Light" series sponsored by the Jewish Theological Seminary, and made it into a cantata with words, music and modern dance. After arranging for the presentation of "The Battle of the Warsaw Ghetto" to the other students at Smith College, Ruchames took the young women on a tour around the state of Massachusetts to other Hillel chapters, and to B'nai B'rith lodges in a dozen small and medium sized towns. Here too, then, a text that memorialized the Nazi catastrophe served Jewish and non-Jewish audiences and demonstrated not the lack of willingness of American Jews to present themselves through the medium of this horrific event but the sense of urgency to do exactly that.

Finally, from April 10-April 14, 1957 the American Jewish Committee conducted a series of meetings, symposia, and lavish dinners at New York's Waldorf-Astoria Hotel to mark its half century of a particular brand of Jewish advocacy, one which emphasized turning to notable gentile Americans of good-will, eschewing militant and overt calls to Jewish self-interest, and quite, behind-the-scenes negotiations over controversial matters. At the opening banquet with the Christian clergymen, government officials, presidents of major universities, and Secretary General of the United Nations Dag Hammarskjold in attendance, the Committee's former president Joseph Proskauer sounded the dominant tone of the jubilee meeting. "Our ethos," he stated, has been to foster "useful, valid, scholarly research into those causes which have operated to make Catholics murder Protestants, Protestants murder Catholics, and both, in turn, from time to time, murder Jews, until we saw its culmination in the Hitler holocaust."

---

18   *Bulletin of Negro History* 19,3 (December, 1955), pp. 63-64.

Proskauer combined various formers of group hatred in his words, but only one form, antisemitism, he argued fostered haters to cross conventional barriers and only it culminated in a "holocaust." Otto Kleinberg, a professor of psychology at Columbia University and formerly in charge of UNESCO's Division of Applied Social Science (and a refugee from Nazi Germany) called on America to solve its race problem in part to allow it to forge positive relationships with the newly emerging nations of Africa. He explained the need for such fundamental reform in light of the fact that "at the time of World War II and preceding it, the internal situation in Germany made a very big difference to its relationship to the outside world. The German treatment of Jews and other minorities modified and transformed the relationships of Germany with the other countries." While Kleinberg, who knew Nazism first-hand asserted, "We, of course are not in anything like as serious a situation as Germany was...we do....face this problem of strengthening democracy at home in order to create a truly democratic alliance abroad." Numerous other speakers invoked the Nazi era nightmare, with Israel's ambassador to the United Nations Abba Eban forcefully recalling that only "ten years ago, as we stood in anguish before the martyred graves of six million of our kinsman," destroyed in an event without precedent, since, "never in all recorded history had any family of the human race been overwhelmed by such a tidal wave of grief and havoc as that which engulfed the Jewish people in the...second World War." Finally, the assembled dignitaries heard the public reading of the American Jewish Committee's resolutions adopted to mark this anniversary. In one set of resolutions, in which the AJC described its obligations for Jewish communities around the world, it acknowledged the "vast changes that have taken place in the structure of Jewish communities," since 1906, particularly "as a result of the holocaust of the Hitler period," in which "the great historic Jewish communities of Europe have been decimated." A lengthy set of resolutions called upon West Germany to make good on all of its restitution promises and to check the troubling rise of "ultra-nationalistic and chauvinistic" groups, and it warned that "further political developments in West Germany will be subject to the test of history." A resolution on Israel, taken by this organization that had long evinced ambivalent feelings about Zionism, declared that "the State of Israel was established nine years ago under the aegis of the United Nations. It has become a place of refuge for hundreds of thousands of victims of Nazi.... persecutions."[19]

These scattered references represent a mere handful of examples of how American Jews used and referred to the Holocaust in the years before the mid-1960's. Knowing that behind these examples there exists a vast trove many times larger of words, objects, and performances that invoked the memory of the slain Jews and which sought to remedy some aspect or another of its cataclysmic impact upon the Jews leads us then to the second part of the project here, to ex-

---

19 *Proceedings of the Fiftieth Anniversary Observance of the American Jewish Committee: April 10-14, 1957: The Pursuit of Equality at Home and Abroad* (N.Y.: American Jewish Committee, 1958), pp. xi, 3, 27, 40, 133, 140, 141,157,199,226, 228,230.

plore the inability or disinterest of historians and later commentators in confronting this empirical material.

ERASING THE EVIDENCE

Scholars from a number of "camps" or cultural orientations have helped create and sustain the scholarly "truth" that American Jews refrained from thinking about or invoking the Holocaust in the post-war decade and a half. One thrust comes primarily from the left and these historians have produced the most widely talked about and broadly received works which have made this assertion central to their argument which stated that the late twentieth (or early twenty-first) century American Jewish emphasis on the Holocaust has been constructed in its mammoth proportion in order to serve a series of fundamentally conservative, and in their assessments, nefarious purposes. Norman Finkelstein's *The Holocaust Industry* has lambasted American Jews, their communal organizations and leaders for investing, "too much public and private resources...in memorializing the Nazi genocide. Much of the output," he bluntly claimed, "is worthless, a tribute not to Jewish suffering but to Jewish aggrandizement." That output indeed he saw as "crass exploitation," in order for American Jews and their organizations and leaders, to push the world to support Israel, a nation state he considers unworthy of that support or recognition.

Notably his argument like those of other critics of contemporary Holocaust culture, pivoted on an historic argument, one that posited that in the post-war period Jews, like other Americans, "paid the Nazi holocaust little heed." Because of the "conformist policies of the American Jewish leadership and the political climate of postwar America," American Jews "hewed closely to official US policy" which emphasized the fostering of cultural assimilation. Since he believed that Israel had not play an important role in American Jewry's political agenda, then they had felt no need or interest in dredging up Holocaust imagery. Rather he saw the period after the end of World War II as one in which Jews emphatically chose to deemphasize the Holocaust because of the emerging struggle between the United States and the Soviet Union. Finkelstein gave particular weight to the fact that, "with the inception of the Cold War" in 1949 and West Germany's emergence as an American ally in the anti-Communist struggle, Germany could not be vilified as the perpetrator of the horrendous crimes that had taken place under Hitler. American Jews collaborated with the United States government in its courting of Germany, its resultant unwillingness to name Germany as the culprit, and in a political project designed to keep public attention diverted from the so recent barbaric behavior of the Germans."[20]

Finkelstein's analysis may have been the most extreme in this contemporary discussion, but it dovetailed well with the sentiments expressed earlier by other critics of the uses of the Holocaust by American Jews. Tim Cole in his 1999, *The Selling of the Holocaust*, depicted the post-War period as one in which "those

---

20   Norman G. Finkelstein, *The Holocaust Industry: Reflections on the Exploitation of Jewish Suffering* (London: Verso, 2000), pp. 4-8, 12-18,42.

Jewish survivors who arrived in Britain, Israel, Canada and the United States tended to remain silent about their experiences," since "silence was a shared reaction." After all, Cole claimed, the Jews who lived in those places and who greeted the refugees believed it would be "detrimental to the best interests of Jewry" to memorialize the Holocaust or draw attention to its horrors. It would have been a shameful "perpetual reminder...that the Jews are a helpless minority whose safety and very lives depend upon the whim of the people among whom they live or the governments who control their destinies." That he understood they did not want.[21]

In the same year that Cole's book appeared, 1999, University of Chicago historian Peter Novick created a stir and brought to himself much attention in scholarly and intellectual circles with his book, *The Holocaust in American Life*. His attack on contemporary Holocaust uses, depended, as he saw it, upon the fact that in the years after the war, and until 1967, American Jews, wanted to make sure "that Jews were not perceived as out of step with other Americans." As such, "In matters having to do with Germany there was a virtual taboo on mention of the Holocaust," and not until the watershed moment of the Six Day War of June, 1967, did American Jews link images of the Nazi cataclysm with the fate of Israel. Novick postulated that among American Jews in the post-war years, only those on the left willingly championed the memory of the Holocaust since they did not, by definition, participate in the anti-communist rhetoric, while for others, engagement with the tragedy existed only "around the kitchen table." Where and when American Jewish publications and mainstream organizations did invoke the images of Auschwitz or Nazism they did so only to engage in the dominant anti-Communist rhetoric of the post-war era, linking developments in the late 1940s and 1950s in the Soviet Union with the history of Jewish suffering under Hitler. Novick as well as those who wrote positive reviews of his book and cited his work as authoritative asserted that when American Jews elided Nazism and Communism in their publications and speeches, they erased the specifically Jewish dimension of the holocaust.[22]

Novick, Cole, and Finkelstein all agreed that 1967 provided the pivotal moment when developments in Israel changed the nature of the American Jewish political agenda and reshaped the ways in which American Jews made their case and the manner in which presented themselves to the American public. In that newly constructed agenda, the Holocaust emerged out of obscurity to play a key role in the American Jewish political project. American Jews, their leaders and organizations, exhumed the Holocaust to appeal to the world's sense of guilt and win support for Israel among those with power and influence in America. For Finkelstein in particular the fact that Israel and its interests catapulted the Holocaust to the top of the American Jewish rhetorical repertoire made the Holocaust observance and consciousness particularly suspect. American Jews

---

21   Tim Cole, *Selling the Holocaust: From Auschwitz to Schindler How History is Bought, Packaged and Sold* (New York: Routledge, 1999), pp. 2, 148.
22   Peter Novick, *The Holocaust in American Life* (Boston: Houghton Mifflin, 1999), for example, pp. 91, 96.

began to claim the Holocaust, these historians have asserted, for narrow, chauvinistic, and non-humane purposes. It had ultimately nothing to do with the victims of the Nazi genocide and everything to do with a particular political agenda of some three decades later.

None of these books rested on a solid base of empirical evidence, systematically and broadly gathered. This absence of data drawn from a wide net of sources, reflected the reality that their "scholarship" emerged from a political agenda, one intended to offer quite harsh criticism of what they found offensive, inappropriate, and misguided in contemporary Holocaust performances, let alone unaesthetic. They set out to show how the culture of Holocaust memory from the late 1960's on reflected what they considered to be the reactionary political project of American Jews, including a defense of Israel's Occupation of Palestinian lands, as well as what they viewed as an increasingly conservative Jewish stance on American domestic matters, particularly vis-à-vis African-Americans and calls for affirmative action in particular. For Novick, the catapulting of the Holocaust to the top of the American Jewish rhetorical repertoire reflected the decline of any other kind of meaningful form of Jewish identity. Religion and ethnic identity, particularly in the form of Jewish secular culture, seemed, he believed to have dried up as sources of meaning to American Jews so organizations concerned with the crisis of Jewish continuity turned to the Holocaust as the sure-fire way to trigger feelings of Jewish solidarity, particularly among the young.[23]

Ironically, to make such moral evaluations of the political posture of a community actually did not require these scholars to consider any aspect of American Jewish history. If they found what American Jews did in the 1970's and beyond to be politically or culturally problematic, they surely could use their books to make that point. Such criticisms would have stood or fallen on their own strengths and the intellectual merits of their arguments about contemporary practice.

Yet history played a key role in these books. They derived much of their political punch from the "fact" of 1950s American Jews' refusal, avoidance, and silence on matters surrounding the destruction of European Jewry. The authors,

---

23 Of the three only Novick made any attempt to provide documentation but his references when studied closely show how his contemporary agenda shaped his scholarship. He made some superficial forays into the records of the American Jewish Committee, but did not survey even the entire corpus of material from that one organization. He saw random bits of American Jewish journalism, but with no thoroughness or consistency, and his lack of interest, indeed utter avoidance of sources coming from the world of Judaism –the religious sphere—as well Zionism, Jewish education, Jewish summer camping, as just a few examples indicate that he engaged with a very superficial set of sources. He had no access to or interest in, it seems, any materials in Yiddish or Hebrew, nor did he survey the vast body of archival material on Jewish organizations' use of radio in the late 1940's and 1950's to refer to the horrors of the Holocaust. He made no use of even easily available material like the *American Jewish Yearbook*, the *Jewish Book Annual*, or scholarly publications like *Jewish Social Studies* which abounded with references to the Nazi catastrophe and which did not require any knowledge of any other language.

Novick, Finkelstein, and Cole, who politically and intellectually functioned well outside of the realm of the American Jewish community, ironically benefited from the reality that Jewish communal activists, historians and others had actually constructed this same argument beginning two to three decades earlier. As far back as the late 1960s internal critics of the Jewish "establishment," young people in the main began to complain that their parents, literally and figuratively, had withheld from them knowledge of the Holocaust and that the previous generation had explicitly avoided talking about the European tragedy in order to strike a bargain with 1950s American culture. Writing, for example in 2001 in a symposium on Peter Novick's book, historian Eli Lederhendler, looked back to his own activist days of "twenty-five years ago." He reported how he as a young "active promoter of Holocaust consciousness" had confronted a Jewish educator –presumably older than himself—who had "offered his opinion in print that it was unwise to "overdo" the curricular treatment of the Holocaust." Lederhendler, remembering himself as an "intrepid youth," then "entered the fray with a response in which I argued that American Jewry had not yet begun to "confront" the Holocaust."[24]

Lederhendler's brief reminiscence pointed to the emergence of a new confrontational, generationally-differentiated debate within American Jewry in the late which made the Holocaust a matter of communal controversy. The Jewish young people who went through the tumultuous era of the 1960's brought to the Jewish world a new consciousness, a product of their particular generation, shaped in large measure by the civil rights struggle, the movement against the war in Vietnam, the campus revolutions launched against "the establishment," assertions of Black pride and cultural separatism, among other powerful and transformative projects. Jewish young people, college students in particular, participated in these enterprises. They also applied the vocabulary of the movements to the Jewish communities in which they lived and which they found wanting.

In the broadest sense these young activists questioned the basic premise on which they believed the Jewish communities functioned. They described in books, articles, manifestoes, newsletters, and alternative newspapers what they saw as an ugly communal truth, one that showed how the institutions of the 1950's, their practices and ways of thinking represented all that the emerging generation found shallow, compromising, and wrong with America and its Jews. In their critique of the suburban congregations which had come to dominate the Jewish landscape, of the affluence of the Jewish community, and its escalating levels of integration, the disaffected youth –and the scholars who grew out of that Jewish countercultural groundswell—saw much that they found wrong with American Jewry.

Whether those influenced by the Jewish counter-culture turned to heightened levels of religious orthodoxy, more militant forms Zionism, more demonstrative public assertions of Jewish distinctiveness, greater involvements in the

---

24 Eli Lederhendler, "On Peter Novick's *The Holocaust in American Life*," *Jewish Social Studies* 7,3 (Spring/Summer, 201), p. 161.

campaign for Soviet Jewry, to the creation of Jewish feminism, or the founding of *havurot* (extra-synagogal religious fellowships), they shared in the assertion that what had preceded them had been obsequious, devoid of intense Jewish content, and collaborative with the larger mainstream culture.

The critique of the older, established community, and the argument that it had prevented the growth of a memorial culture united Jews along a wide political spectrum. It put Meyer Kahane, of the Jewish Defense League, clearly a group far to the right, with Jews for Urban Justice, a progressive organization on the left. Both not only used Holocaust imagery for their very different political purposes, but both critiqued the community's leaders for suppressing any kind of meaningful and deep confrontation with that history. Across the political spectrum, they challenged the communal leadership. Both not only infused their rhetoric in general with graphic Holocaust images, but they directed their anger at the organizations, leaders, and practices which predominated in American Jewish life. The rage they expressed focused on contemporary issues, but segued easily into historical diatribes, claiming that in the face of the Nazi menace American Jews did little and in the aftermath of the catastrophe, went about their business as though nothing cataclysmic had transpired.

Kahane, in his manifesto, *Never Again*, claimed, "millions in Europe went to their gas chambers and crematoria, and we knew of it. We knew of it and were worse than silent, for he who knows of horror and limits himself to tepid, useless, respectable, occasional efforts is worse than the one who knows and does nothing." Kahane realized that his words would offend many in the "Jewish establishment," a phrase who invoked repeatedly, and "there re those who will be upset. Why raise such a painful subject? That which was done is done and buried and what can be gained by going back over this most terrible of Jewish historical periods?" In answer to his own question he made clear that the leadership which attacked him "still shepherds us and still speaks in our name and gives us guidance." His Jewish Defense League would do what had not been done by those responsible for the "moral bankruptcy" that ran rampant in the American Jewish community. It would make sure that "Jewish heroes and martyrs" would "be brought to the attention of Jewish youngsters. It would sponsor "in-depth study of the Holocaust, the Jewish partisans and resistance in Nazi Europe," and it would create programs of Jewish self-defense, overtly based on the truth that "the death of six million Jews has in no way lessened the thirst of the world for Jewish blood," a point that the leadership of the community refused to acknowledge as it continued its morally suspect assimilationist behavior.[25]

At the other end of the political spectrum, but reflecting the same assault on the American Jewish status quo, *The Freedom Seder: A New Haggadah for Passover*, edited by Arthur Waskow—published in 1969—also merged Holocaust imagery with biting attacks on the prevailing Jewish practices. It offered a reading from Emmanuel Ringelblum's diary of the Warsaw Ghetto and the "Ani

---

25 Meir Kahane, *Never Again! A Program for Survival* (Los Angeles: Nash Publishing, 1971).

Ma'amin, neither which would have been out of place in American Jewish texts of the time, or of the previous two decades. But it went on to offer in the pages of the sacred work a frontal attack on the politics of American Jewry. "In America," the *haggadah* declaimed, "we"—presumably American Jews—"have been both coerced and cajoled into abandoning the prophetic legacy," while, "or the sake of a mess of pottage, they,"—presumably the leadership—"have abandoned their birthright in the Prophets and the Covenant." "Our people," the seder reader was instructed to intone, "have been frightened into allowing themselves to be purchased, and they have been purchased at such affluent prices that they have forgotten to be angry." That amnesia, the redactors predicted, will come with a price, because "we know the cost of hushing; we counted it in millions dead. So we shall choose the risks of freedom." One contributor to the *Freedom Seder* played this theme out further in an editorial note as to "What's wrong with the American Jewish establishment." Its flaws consisted of having "completely lost track of what being Jewish is—in the pursuit of safety and material gain....American Jewish life is largely geared toward defense and chauvinistic fund-raising." In "the willingness of the Jewish Establishment to compromise their own ethical/moral posture for the sake of what they think is the best interest of Israel," it has adopted the position of, "Don't rock the boat or give the (goyishe) Establishment any trouble or they'll pull the rug out from under Israel." On the following page the text offered a quote "From Adolf Eichmann: I sat at my desk and got on with my job."[26]

Clearly these works represented a challenge to the American Jewish status quo and in that challenge the imagery of the Holocaust played a pivotal role. Not that it had not been there before in art, sermons, liturgy, ceremony, and communal rhetoric, but it came to be one of the events or phenomenon which could be used by the rising generation, the "new Jews" who hoped to create from scratch novel forms of Jewish communal rhetoric and practice. As they saw it, much of that which came before them, that which had been produced by the "Jewish establishment" had no resonance in part because it lacked sting. They considered so much of 1950's American Jewish culture as thin and weak, without the intensity which they believed Judaism and Jewish life needed. They took upon themselves the challenge to the American Jewish *status quo* and made the Holocaust part of that challenge.

That critique of 1950's American Jewry dismissed as trivial the texts and practices, artifacts and ceremonies which had been created in the United States beginning immediately after World War II ended and stretching into the early 1960's to remember the Jewish victims of the Nazi era. They saw little in the post-war doings of the organizations which had monitored the Nazi war crimes trials and reported upon them in detail in the press, which had pressed for Germany to make payment to the survivors and root out resurgent Nazism, and which had called upon the United States government to help make possible and support Israel as a place of refuge for the survivors, that they considered ade-

---

26   Arthur I. Waskow, *The Freedom Seder: A New Haggadah For Passover* (Washington, D.C.: Micah Press, 1969), pp. 17, 19, 54, 45-47.

quate Holocaust work. Indeed, the young people of the late 1960s, at the time and later as they went on to write their books and create new texts

In their critique of 1950's American Jewry, the insurgents paid scant attention to the texts and practices, artifacts and ceremonies which had been created in the United States beginning immediately after World War II ended and stretching into the early 1960's to remember the Jewish victims of the Nazi era. They saw little in the post-war doings of the organizations which had monitored the Nazi war crimes trials and reported upon them in detail in the press, which had pressed for Germany to make payment to the survivors and root out resurgent Nazism, and which had called upon the United States government to help make possible and support Israel as a place of refuge for the survivors, that they considered adequate Holocaust work. The young people of the late 1960s, at the time and later as they went on to write their books and create new forms of Holocaust observance played a crucial role in erasing from public consciousness all that had been said, done, written and created about the catastrophe in the period from 1945 to 1962.

The process of white-washing out of existence a period of time in American Jewish cultural and political action vis-à-vis the Holocaust and its victims continued a pace in the work of scholars who began in the 1970s to write the history of American Jewry. Many historians of the Jewish experience in America, some them religiously observant individuals, deeply involved in the inner life of the Jewish communities where they lived, and enthusiasts for Israel, in fact provided the imprimatur of scholarly authenticity to the assertions which Novick and Finkelstein were to make by the latter part of the 1990s.

The works that might be considered "insider" writings about American Jewish history fall into two broad categories, one, the key works in the field of American Jewish history and culture and the other, memoirs by American Jewish intellectuals and activists written at the end of the twentieth century, but looking back to the post-war era. Both set of sources have asserted directly and indirectly that the Holocaust did not exist as part of the expressive repertoire of American Jews in the fifteen years after the end of World War II, and only the Israeli victory in 1967, brought the Holocaust out of historical hiding.

A few examples from the historical scholarship since the early 1990's demonstrate the currency of this thinking and the degree to which it represents an academic and communal assumed truth. Until the 1990's no historian studying American Jews actually tackled the post-war period. In the 1970's and 1980's, the few works of history which dealt with this era treated it as contemporary studies and painted it with a broad-brush. Scholars like Henry Feingold and Arthur Goren who treated the era, "1945 to the Present," made nearly no reference to the ways in which American Jews in those years had remembered the Holocaust and its victims, concentrating instead on suburbanization, the decline of anti-semitism, the movement of Jews into the upper middle class, and the like. Where these historians dealt with cultural matters, they focused instead on the great panache with which American Jewish novelists and dramatists created works which explored Jewish themes to American audiences.[27]

By the 1990s, though, American Jewish historians did in fact begin to pay attention to the post-war period and in their treatment of that era, they played a pivotal role in excising the history of Holocaust commemoration as a factor in American Jewish life and culture. In 1992 the American Jewish Historical Society released a five volume history of Jewish life in the United States, "The Jewish People in America." The fifth volume, which spanned the years from 1945 through the 1980s, written by Edward Shapiro, not only documented nothing that had been created before 1967 to recall the lives of the Jews of Europe who perished at the hands of the Nazis, but he assertively stated, "for the first decade and a half after the end of World War II, Jews were reluctant to discuss the Holocaust." With no empirical data at his command, with no evidence drawn from any archives or published primary sources, he firmly stated that, "During the 1950s, Jewish communities did not sponsor Holocaust commemorations, the Jewish lecture circuit did not feature speeches on the holocaust....and there was little public discussion among Jews regarding the fate of European Jewry." This assertion, which has been recycled by numerous other historians, including Finkelstein and Novick not only then failed to treat what had taken place vis-à-vis American Jewish confrontations with the European catastrophe, but it positively concluded that that which had taken place did not. Shapiro additionally offered a number of explanations as to what finally shook American Jewry out of its muteness. None proved to be as important as the Six-Day War, a lightning bolt which made it possible for "repressed memories of the Holocaust" to spring "out in the open."[28]

The same year that Edward Shapiro made his pronouncement on the pre-1967 Holocaust silence and the importance of 1967 in bringing about the change in American Jewish willingness to engage in Holocaust talk, Howard Sachar in a one-volume history of American Jews, made the same point. While he did offer a few examples from the late 1940's, the very immediate aftermath of World War II, he saw the 1950s as the era of silence, one in which "the sheer density...inhibited Jewish writers and philosophers, no less than Jewish communal leaders, from coming to grips with the Holocaust." In Sachar's analysis, the

---

27 Arthur A. Goren, "The Jews," in, Stephan Thernstrom, ed., *Harvard Encyclopedia of American Ethnic Groups* (Cambridge: Belknap Press of Harvard University Press, 1980), 592-598); Stanley Feldstein, *The Land I Show You: Three Centuries of Jewish Life in America* (Garden City, New York: Anchor Press, 1978), pp. 416-471; Henry L. Feingold, *Zion in America: The Jewish Experience for Colonial Times to the Present* (New York: Hippocrene Books, 1974). Pp. 299-357. Feingold began his final chapter, "The American Jewish Condition Today" which a philosophic statement that indicated that the Holocaust had come to be a crucial element in American Jewish self-consciousness, "the touchstone of all contemporary sensibility," but he did not historicize this statement and explore how American Jews went about the process of weaving it and images of it into their communal practices. (p. 299).

28 Edward Shapiro, *A Time for Healing: American Jewry since World War II* (Baltimore: Johns Hopkins University Press, 1992), pp. 213-216.

"economic and political advancement" enjoyed by American Jews and the "preoccupation with the birth and growth of Israel" pushed the European catastrophe to the margins of public consciousness, only to re-emerge with vigor after 1967.[29]

It surely would not be interesting or useful to cite and quote from every work of American Jewish history and culture which has bought into this paradigm. After all this thinking represents so broad a truth in the field that such an endeavor would basically consist then of quoting from the entire corpus of literature.[30] Let me then just a few subsequent examples to indicate how widely this thinking pervades the field, how little evidence supports it, and how scholars from within the world of American Jewish history or, Jewish history more broadly, have concurred with the analysis that fundamentally indicts American Jews of the 1950s for failing to put the Holocaust into the foreground of their communal culture.

Two works of 1997 presented cases in point. Gerald Sorin's *Tradition Transformed* emerged as probably the best single volume history of American Jews and one that has widely adopted for use in undergraduate courses on the subject. Sorin leaned heavily on Edward Shapiro's *A Time for Healing* to fashion his final chapter and in it deviated not at all from Shapiro's analysis. If anything, he went beyond him in condemning post-war American Jews for their inability or disinterest in engaging in acts of public mourning or in making use of the Holocaust in their communal culture. He described American Jewish culture of the 1950s as based on a "conspiracy of silence," with the survivors who refused to talk and American Jews who would not listen as collaborators in a project that would last until the 1970s when "the consciousness of its [Holocaust's] enormity and the struggle with its meaning—took a place as one of the pillars supporting identity." The "historical amnesia" of the 1950s persisted until the "Six Day War...ended the silence."[31]

Lastly, in 1997 Stuart Svonkin published his dissertation under the title, *Jews Against Prejudice*, one of the first book length historical works on American Jewish political culture of the 1950's. Here in a study of the involvement of Ameri-

---

29 How Sachar, *A History of the Jews in America* (New York: Knopf, 1992), pp. 839, 844, 847.
30 Jacob Neusner, "How the Extermination of European Jewry Became "The Holocaust," in, *Stranger at Home: "The Holocaust," Zionism, and American Judaism* (Chicago: University of Chicago Press, 1981), pp. 82-91, see, p. 84; Rona Sheramy, "Defining Lessosn: The Holocaust in American Jewish Education," unpublished Ph.d. dissertation, Brandeis University, 2001; Michael Staub, *Torn at the Roots: The Crisis of Jewish Liberalism in Postwar America* (New York: Columbia University Press, 2002) are a few examples of pieces of scholarship which have in one way or another chipped away at the prevailing paradigm. Neusner's piece was an article with no documentation, Sheramy's is a dissertation which focuses on the uses of the Holocaust in American Jewish pedagogic material and has several chapters on the pre-1967 period, while Staub, although he has much material on the pre-1967 period and the invocation of the Holocaust, never strayed beyond a few sources, particularly *Commentary*.
31 Gerald Sorin, *Tradition Transformed: The Jewish Experience in America* (Baltimore: Johns Hopkins University Press, 1997), pp. 194-195, 217.

can Jewry's "big three" defense organizations, the American Jewish Committee, the American Jewish Congress, and the Anti-Defamation League and how they created a role for Jews in the arena of liberal politics, Svonkin focused on the Jewish organizational tendency to universalize rather than particularize, to create programs and texts to fight prejudice in general, rather than to point out the specifics of anti-semitism. In that political project, Svonkin assumed as true that the organizations had no reason to single out, name, or refer to the European catastrophe unleashed against the Jews. The era which Svonkin studied, he asserted, came to an end with the late 1960's and the "new concerns about...the Holocaust." Citing and quoting Shapiro, Svonkin stated that the organizations' behavior could be explained in light of the fact that, "American Jews seemed to have been reluctant, or unable, to come to terms with the mass destruction of European Jewry." Both Sorin and Svonkin saw the 1950's as the nadir of Holocaust consciousness, a period of time in American Jewish history when outside pressures, particularly the Cold War and the desire of Jews to participate in the bounty of the decade's suburban affluence, as well as their own shame and embarrassment at having a mournful history, closed off the wellsprings of any kind of commemorative memorial culture.[32]

One final example from the early 2000's demonstrated the hardiness of the paradigm and the absence of systematic scholarship behind it. In 2001 Alan Mintz, a professor of Jewish literature at the Jewish Theological Seminary in a series of lectures at the University of Washington, explored the contours of Holocaust memory in the United States. He focused on the role of the larger American popular culture in spreading a distinctively American set of images and tropes. He quite categorically dismissed anything American Jews produced in the 1950's, a period of time in their history that amounted to, a "celebration" of American liberalism, "at which the Holocaust and everything we now associate with it were not welcome guests." Mintz acknowledged that at the immediate end of the war newsreels shown in movie theaters made it impossible to utterly avoid the subject in all of its gruesomeness but "an acute awareness of the Holocaust was not part of the American Jewish experience during the first two decades after the event because it impeded the process of Americanization" and so Jews went out of their way to avoid performing it in public, since they were "too deeply engaged in the energetic enterprise of entering American society and seizing the opportunities offered to them to be available to make the subversive sadness provoked by the Holocaust." Mintz wrote his book after the publication of *The Holocaust in American Life* and he praised Peter Novick, not-

---

32   Stuart Svonkin, *Jews Against Prejudice: American Jews and the Fight for Civil Liberties* (New York: Columbia University Press, 1997), particularly pp. 180, 185-186; a number of other works on Holocaust memory and Holocaust memorial projects give some attention to efforts to commemorate the tragedy in the late 1940's but do not extend their analyses and consider the 1950's at all. See, James Young, *The Texture of Memory: Holocaust Memorials and Meaning* (New Haven: Yale University Press, 1993), pp. 287-290; Edward Linenthal, *Preserving Memory: The Struggle to Create America's Holocaust Museum* (New York: Viking, 1995), pp. 5-9.

ing that "the book's most valuable sections...deal with the forties and fifties and the role of the Cold War" in making Holocaust silence the norm in American Jewish culture.

Mintz, like all those who have participated in the dissemination of this truth, presented his definitive assertions on American Jewry's avoidance of the subject of the Holocaust in their expressive culture in the late 1940's and particularly the 1950's with little empirical documentation. Although he suggested in a footnote that "there is much work to be done in fleshing out our picture of the late forties and fifties," he like Sorin, Shapiro, Novick, Finkelstein, among others, have relied on the truth of a community memory, rather than consulting the massive amount of empirical material available on this time period. In relying on this assumption, historians from across the political spectrum, with very different positions vis-à-vis Judaism and Jewish culture, have met and shared in the erasure of history.[33]

In this they have likewise joined with, or been joined by, a number of scholars and other communal commentators have invoked their own personal memories of the period before 1967 to prove just how much has changed since that watershed moment. They have told their personal stories along the lines of this narrative trope which has dominated the scholarship. In so doing these memoirists demonstrated that despite available empirical evidence to the contrary, the truth of Holocaust erasure in the 1950's functions as more than the construct of historians. It exists as the over arching orthodoxy. Arthur Hertzberg, rabbi, historian, Jewish communal activist, on of the memoir writers, reflected in book form on his long life as *A Jew in America* in 2002. Firmly, he stated, "The measure of how much the times were changed was the suddenly revived memory of the Holocaust," in the 1970's. Before that moment "American Jews did not want the mass murder in Europe to be much mentioned in public." He recalled how he had spoken from the pulpit about the Warsaw Ghetto uprising, and "the father a young woman whose Bat Mitzvah was being celebrated that Sabbath went to the board of the synagogue to complain that I had ruined a happy family occasion by bringing up so sad a topic." Besides the analytic problem of conflating one person's reaction—the complaining father—with all of American Jewry (we do not learn how the board reacted), Hertzberg's anecdote stands in sharp contrast to, for example, the bat mitzvah gift book with its pages and pages specifically dedicated to telling the story of the six million, the Rabbinical Assembly *mahzor* with its Yom Kippur dirge "To the Six Million" or the large numbers of articles which appeared in *Conservative Judaism*, the movement's official magazine to indicate that that the denomination had incorporated the tragic events into its religious projects.[34]

Political scientist Daniel Elazar, an American-born scholar who emigrated to Israel and wrote extensively on American Jewish communal politics, remi-

---

33 Alan Mintz, *Popular Culture and the Shaping of Holocaust Memory in America* (Seattle: University of Washington Press, 2001), pp. 5-8, 187.
34 Arthur Hertzberg, *A Jew in America: My Life and a People's Struggle for Identity* (San Francisco: harper San Francisco, 2002), pp. 403-404.

nisced about his years in Habonim, the Labor Zionist Youth movement. As he remembered the postwar period from the vantage of 1993, the Holocaust had gotten scant mention in the activities of the group. He recalled that the Americans who had gone off to fight in the Abraham Lincoln Brigade on the Republican side of the Spanish civil war had been their heroes while the partisans and ghetto fighters did not.[35] Peter Novick, in fact, cited this particular memory of the early 1950's as a forceful piece of ammunition in his arsenal of evidence.

While there can be no question as to why Novick found this statement appealing, it is harder to explain why Elazar remembered the past the way he did, because in actuality, his memories stood in direct conflict with material in the Habonim archives which include much in the way of handbooks for group leaders and counselors and descriptions of actual programs held in both the various summer camps and the city clubs which showcased the Holocaust. The summer camps in particular used the destruction of European Jewry as a way to mark the summer holy day of Tisha b'Av, a moment in the liturgical year that recalled the Babylonian and Roman destructions of the Temple in Jerusalem.

Habonim in fact published a history of its camping activities in 1957, *Adventures in Pioneering*, and in that silver anniversary book, graduates of the various camps enumerated how they as staff had grafted Holocaust imagery on to the summer fast day programming or as campers how they had experienced the heightened emotions of the day. One writer chronicled the activities of the summer of 1956 at Camp Kvutzah in California. "Our general camp theme," wrote David Yaroslavsky, "was: "Jewish Heroism through the Ages." Through lectures, discussions, literary trials, models, games, and the arts, the children at camp became acquainted with the heroic moments in Jewish history beginning with our ancient struggles for freedom and independence down to the modern deeds of courage and valor of the defenders of the Warsaw Ghetto and of the Hagana."

Elazar, who remembered no programming on the Holocaust in his Habonim days—and Novick who accepted Elazar's memories—might have been interested in, as well, the ceremony staged at the movement's national convention of 1945 and then reprinted in the 1957 anniversary book. That 1945 *ve'ida* began with a poetic presentation of remembrance, *Hazkara*, which declaimed:

> Over the blood-soaked plains of Poland, the sound of firing still is heard.
> And the dazed survivors of your people flee before the same pursuing mob.
> Only in a brief moment of council, we pause to consider a fitting monument
> And to tell our losses.
> The hundreds upon thousands upon millions, yet calls afresh each loved one
> Gone.
> From ghetto and from concentration camp, from Warsaw, Bialystok, Lublin,
> Majdanek, Auschwitz and Stryi.
> Brothers, from your graves look out!
> Look upon your people!

---

35 Daniel J. Elazar, "Detroit, the Early 1950s: "Habonim Was Looked at a Bit Wild," in, J. J. Goldberg and Elliot King, eds., *Builders and Dreamers: Habonim Labor Zionist Youth in America* (New York: Habonim Dror, 1993), p. 173.

> Look into the ghetto, to the camp, into the ship that bears
> Illegal freight out of the graveyards of Europe.
> Look and say, oh brothers, will they live?
> Will this your people, these dried bones yet live?[36]

Lastly, Alan Dershowitz's *Chutzpa*, a 1991 memoir-manifesto, dedicated to the premise that "American Jews need more chutzpah," or willingness to vociferously assert that "we are entitled to first-class status" told of his elementary and high school years at Brooklyn's Etz Chaim Yeshiva, where "many of our teachers –especially in our religious subjects—were right off the boat from the European displaced persons camps." Despite their experiences and those of "several of our classmates [who] had also experienced Hitler's concentration camps," the classrooms and playgrounds proved to be places where talk of those traumas never took place. Yes, he admitted, "it was in the air," but never became entered into the realm of the concrete in terms of curriculum or conversation.[37]

Yet in the 1953 yearbook put together by the eighth graders at a nearby school, not terribly different from Etz Chaim, the Yeshivah Flatbush, children committed to writing exactly what Dershowitz –who would have been in the tenth grade that year—claimed only hovered amorphously in the atmosphere. In the yearbook, no doubt edited by teachers and approved by administrators, autobiographical pieces recounted the horrors of the Nazi era and tales of rescue and survival. One boy, Kenneth Wetcher, a sixth-grader, in a story, "Here, There and Everywhere," stated in the yearbook directly, "I am the only child in my family. I was born, April 16, 1941....At the age of one and one half, we went by cattle train from Russia to Poland. On the way soldiers made signs at us that they would slit our throats. In Poland many people hated Jews and threatened to kill us." Abraham Fuksman, "born May 1, 1940 in Barawich, Poland," told his teachers, school mates, and whatever adults may have perused the yearbook, that "at the time, the Nazis started to attack Poland. I stayed with my parents," but, "on the sixteenth month, my parents gave me away to a Christian woman in order to save me....I did not know I was a Jews....As soon as the war ended with a casualty list of over 6,000,000 people my mother and father came to take me back." Other Yeshiva Flatbush children used Holocaust imagery in their poems, drawings, and vignettes about Jewish holidays, particularly Hanukkah, Purim, and Israeli Independence Day. Where Dershowitz remembered his Etz Chaim days as devoid of Holocaust-talk, the words on paper, penned by the children of the other Brooklyn Orthodox day, cast grave doubt on those later memories.[38]

Clearly a large chasm separates how American Jews –academics among them, and other political commentators from a variety of ideological positions, think about the post-war period and the actual data which exists in archives, publications, books, and articles. The first considers it to be true that American Jews could not, would not, and did not weave the images, words, and metaphors

---

36 David Breslau, ed., *Adventures in Pioneering: The Story of 25 Years of Habonim Camping* (New York: Chay Commission of the Labor Zionist Movement, 1957), pp. 98-100, 159-162.
37 Alan M. Dershowitz, *Chutzpa* (Boston: Little, Brown, 1991) p.42.
38 *Yeshivah Yearbook: 1953*, pp. 28, 30, 34, 36, in the possession of the author.

of the European destruction of the Jews into their communal culture in the first decade and a half after World War II ended. The other consists of a vast and only barely sampled repertoire of words, music, and graphic images for Jewish and non-Jewish audiences that confronted the calamity. How can this disjunction be explained?

Perhaps in the face of the mammoth edifice of Holocaust-performance of 1970's, 1980's, and 1990's, the post-war references and invocations seem paltry enough as to have caused scholars and activists in dismissing them from the historic record. The ways in which American Jews remembered the tragedy of the Nazi era in the earlier era may have seemed so pale to memoirists like Dershowitz, Hertzberg, and Elazar, as well as historians like Svonkin, Shapiro, and Sorin, when compared to such contemporary phenomena as the U.S. Holocaust Memorial Museum in Washington, D.C., movies like "Schindler's List" and "The Pianist," as well as projects like the March of the Living where thousands of Jewish teenagers from around the world converge on Auschwitz and march through it on Yom Hashoah —Holocaust remembrance day—as to literally excise from personal and communal memory what came before.[39]

Secondly, for the communal insiders and the critics of American Jews alike, seeing Holocaust observance as an historically continuous phenomenon, which only changed and grew over time, diminishes the significance of the June, 1967 war in Israel. By looking at Holocaust observance as an evolving phenomenon which began immediately (and indeed grew out of communal practices during the war itself) after the end of the war, and then developed through as writers of prayerbooks, compilers of song books, and the creators of a whole range of other texts, experimented with images and tropes, minimizes the role of Israel's victory in stimulating American Jewish consciousness. The idea that that event represented a momentous turning point in American Jewish political and cultural life has become thoroughly embedded in historical consciousness. To assert that it did not represent a watershed, that American Jews had found many times and places to remember the catastrophe before June, 1967, then implies that modern American Jewish history need not be divided into a pre-1967 and post-1967 period.[40]

---

39 Irving Howe made a point in this vein in his autobiography, *A Margin of Hope*. When in the memoir he explored his own political and intellectual engagement with the Holocaust he admitted that he did in fact react slowly, but "would add mildly that now, when incessant talk about the Holocaust risks becoming a media vulgarity, we may value silence a bit more than anyone could have supposed in earlier years." Howe in fact participated in 1950's remembrance in as much as his anthology of Yiddish short stories put the tragedy on to the front page. Irving Howe, *A Margin of Hope: An Intellectual Biography* (New York: Harcourt Brace Jovanovich, 1987), pp. 247-248.

40 This point and the need to rethink the significance of 1967 has been made by Eli Lederhendler, *New York Jews and the Decline of Urban Ethnicity, 1950-1970* (Syracuse: Syracuse University Press, 2001). Here I need to plead a bit guilty myself. In my book, *The Jews of the United States* (Berkeley: University of California Press, 2004) I have built my final chapter around the date 1967.

Most importantly, though, since the late 1960's American Jewish engagements with the Holocaust have taken place in a very different kind of America. In that earlier era, American Jews stood alone as the creators of books, poems, paintings, musical compositions, prayers, articles in magazines for children and adults, public ceremonies, and other kinds of texts which spoke of gas chambers, crematoria, annihilations, liquidations, mass murders of millions, genocides, and destructions of total communities and cultures. In those earlier years, immediately after the war and into the early 1960's American Jews had no "partners" or competitors in this kind of rhetoric.

After the 1960's a new kind of tone and texture came to dominate American public culture, one which venerated and validated discussions of group suffering. American Jews who had been lamenting in their particular ways the tragic fate of the six million now did so alongside other Americans, from other ethnic backgrounds, who also created texts and practices that memorialized tragedy.

Additionally after the 1960's the language of "Holocaust" and the appearance of the word itself in capital letters, came to be used to describe so many other historical outrages and horrendous calamities against so many other people. The tendency of many others to refer to their own "Holocausts" gave Jews in the United States a particular cultural project, designed to make sure that they did not lose that word and idea, that their very particular history would not be lost. The massive Holocaust memory project which American Jews launched in the 1970's and beyond, the development of programs designed to inspire "Holocaust consciousness," and the magnetic draw of the Holocaust in American popular culture well beyond the boundaries of the Jewish community, all have histories which grew out of the concerns and contours of late twentieth century America, a very different American than that of the years 1945 to 1962.

The differences between those two eras and the differences in the context of their Holocaust performances deserve to be studied in a comparative fashion. Whatever conclusions would emerge in such a study, it should not blind historians—as it has heretofore—to the efforts of American Jews, writers, teachers, summer camp counselors, rabbis, artists, as well as the consumers of these texts to remember the six million. American Jews did not experience a period of amnesia, nor did they go about their post-war lives silent or impervious to the recent tragedy. They cobbled together a set of communal practices that reflected their sense of identity and those deserve not to have been air-brushed out of the historical record.

References

Bernstein, Philip S. *What the Jews Believe*. New York: Farrar, Straus, and Young, 1951.
Breslau, David, ed. *Adventures in Pioneering: The Story of 25 Years of Habonim Camping*. New York: Chay Commission of the Labor Zionist Movement, 1957.
Cole, Tim. *Selling the Holocaust: From Auschwitz to Schindler How History is Bought, Packaged and Sold*. New York: Routledge, 1999.
Dershowitz, Alan M. *Chutzpa*. Boston: Little, Brown, 1991.
Diner, Hasia. *The Jews of the United States*. Berkeley: University of California Press, 2004.

Elazar, Daniel J. "Detroit, the Early 1950s: "Habonim Was Looked at a Bit Wild," in *Builders and Dreamers: Habonim Labor Zionist Youth in America*. Ed. J. J. Goldberg and Elliot King. New York: Habonim Dror, 1993.
Feingold, Henry L. *Zion in America: The Jewish Experience for Colonial Times to the Present*. New York: Hippocrene Books, 1974.
Feldstein, Stanley. *The Land I Show You: Three Centuries of Jewish Life in America*. Garden City, New York: Anchor Press, 1978.
Finkelstein, Norman G. *The Holocaust Industry: Reflections on the Exploitation of Jewish Suffering*. London: Verso, 2000.
Goren, Arthur A. "The Jews," in *Harvard Encyclopedia of American Ethnic Groups*. Ed. Stephan Thernstrom. Cambridge, Massachusetts: Belknap Press of Harvard University Press, 1980.
Hertzberg, Arthur. *A Jew in America: My Life and a People's Struggle for Identity*. San Francisco: Harper San Francisco, 2002.
High Holiday Prayer Book. New York: Reconstructionist Foundation, 1948.
High Holiday Prayer Book. United Synagogue of America, Hartford, Connecticut: Prayerbook Press, 1951.
Howe, Irving, and Eliezer, Greenberg. *A Treasury of Yiddish Stories*. New York: Viking, 1954.
Howe, Irving. *A Margin of Hope: An Intellectual Biography*. New York: Harcourt Brace Jovanovich, 1987.
Kahane, Meir. *Never Again! A Program for Survival*. Los Angeles: Nash Publishing, 1971.
Lamm, Norman. "The Need for Tradition: The Editor's Introduction to a New Journal." *Tradition: A Journal of Orthodox Jewish Thought*, 1, 1 (Fall, 1958).
Lederhendler, Eli. "On Peter Novick's The Holocaust in American Life." *Jewish Social Studies* 7, 3 (Spring/Summer, 2001).
Lederhendler, Eli. *New York Jews and the Decline of Urban Ethnicity, 1950-1970*. Syracuse: Syracuse University Press, 2001.
Levinger, Elma Ehrlich. *Jewish Adventures in America: The Story of 300 Years of Jewish Life in the United States*. New York: Bloch, 1954.
Linenthal, Edward. *Preserving Memory: The Struggle to Create America's Holocaust Museum*. New York: Viking, 1995.
Mintz, Alan. *Popular Culture and the Shaping of Holocaust Memory in America*. Seattle: University of Washington Press, 2001.
Neusner, Jacob. *Stranger at Home: "The Holocaust," Zionism, and American Judaism*. Chicago: University of Chicago Press, 1981.
Newman, Louis I. *Pangs of the Messiah and Other Plays, Pageants and Cantatas*. New York: Bloch Publishing Company, 1957.
Novick, Peter. *The Holocaust in American Life*. Boston: Houghton Mifflin, 1999.
Proceedings of the Fiftieth Anniversary Observance of the American Jewish Committee: April 10-14, 1957: The Pursuit of Equality at Home and Abroad. N.Y.: American Jewish Committee, 1958.
Rabbinical Council. *Manual of Holiday and Sabbath Sermons*. New York: Rabbinical Council Press, 1957.
Roskies, David. *Against the Apocalypse: Responses to Catastrophe in Modern Jewish Cutlure*. Cambridge: Harvard University Press, 1984.
Ruth, Rubin. *A Treasury of Jewish Folksong*. New York: Schocken, 1950.
Sachar, How. *A History of the Jews in America*. New York: Knopf, 1992.
Shapiro, Edward. *A Time for Healing: American Jewry since World War II*. Baltimore: Johns Hopkins University Press, 1992.
Sheramy, Rona. "Defining Lesson: The Holocaust in American Jewish Education." Unpublished Ph.D. dissertation, Brandeis University, 2001.
Sorin, Gerald. *Tradition Transformed: The Jewish Experience in America*. Baltimore: Johns Hopkins University Press, 1997.

Staub, Michael. *Torn at the Roots: The Crisis of Jewish Liberalism in Postwar America*. New York: Columbia University Press, 2002.

Svonkin, Stuart. *Jews Against Prejudice: American Jews and the Fight for Civil Liberties*. New York: Columbia University Press, 1997.

Uris, Leon. *Exodus*. Garden City, N.Y.: Doubleday and Company, 1958.

Waskow, Arthur I. *The Freedom Seder: A New Haggadah For Passover*. Washington, D.C.: Micah Press, 1969.

Waxman, Meyer, Sulamith Ish-Kishor, and Jacob Sloan. *Blessed is the Daughter*. New York: Shengold Publishers, 1957.

Young, James. *The Texture of Memory: Holocaust Memorials and Meaning*. New Haven: Yale University Press, 1993.

Neighbourhood on a Hill: the Traditional Polish American Neighbourhood: Has it Changed Forever? Has it a Future? The Examples of Worcester and Webster, Massachusetts

David A. Jones (University of Warsaw)

Neighbourhoods were very important to Polish Americans from before World War II until well into the 1980s and beyond. Frequently, Polish-American neighbourhoods were built on a hill, much as was the Massachusetts state capitol on Beacon Hill in Boston, that prompted colonial governor John Winthrop to portray Boston (and America) as being a "city upon a hill" (Winthrop, 1630), the imagery of American exceptionalism and of America as a "Redeemer Nation" (Tuveson, 1980).

Indeed, one could argue that the Polish-American communities of central Massachusetts were built on hillsides, often physically but always metaphorically, because they stood out and apart from other ethnic communities in terms of their superior values. They were, they are, a cut above other ethnic neighbourhoods in America: cleaner with far more visible flowers in window boxes, almost crime free. As important, perhaps even more so, one could discern Polish-American homes in Worcester and Webster by the newspapers delivered to the porches of their homes (sometimes weeks after publication), written in Polish, German, Russian Cyrillic, and sometimes Yiddish languages, in addition to the global and local newspapers written in English. First generation Polish-Americans read all of these languages fluently, and this ongoing connection with Eastern Europe helped the Polish diaspora settling in central Massachusetts to recreate their own civil society there across the 20th century. Today, many aspects of Polish neighbourhoods seem to have vanished, and with them a part of both America and Poland. Not every aspect has vanished, of course, because the houses themselves, or many of them, still exist, although no longer are they Polonia. The questions this paper poses: Has the Polish-American neighbourhood changed forever? Has it a future? The author's answer to these two research questions is clearly Yes and Yes, for reasons that follow, based in large part upon the author's participant observation.

Polish-American neighbourhoods in central Massachusetts have changed over the course of the second half of the 20th century. The 2000 U.S. Census lists 323,210 residents of the Commonwealth of Massachusetts as having declared themselves to be of Polish origin, making that state the 10th largest location of Polish diaspora among the 50 United States (Brittingham, de la Cruz, 2004; U.S. Census Bureau, 2000). In 1945, at the end of World War II, the Polish neighbourhood of Worcester, Massachusetts centred around Water Street as Vernon Hill rose above Kelley Square and "The Island" in downtown Worcester. There sprung up the clubs of Polish America, including the Polish National Alliance Hall on LaFayette Street, and on parallel Green Street the Polish Falcons in White Eagle Hall and the Polish-American Veterans Association of World War

II. Nearby, there was an area along Millbury Street not far from where were located the major factories that employed Polish-Americans as labourers, many of whom rose to levels of management over time. The long, flat area that stretched from Quinsigamond Avenue and Cambridge Street was the location of American Steel and Wire Company's South Works and of the Crompton and Knowles Corporation. American Steel and Wire was the largest employer of Polish (and Lithuanian) American diaspora in central Massachusetts, followed by Crompton and Knowles Corporation. American Steel and Wire made the barbed wire fences that carved out homestead land along the "frontier" of the American west. Crompton and Knowles was the manufacturer of giant textile looms for the world (Proko 2009).

The Polish American neighbourhood in central New England revolved around its very ethnic Roman Catholic churches and slightly less ethnic synagogues that formed its core. To these religious institutions, symbolised by their edifices, were joined shoppes selling foods and merchandise peculiar to the tastes of the Polish American family, delicatessens and restaurants serving Eastern European sandwiches, lunches, and dinners, social clubs, and of course the very noticeable architecture of the three storeyed wooden frame house, known colloquially as the "triple decker" that was home to most first, many second, and some third generation Polish American working class families some of whom rose to become the proprietors of small delicatessens, restaurants, and stores. In these structures several generations of Polish Americans tended to live together, for a time, sometimes within one flat, usually in their own flats, one above the other.

Polish American neighbourhoods have changed the way all of society changes. Beyond the second generation, and especially beyond the third generation, many of the descendants of the original Poles who had sailed to America during the first quarter of the 20th century had "married out" and lost their Polish identity along with their Polish names. Women took the surname of their non-Polish spouse. Some men made slight changes in their surnames, such as from Burowicz to Buroway. As they entered the ranks of the middle class, Polish Americans moved toward or into the suburbs, almost as classically as Robert Park and Ernest Burgess had projected in their urban ecology studies of the mid-1920s (Park, Burgess, 1925), but seemingly without the negative aspects of social disorganisation leading to crime identified by Clifford R. Shaw and Henry D. McKay as they studied Chicago (Shaw, McKay, 1969). The neighbourhoods the Polish American families of central New England left behind, however, did not decay but have become home to newly arrived people from the Middle East and elsewhere.

Early Worcester County Polish American Neighbourhoods

Polish people began to settle in central Massachusetts from late in the 18th century, following the partition of Poland amongst its neighbouring countries: Austria, Prussia, and Russia. The first flock of Polish persons came to America late in the 1860s, mostly from Northwestern Poland that was occupied by Prussia. Many Polish persons who arrived in Worcester in the late 1860s were Jewish and built their first synagogue on Grafton Hill (Jewish Virtual Library). All synagogues in Massachusetts are said to have evolved from Temple Ohabei Shalom, formed in 1842 in Brookline (between Boston and Worcester), but what is interesting is that although Jewish Poles lived harmoniously with Catholic Poles on Grafton and Vernon Hills (parallel streets) respectively in Worcester, German Jews who had founded Temple Ohabei Shalom, then withdrew from it 12 years later in 1854 to form Temple Israel in Boston, because they resented so many Polish Jews becoming members of Temple Ohabei Shalom (Sarna, Smith, 1995, 169).

The centre of Polish American Roman Catholic community life was the Church. The first community effort, not surprisingly, was to form a committee of clergy and laiety to construct a Roman Catholic Church for the Polish community. The first Polish church in New England was St. Joseph's Roman Catholic Church in Webster, Massachusetts, about 15 miles (24 kilometres) south of Worcester and 60 miles (90 kilometres) west of Boston, near the Connecticut state line, consecrated in 1887. Destroyed by fire in 1914, it was completely rebuilt. The Church of St. Joseph sits today as the centre of Webster's Polish-American neighbourhood atop a hill above the city centre of Webster amongst a cluster of single-family detached houses (mostly white and pastel coloured), a red brick double-steepled edifice with separate accompanying edifices for housing priests and nuns. Known now as St. Joseph's Basilica, it serves a congregation of about 1,200 parishioners.[1] Other Polish parishes followed as the diaspora moved into newer suburbs, including St. Andrew (Św. Andrzej) Bobola Church in contiguous Dudley, Massachusetts.

Half a generation after the completion of St. Joseph's, Polish Americans from the Prussian section of Northern Poland helped newer arrivals from the Russian and Austrian sectors to settle and build their churches, beginning with Our Lady of Częstochowa Parish, built in 1903 at 34 Ward Street in Worcester, just off Belmont Street near the intersection of Main and Highland Streets. Today, this is the area of the Worcester Polytechnical University, and Highland Street climbs up a hill on which repose many fashionable homes. Although the Roman Catholic Diocese of Worcester has closed many churches due to falling attendance, all seven of its Polish churches remain active and open today. The second wave of Polish newcomers to the Worcester area came from Poland's northeastern Łomża and Suwałki Voivodeships (now Podlaskie Province) and part of what today is the Republic of Lithuania, from which they had emigrated to avoid taxes they felt Imperial Russia levied on them unfairly and disproportionately as affluent farmers, known pejoratively as the "rich peasants" or as "great peasants" (Kruzka, 1998). Frequently, they were able to own their own

---

[1] See http://www.prthatrocks.com/articles/stjoe.html. The author was married at St. Joseph's Roman Catholic Church to a Polish-American woman, and all six of their children were baptised there also, perhaps a further testament to the Polish and American nationalism of the Polish-American diaspora in the last quarter of the 20th century.

homes ("triple deckers," sometimes also called "three deckers") in the Worcester area because they brought with them to the New World enough money for a down payment, and sometimes even enough money to purchase a home outright. That money came from the sale of their farmlands in Poland, sometimes purchased from them by their siblings who chose to remain in Poland. Many faced the choice of purchasing their home outright or making a down payment on a mortgage and using the balance of their savings to open a delicatessen, a restaurant, or a store, as some of the author's relatives did.

One must remember that Lithuania and Poland have shared a common heritage across some centuries: Lithuania was a part of the Kingdom of Poland, and Poland was a part of the Kingdom of Lithuania. In Worcester County, Massachusetts, many persons who consider their heritage to be Lithuanian married Polish Americans (Wolkovich-Valkavicius, 1980). The principal Lithuanian church in Worcester across the 20th century, St. Casimir Roman Catholic Church at 41 Providence Street, still stands where it was built in the Lithuanian section that rises from downtown Worcester,[2] but the diocese closed it on 01 July 2008, due to declining membership. Since closing St. Casimir's, much of the Lithuanian community that continues to reside within that parish has come to attend St. John's Roman Catholic Church, the oldest in New England outside of Boston, where a Lithuanian priest has been posted as the associate pastor. Another Lithuanian-American Roman Catholic Church, Our Lady of Vilna at 153 Sterling Street, Worcester, continues to operate as an active parish under its original name, honouring the Blessed Virgin in the capital city of the present Republic of Lithuania, Vilnius, but has become a Vietnamese congregation, reflecting the new occupants of a part of the traditional Polish and Lithuanian-American neighbourhoods of Worcester, Massachusetts.

Worcester's "Triple Decker" Homes

Worcester is replete with wooden frame three storey apartment buildings known as "triple deckers," and these are very visible even today from Interstate 290 ("Worcester Expressway") as it cuts across downtown Worcester below Grafton Street and Vernon Hill. They have three decks, each surrounded on at least two sides by a rather copious porch. An external staircase led from one floor to the next as did an internal staircase, the latter rarely used by traditional Polish-American families. Almost all residents and guests entered and exited through the rear door to the kitchen, rather than the front door that lead through a front hallway and into the parlour. Usually, there were two bedrooms off the parlour, and a third off the kitchen.[3] Families tended to gather around the kitchen table, sometimes because the flat was heated almost exclusively

---

2 See *http://lithuaniangenealogy.org/databases/ma/st_casimir.html* (Accessed 11/30/ 2010) for a silhouette of the Church and a list of its members in 1920.

3 For pictures of the "triple decker" home in Worcester, Massachusetts, see "Vistadome Views," *http://www.vistadome.com/worcester/triple_deckers/index.html* (Accessed 11/30/ 2010).

from the kitchen stove, but the parlour began to be used more widely as the radio gained popularity in the 1930s, and even more widely as the television came into fashion in the late 1950s and 1960s.

One significant feature of the Polish-American family in Worcester was that most triple deckers were owned by a senior member of the family who occupied one of its three floors, and junior members of the family (children, grandchildren) occupied the two other floors, usually the higher ones. This distinguished Polish-Americans from other ethnic inhabitants of the area, many of whom rented their housing units from absentee landlords. What this meant in practice was that Polish triple deckers, unlike their counterparts that housed American minorities from other ethnicities, stayed in pristine condition due to pride of ownership. As one generation of a Polish-American family moved out of the triple decker to start a new family, often in a suburb and quite frequently in a single family detached dwelling, the triple decker flat quickly became inhabited by another family member, a younger member of the same generation that moved out, or the next generation. The point is these apartment units remained in the same family and remained Polish-American across the 20th century. Even nowadays, in the 21st century, the same formerly Polish-American triple decker homes tend to be owned by newcomers to America such as the Vietnamese who continue to share the same values as did the Polish-Americans who previously owned their homes: pride of ownership. So these neighbourhoods remain today both clean and safe, and most of the triple decker houses seem to be in surprisingly good repair, given their age.

Changes After The War

The Polish community in Worcester County changed after World War II, then it changed again during the 1970s-1980s, and in turn again during the transition from the 20th to the 21st centuries. No longer is the Church really the centre of the Polish community, although churches remain located physically near the centres of the neighbourhoods that once formed the Polish-American communities. There is quite a difference between the Church at the centre of a community in spirit, and the Church building located physically near the centre. The Church stopped functioning at the centre of Polish-American community life as more and more Polish-American men, very gradually, stopped attending church regularly, then stopped attending altogether or began to "attend" by congregating outside of the church on its steppes or in its parking lot, smoking and discussing work or political issues whilst their wives and children attended Mass inside the church.

After World War II, the centre of Polish-American community life in Worcester may be said to have become "The Island." This is an area of downtown Worcester not far from the College of the Holy Cross, contoured by Kelly Square and Water Street, the latter so named because it stands atop what used to be a canal. Today, this area is an "island" in name only, because the streams that once formed its boundaries have been rerouted in pipes underground. The Worcester

Expressway passes high overhead as it connects traffic from Webster near the Connecticut line to Northborough and the Massachusetts Turnpike ("Mass Pike"). Also, Kelly Square was the round about for trolley cars (European "trams" on tracks) until the War, when trolleys were taken out of service and replaced by buses, as yet another hallmark of Europe vanished from America.

"The Island" was a magical neighbourhood, almost entirely ethnically Polish and Polish Lithuanian, that reflected the interface of the Polish diaspora with the "white Anglo-Saxon Protestant" or "WASP" community, but also reflected the interface of Poles and Lithuanins who were Roman Catholic and who intermarried frequently (Wolkovich-Valkavicius, 1980) with those who were Jewish, and of both groups with Muslims and Christians from the Middle East, especially Lebanon. In fact, probably, the two most prosperous eating establishments within this Polish community were Weintraub's delicatessen, located at 126 Water Street, and El Morocco, a restaurant on 100 Wall Street off Grafton Street that rose above "The Island." Almost every Polish-American family, regardless of religion, patronised Weintraub's at least once per week during the second half of the 20th century, particularly on Sundays when other stores were closed, to purchase Polish food, especially bagels, kielbasa and bulkie rolls. Weintraub's was closed on Saturdays until dark in observance of the Jewish Shabbat. El Morocco did not serve alcoholic beverages, but allowed its customers to bring their own bottles. Legend is that "big band" leader Tommy Dorsey ate at El Morocco and loved it so much he recommended it to his Hollywood friends. It had autographed photographs along its walls of almost every American singer who ever performed there, and the list included almost every "star" who lived between the war and the end of the third quarter of the 20th century: Italian-Americans Frank Sinatra and Tony Bennett, Jewish Americans Eddie Fisher and Danny Kaye, African Americans Louis Armstrong and Count Bassie, among very many others including Mick Jagger and of course Bobby Vinton, known as the "Polish Prince of Pittsburgh." The point was that this Polish-American neighbourhood was a melting pot that reflected America itself, big time in its own unique way.

In Webster, the Church of St. Joseph remained the centre of the Polish-American community down through the 20th century, but not entirely due to the church itself. Long after many Polish Americans who were American born stopped attending church ritually, their children continued to attend St. Joseph's School, and the school became the new centre of Polish-American culture as much as, or even more than, the centre of Polish Catholic religion. St. Joseph's School became a place where children of at least one Polish-American parent tried to learn the rather complicated basic structure of the Polish language, both spoken and written, together with the fundamental history of Poland as a country and as a culture. Polish-American families in America during the second half of the 20th century tended to prefer Roman Catholic parochial schools for their children over public schools, as one tool for preserving Polish culture, but also because the quality of the education supervised by nuns was considered superior to what public schools offered.

The age of Polish-American clubs may be said to have reached a zenith in the 1960s. Of course, many such establishments existed well before that time, but by the 1960s and continuing through the 1980s and afterwards, "Polish clubs" provided their members with a social and a political environment within which to drink alcohol and debate controversial issues including local and national American politics as well as the Solidarity movement as it rose to favour in Poland. Members included both men and women, but more men than women, and perhaps not surprisingly mainly men who were married and women who were not. Examples of the Polish-American club were the "Polish Naturalization Club" in Worcester and the "Booster Club" in Webster. Many members had Polish surnames, but increasingly many did not, reflecting the increasing rate at which the children of the Polish diaspora in Massachusetts married outside of their own ethnic group.

One reason for the changes in activities within Polish-American neighbourhoods during the second half of the 20th century was the change process that occurred inside Polish-American families during the same period. The reason for the change seems to have been largely due to the increasing role organised labour played in improving the wages paid to working men in America, coupled with the "G.I. Education Bill" under which veterans of World War II who had been discharged honourably from military service received government funding that allowed them to attend college or trade school, thereby increasing their education and earnings potential. With this came mobility upwards in terms of income and social class. With the same emerged the opportunity for Polish-American families to apply for veterans' loans, often through company credit unions and Polish-American controlled banks such as the Polish National Credit Union,[4] established in 1921, to finance modern single family detached housing in the suburbs of Worcester County, along with an automobile. This meant that many Polish-American families moved out of Worcester's "triple decker" apartment dwellings and into new housing then being constructed by the thousands in neighbouring towns such as Oxford (between Worcester and Webster) or Dudley (between Webster and Connecticut), where they built or bought single family detached homes common to the emerging middle class of the 1950s and 1960s. The new planned communities that sprung up formed a new set of Polish-American communities, but these were not entirely Polish at all.

These new neighbourhoods were different in many ways from the older inner city Polish-American neighbourhoods. Not only were they largely single family detached houses on a small plot of grass land in contrast to Worcester's inner-city three storeyed "triple decker" buildings that offered only a flat with no land, but also these neighbourhoods were "mixed" in terms of the diverse ethnicity of their occupants. Polish-American families began to live side by side with Irish or Italian and sometimes even WASP families, instead of living almost entirely among other Eastern Europeans as had been the case with the "triple decker" neighbourhoods until after World War II. The result was both construc-

---

4   See http://www.compasscg.com/banking_links/massachusetts.html (Accessed 09/09/2010).

tive and destructive: it led to assimilation through intermarriage between Polish-American children and the offspring of families from vastly different backgrounds, considered constructive, but it also signaled the beginning of the end of the Polish-American neighbourhood and, to a lesser extent, of the Polish culture itself in America, considered destructive by many. The Polish Americans who came to occupy houses in these middle class suburban towns held supervisory or skilled labour positions at factories large and small, sometimes including where their parents had worked mainly as unskilled blue collar workers. Such factories included Norton Company in addition to American Steel and Wire Company and Crompton and Knowles Corporation.

Polish-American neighbourhoods in Worcester extend literally to the doorsteps of its major colleges and universities: The College of the Holy Cross that most people rate as America's fourth best Roman Catholic college (after Notre Dame, Georgetown, and Boston College), and Clark University. Yet, the Polish diaspora have never seemed to matriculate at these institutions of higher learning as well as other ethnic minorities have done. There could be some plausible reasons for this. Outright discrimination may explain why students having Polish or Lithuanian surnames are not as plentiful at these schools as students bearing Irish, Italian, or other ethnic minority surnames, but it would be less likely to explain why children of Polish diaspora whose surnames are not Polish tend to be underrepresented. What might explain this phenomenon could be that for parents who are first, second, or third generation Polish-Americans a state university is more attractive because it seems to be better than a private university for their children. This is true factually in Poland itself, of course, where the University of Warsaw ranks first and is followed mostly by other state universities. Perhaps this tradition carried over into the United States for some Polish-Americans. With a few exceptions such as the University of Michigan, the University of California at Berkeley, the University of North Carolina and the University of Texas at Austin, the best universities in the United States are private. The author's alma mater, Clark University, does have a significant Jewish faculty and student population, but most surnames do not appear to have been Polish across the final quarter of the 20th century. It is only fair to point out, however, that both Hillel and Newman clubs are popular both at Clark and at Holy Cross, so that if it does exist the discrimination is not overtly religious.

The neighbourhoods the Polish-American diaspora occupied for a generation or longer before World War II and for two or three generations afterward in Worcester and Webster, Massachusetts have changed. Their future is secure. True to the theory of McKay and Burgess (1925), as one set of occupants moved into the suburbs or to another area entirely, newer ethnic arrivals occupy the housing units. In Worcester, the newer arrivals include some Hispanics, many newcomers from the Middle East, and Vietnamese Americans. The new occupants of the old Polish-American neighbourhoods seem to be maintaining them much in the manner that the Polish diaspora were accustomed to doing: the "triple deckers" are not rotting but thriving. A large part of the explanation for this fortuitous circumstance seems to be the fact that over the years, from generation to generation, Polish-American neighbourhoods of Worcester, Webster, and Dudley Massachusetts, have fulfilled the vision Governor John Winthrop enunciated almost 400 years ago in referring to Boston and to America as a whole: a "city upon a hill" (Winthrop, 1630).

References

Brittingham, Angela, and G. Patricia de la Cruz. "Ancestry 2000." Washington: U.S. Census Bureau (Jule 2004). http://www.census.gov/prod/2004pubs/c2kbr-35.pdf (Accessed 07/04/2010).
Friedman, Lee Max. *Early American Jews.* Cambridge, Massachusetts: Harvard University Press, 1934.
Friedman, Lee Max. *Early Jewish Residents in Massachusetts.* Charleston: BiblioLife (2009 07 17).
Friedman, Lee Max. *Jewish Pioneers and Patriots.* Philadelphia: Jewish Publication Society, 1945.
Freidman, Lee Max. *Pioneers in a New Land.* Philadelphia: Jewish Publication Society, 1948.
Jewish Virtual Library, Massachusetts http:// www. Jewishvirtuallibrary .org/ jsource /judaica /ejud _0002_0013_0_13387.html (Accessed 07/29/2010).
Kruszka, Waclaw. *A History of the Poles in America to 1908.* Part III: Poles in the Eastern and Southern States. Washington, D.C.: The Catholic University Press of America, 1998.
Marcus, Jacob Rader. *Early American Jewry. (*Philadelphia: Jewish Publication Society of America, vol. 1 1951, vol. 2 1953).
Park, Robert E., and Ernest W. Burgess. *The City.* Chicago: University of Chicago Press, 1925.
Proko[powicz], Barbara. "Basia's Polish Family: From Vilno to Worcester: Researching the Genealogy of the Prokopowicz, Ruscik, & Blaszko Families," August 17, 2009. http://wilnoworcester.blogspot.com/2009/08/worcesters-polish-neighborhood-1945.html (accessed 04/04/2010).
Proko[powicz], Barbara, and Janice Baniukiewicz Stickles. *Images of America: Worcester County's Polish Museum.* Charleston: Arkadia Publishing, 2007. http://www polartcenter. com/Images_of_America_Worcester_County_p/9702845.htm. Accessed 04/07/2010).
Rawinski, Stasia Obara, and Joseph Kuras. A History of the Polish American Community of South Grafton, Massachusetts. December 27, 1998. http://polishhistorysouthgrafton.s5. com/PolishHistory.pdf. (Accesed 04/07/2010).
Sarna, Jonathan D. and Ellen Smith, eds. *The Jews of Boston.* New Haven: Yale University Press, 1995.
Shaw, Clifford R. and Henry D. McKay. *Juvenile Delinquency and Urban Areas.* Chicago: The University of Chicago Press, 1969.
Tuveson, Ernest Lee. *Redeemer Nation: The Idea of America's Millennial Role.* Chicago: University of Chicago Press, 1980.
U.S. Census Bureau, Population Profile of the United States, 2000. http://www.census. gov/population/www/pop-profile/profile2000.html. (Accessed 07/04/2010).
Winthrop, John. "City Upon A Hill," 1630. http://www.mtholyoke.edu/acad/intrel/ winthrop.htm (Accessed 04/06/2010).
Wolkovich-Valkavicius, William. "Lithuanians of Worcester, Massachusetts: A Socio-Historic Glimpse at Marriage Records, 1910-15 and 1930-34," in *Lituanus: Lithuanian Journal of Arts and Sciences,* Vol. 26, No. 2 (Summer 1980).
Wytrwal, Joseph. *America's Polish Heritage.* Detroit: Endurance, 1961.

The Role of Religious Institutions in Building the Polish Community in Windsor, Ontario

Agata Rajski (Jagiellonian University)

The Rise of Windsor

Windsor is Canada's southernmost city, located in the Province of Ontario, in the Great Lakes region. It is situated on the left bank of the Detroit River and on the shore of Lake St. Clair, bordering on the American city of Detroit, Michigan.

The first references to the region, in which Windsor is now located, date back to August 1679, when the French voyager Rene-Robert La Salle reached the mouth of the Detroit River. He arrived at the lake and named it St. Clair. The efforts at European settlement in Detroit-Windsor region began in 1701, when Sieur De Larnothe Cadilac came and founded Fort Pontchartrain at the river, on the Detroit side.[1] In the years 1748-1760, on both sides of the river, the French settlement grew. In 1760, the British captured Fort Pontchartrain and held control over these lands, but the majority of the settlers was still the French population. The lands formed part of a larger area, negotiated from the Indians and governed by the British.

In the year 1797, the settlement of Sandwich was established.[2] Its main inhabitants were people of French and British origin from Detroit, who wanted to remain under British sovereignty after the occupation of the city by American forces. This fact provided a beginning for the first local settlement and took the form of the first English migration into the region.

In the 1820s the small ferry landing opposite Detroit began to emerge. The future Windsor blossomed as the major transportation centre and border crossing in the region. Business activities that focused upon the local trades and customers from Detroit led to the creation of a municipality. In 1836, James Dougall gave the settlement the name of Windsor.[3] The rebellions of 1837-1838 stopped the economic growth of the area, however, by 1850s the construction of railway provided a stimulus to immigrant workers. The arrival of the Great Western Railroad gave Windsor the importance as the main rail crossing to the United States along the New York-Chicago corridor. In 1854, Windsor was formally registered as an independent Village, and in 1892 achieved city status.[4] The three small towns, Windsor, Sandwich and Walkerville, known as Border Cities, were soon to be joined by a fourth, Ford City. In 1935, the Border Cities constituted an urban entity of Windsor.

From earliest times, the region had hosted a diverse population. The first inhabitants were Native people, followed by French Canadians. Fur traders and

---

1 *The Town of Sandwich*, 1979, Windsor: the Essex County Historical Association, p. 135.
2 Ditto, p.137.
3 *Windsor Panorama*, 1974, Windsor: Windsor Separate School Board.
4 Ditto.

merchants of different nationalities worked with the military contingents, French or British, who were established at Fort Detroit. In the wake of the American Revolution, Loyalists from the South poured into the colony of Upper Canada. After 1815, these pioneers were joined by a new wave of British immigrants. The massive Irish influx took place in 1840s and 1850s. Windsor, as a railway center and international border crossing, received a significant volume of the immigrants heading for the United States.

The Fugitive Slave Act of 1850, caused the arrival of black residents seeking freedom and a new life in Canada. Civil War pressures and border incidents provoked nationalist responses on both sides, which led to the imposition of a restrictive passport system. By the time of Great Migration of the 1880s, Windsor had developed to be attractive to newcomers. The flat, but fertile agricultural lands of Essex County and border location made Windsor the market centre of a growing agricultural economy.

The first decade of the twentieth century brought dynamic urbanization and industrialization of the city. The establishment of Ford Motor Company in Windsor in 1904, created new jobs in motor industry and stimulated the development of the city.[5]

Windsor's ferry service expanded, developing its position as a transportation centre and border gateway. By 1907, the Sandwich, Windsor and Amherstburg street railway (SWA) that connected the Border Cities expanded into the electric railway. Eventually, the Windsor, Essex and Lakeshore Railway brought other counties into the Border Cities region. In 1910, the first railway tunnel under the Detroit River was opened. It carried not only passengers but also freight.

The industrial growth of the city gave an opportunity for American firms to invest in Windsor. In 1920, General Motors and Chrysler were built. In 1930, the Tunnel and the Ambassador Bridge were constructed, connecting Canada and the United States.

The growth of automotive industry not only changed the city to rapidly developing urban centre, but also brought about the migration of national minorities, among them the Polish ethnic group, to Windsor.

The establishment of automotive branch induced the economical growth, especially after the World War II and the following decades. Today, the city is known as the Canadian capital of the motor industry. It is the largest Canadian border city and one of the most important transportation centres in North America. It is also an essential academic and cultural centre with the University of Windsor and St. Clair College of Applied Arts and Technology.

During the past decades, Windsor became a modern city with many recreational and cultural facilities.

---

5   Ditto.

Building the community

During the course of the past century several waves of Polish settlement can be distinguished in Windsor. Each wave had different character, based on the volume of immigration, and dominant type of arriving people. The first wave started in the beginning of the twentieth century and lasted to the outbreak of the World War I. The next one can be distinguished by the years of 1919-1939. The following wave began after the end of the World War II, and lasted to 1956. The next wave appeared between 1960 and 1980. The biggest in size, known as the "solidarity wave" started in 1980 and lasted to the end of decade. The last noticeable wave of immigrants heading for Windsor occurred between 1991 and 2001. During the last decade the immigration movement was still in process, although in less intensive occurrence.

The first wave of Polish immigrants appeared in the first decade of the twentieth century, however, in 1878, before Poles established a stable community in the city, the first group of Eastern European Jews settled in Windsor. They arrived mostly from Suwałki and small Russian-Polish towns in Białystok province, close to the Lithuanian border. The first Jewish immigrant, who came to Windsor from Poland was Aaron Meretsky. He was born in Sztabin in 1854, as the second son of a simple family of four boys and three girls. Aaron married Katherine Barowsky. She was born in 1856 and came from a wealthy family who had owned a tannery in Poland.[6] Seven years later she joined her husband in Windsor with their son Simon.

The first Polish Christian family arrived in Windsor in 1908.[7] It is not clear where they came from, but they provided the beginning of Polish settlement in the city. The arrival of Poles in Windsor was closely connected to the Polish settlement of Detroit, where immigrants began to stream in, around 1850. A larger influx of Poles occurred after 1914, when the car factories began to appear in Windsor. A significant number of immigrants migrated from the Prairie Provinces. In 1915, about 300 Poles lived in the city.[8] These pioneers came mainly from the Austrian and Russian annexed territories, and found work on the lowest rung of the social ladder.

The first group of settlers did not have a Polish priest. In 1915-1916, the spiritual needs of Poles received attention from Father Raphael Hubert Dignan, who had the responsibilities of Vicar in the English Parish of the Immaculate Conception of the Most Holy Virgin Mary.[9] He delivered his sermons in English,

---

6   J.V. Plaut, L. Kulisek, 2007, *The Jews of Windsor, 1790-1990: a historical chronicle*, Toronto: Dundurn Press Ltd., p. 43
7   *Pamiętnik Czterdziestolecia Parafii św. Trójcy w Windsor 1916-1956 (Diary of the Fortieth Anniversary of the Holy Trinity Parish in Windsor 1916-1956)*, Windsor 1955.
8   *Annual Report of the Parish of Holy Trinity Church*, Archives of the Diocese of London, London 1916.
9   J. Plewko, 1992, Parafia św. Trójcy [w:] *Leksykon geograficzno-historyczny parafii i kościołów polskich w Kanadzie (The Holy Trinity Parish, In: A Geographical-Historical Lexicon of Polish Parishes and Churches In Canada)* t. 1, pod red. E. Walewandra, Lublin: Instytut Badań nad Polonią i Duszpasterstwem Polonijnym, p. 324.

which was not understood by most of the new immigrants. The difficulties of communication of Father Dignan with the Polish immigrants influenced the decision of the bishop M.F. Fallon, to assign a priest of Polish descent.

In October 1916, Father Jan Andrzejewski began ministry in the Polish language. In 1918 the Polish immigrants built their own church on the land donated by a Protestant Mr. Walter Boug. The Holy Trinity Church arose as the fifth in Windsor and also as the fifth Polish church in Canada. It was also the first Polish church in the London Diocese.[10] The church became a centre of spiritual and secular life. It concentrated the lives of the first immigrants. Poles started to build the institutional completeness within their community.[11] They formed first ethnic organizations of social, educational and cultural character. They built houses within polish community (mainly in the area of Moy, Langlois, Parent, Ottawa, Walker Road), and established small family businesses in the neighborhood of the church. Most of the first organizations started their activities in the basement of the church. Among them: The Polish People's Home Association, Post 126 of the Polish Army Veterans Association, and the Polish Language School. In 1930 the Polish Hall was built and became the place of sociocultural life of Polish immigrants and location of the Polish Language School.[12] According to the Statute of the Polish People's Home Association, not changed since 1925, the Association stands for leadership in cultural-educational activities among its members and all of Polonia, and collaboration with other Polish organizations in the field of promotion of Polish culture.[13] In 1931,the size of Polish immigration amounted to 1,495 people.[14]

The outbreak of the World War II stopped the wave of settlement from Poland. However, the need of the Canadian arms industry for qualified technicians and engineers made possible the immigration of specialists, travelling to Canada on contracts.[15]

The war time was a specific period in the history of Polish immigration and particularly the Polish ethnic group in Windsor. In the years 1941-1942 there was the Recruitment Unit of the Polish Armed Forces located in Windsor. It was established under the commandment of General Bronisław Duch (1. Division of Grenadiers), the leader of the Polish Armed Forces in Canada.[16] The Chief of

---

10   *Pamiętnik Pięćdziesięciolecia Parafii św. Trójcy w Windsor, Ontario 1916-1966 (Diary of the Fiftieth Anniversary of the Holy Trinity Parish in Windsor, Ontario 1916-1966)*, Windsor 1966.
11   R. Breton, *Institutional Completeness of Ethnic Communities and Personal Relations of Immigrants*, [in:] "The American Journal of Sociology", 1964, vol.70, nr 2, p. 193-205.
12   *Pamiętnik 75-lecia Stowarzyszenia Polskiego Domu Ludowego w Windsor (Diary of the 75th Anniversary of the Polish People's Home Association in Windsor)*, Windsor 2000, p. 13.
13   Constitution of the Polish People's Home Association, Windsor 1925.
14   Canada. Statistics Canada. Canada Year Book, Population by ethnic groups, for Canada, years 1901-1971, [Windsor].
15   A. Reczyńska, 2001, *Diaspora polska w Kanadzie* [w:] *Polska Diaspora (The Polish Diaspora In Canada, In: The Polish Diaspora)*, pod red. A. Walaszka, Kraków: Wydawnictwo Literackie, p. 35.
16   *The Windsor Star*, July 21, 1941, Vol 46, No 121.

Staff of General Duch was Colonel Zenon Wzacny. The leadership comprised: the Army Mission with Colonel F. Rola-Arciszewski, the Air Force Mission with Colonel Stefan M. Sznuk, and the Navy Wartime Mission with Commander W. Zajączkowski. The Quartermaster was Major W. Tysowski and the Chief of the Chaplaincy was the Reverend Deacon Ludwik Bombas.[17]

The city of Windsor handed over at no cost two deserted buildings for use by the military, the residence known as "Henkel House", and the former town hall of East Windsor. The Henkel House was designated as the Headquarters, the other one for the Administration of the Polish Armed Forces. The office equipment company Burroughs offered one floor of its factory, for the quarters of the Army.[18] The training camp for the volunteers was located in Owen Sound, Ontario (200 km to the North-West of Toronto).[19] In accordance with the Polish-Canadian agreement, the volunteers were trained there from 6 weeks to 3 months and then sent to the Polish Army in England.

The location of the Recruitment Centre proved to be the great honor and privilege for the city of Windsor and the Polish ethnic group. It raised the standing of Polonia in the eyes of the local population. The inhabitants of the city, before the opening of the Recruitment Centre, took a critical approach to the fact that the detachment of the Polish Armed Forces was established in the city. They feared an increase in criminality and an influx of foreigners.[20] After several months, they referred with enthusiasm to every action of the Recruitment Centre. Marches through the city by detachments of the Polish Army with its orchestra, especially to services at the Holy Trinity Church, were applauded by people, gathered along the sidewalks. The campfires in front of the headquarters enjoyed popularity, with the Polish ethnic group from Windsor and Detroit and also with the inhabitants of the city. Meetings with the soldiers in Polish Hall, concerts of music by Polish composers, lectures, and other undertakings convinced the inhabitants of Windsor that Poles are a nation, capable of not only hard, physical labour, but a nation displaying a rich history and culture. The image of poor and not intelligent Polish immigrants began to change also by sociocultural activities undertaken by Polish organizations.

During the activity of the Recruitment Centre, a weekly publication was released in Windsor, with the bilingual title *Odsiecz - Polska Walcząca w Ameryce - Fighting Poland (Relief Force-Fighting Poland in America)*.[21] Its main task was the popularization of enlistment in the Polish Armed Forces in Canada, as well as informing about the situation on the front. The magazine was published in the graphics departments of the local newspaper *The Windsor Daily Star*. At the beginning, the editorial office was located in the headquarters of the Polish

---

17   F. Kmietowicz, 1984, *Polskie Siły Zbrojne w Kanadzie podczas drugiej wojny światowej (The Polish Armed Forces In Canada during the World War II)*, Windsor, p. 14.
18   *Board of Control Minutes*, Archives of the Public Library in Windsor, Nr 949, p.4.
19   F. Kmietowicz, op.cit., p. 13.
20   *Odsiecz-Polska Walcząca w Ameryce, Relief Force-Fighting Poland In America)*, 19 IV 1942, Vol. 2, Nr 16(38), Windsor, Kanada.
21   F. Kmietowicz, op.cit., p. 49.

Armed Forces, and later in rented house at 849 Kildare Road.[22] The group of editors composed of professional journalists. The Editor-in-Chief of the magazine was Lieutenant Wacław Drzewiecki. Between July 1941 and April 1942, 38 issues of *Relief Force* came out and the circulation exceeded 20 000 copies. The weekly had 79 sales locations in the United States, 10 locations in Canada, and one in Great Britain.[23]

In the Recruitment Centre in Windsor, 1,250 recruits were registered. Between December 1941 and November 1942, after the introductory training, 903 volunteers, as well as 40 instructors of the Polish Army, were sent to Great Britain in seven transports. Altogether 550 volunteered from the United States, 250 from Canada, 150 from Latin America, and 50 from Poland (they reached Canada from Spain, and even from Russia through Japan).[24] The number of volunteers was relatively small. It did not reach equal the numbers of those, who previously had completed their registration at the consulates. The entry of the USA into the war, as well as activities related to the creation of the Polish Army in the Soviet Union, brought about a change in strategy on the part of the Polish leaders.

After the liquidation of the Polish Military Mission in Canada, recruitment into the Polish Army was not halted. The Rallying Station remaining in Windsor continued recruiting. According to some sources, it accepted and sent to Great Britain 323 more candidates to be soldiers.[25]

In the columns of the last issue of the weekly Relief Force, General B. Duch said farewell to the Canadian Polonia with these words: "The entry of the United States into the war and, connected to this the process of mobilization of all forces and reserves with regard to the war effort of the United States, were the deciding factor, which influenced such a reorganization (...). In saying farewell to the American Polonia, I want to emphasize that the memories of our stay in the western hemisphere are deeply engraved in our mind and heart. I know today, even better than I knew before I came to America, that on this side of the Ocean millions of Polish hearts are beating, sincere and warm. I know and I deeply believe in it, that the American Polonia remains for all time a huge reserve of our proud and noble People".[26]

After the war, there was a substantial proportion of the refugees, who came to Windsor from United Kingdom. Among this group there were inhabitants of the eastern territories of Poland, which was taken over by the Soviet occupation. The Poles from that area (the former Stanisławów, Tarnopol and in part Lwów) were driven out and deported to Siberia. Some of them escaped to south of Russia, and together with the Army of General Władysław Anders were directed in-

---

22 Ditto, p. 50.
23 Ditto, p. 54.
24 Ditto, p. 57.
25 A. Reczyńska, 1997, *Piętno wojny, Polonia kanadyjska wobec polskich problemów lat 1939-1945 (The Stamp of the War, Polish-Canadians Facing Polish Problems)*, Kraków: Zakład Wydawniczy "Nomos", p. 108.
26 "Odsiecz-Polska Walcząca w Ameryce, Relief Force-Fighting Poland In America", 19.04.1942, Vol. 2, Nr 16 (38), Windsor.

to the Persian Gulf region, where they reached camps for refugees. Next, the Polish refugees were transported to Teheran and later to Pakistan and Africa. During their stay in Africa the children went to schools for refugees. They completed the basics of education at primary schools and high schools. In Teheran the youths under 16 years of age were assigned to "youth brigades", military schools, which trained them for the army. Young soldiers traveled from Teheran, through Iraq, to Palestine and then to Italy. Many fought in the II Corps of General Władysław Anders at Monte Casino.[27] After the war, Polish soldiers and refugees traveled to England and from there, to South America, United States and Canada. Some of them, as demobilized soldiers came to Windsor.

In 1952, there was admission still for demobilized soldiers, former prisoners of war and others, who chose immigration to North America instead of returning to Poland governed by communists. At this time, which witnessed the end of immigration of DPs (Displaced Persons), the number of Polish immigrants in Windsor amounted to 3,819 people. This wave of immigration was represented by almost all social groups with high professional qualifications, as well as high school or higher education. Some of them knew one of the official language of Canada. All of this distinguished the new arrivals from the earlier immigrants from Poland. The start of the new wave in Canada, although difficult, was without comparison easier than the start of the pioneers at the beginning of the century or even of the emigration between wars.

In 1940s and 50s, besides already existing Polish organizations in Windsor, such as: the Polish People Home Association (established in 1925)[28], the Border Cities Polish-Canadian Club (1930), and Post 126 of the Polish Army Veterans Association (1932)[29], Polish ethnic group joined in other organizations. The Polish Alliance of Canada, Group 20 (1943)[30], the Polish Women's Circle of the Polish Alliance of Canada, Group 20 (1944), the Youth Group of the Polish Alliance of Canada, Group 20 (1952)[31], the Canadian-Polish Congress (1944)[32], the Polish Social Club (1951)[33], the Sports Club – Polish Vets (1951)[34], the Scout Troops (1953)[35].

27 Interview with the members of Post 126 of the Polish Army Veterans Association in Windsor, Windsor, August 2005.
28 *Memorial Album, Księga Pamiątkowa Stowarzyszenia Polskiego Domu Ludowego w Windsor, 1925-1950 (Memorial Album, Polish People's Home Association In Windsor, 1925-1950)*, Windsor 1950, p. 20.
29 *Pamiętnik 50 zjazdu Okręgu 6-go Stowarzyszenia Weteranów Armii Polskiej (Diary of the 50th Meeting of Branch 6 of the Polish Army Veterans Association)*, Windsor 1979.
30 *50 lat Grupy 20-tej Związku Polaków w Kanadzie, Windsor 1943-1993 (50 Years of the Polish Alliance In Canada, Group 20, Windsor 1943-1993)*, Windsor 1993, p. 6.
31 *Diamentowy Jubileusz Związku Polaków w Kanadzie 1907-1982 (The Diamond Jubilee of the Polish Alliance of Canada 1907-1982)*, Windsor 1982, p. 50.
32 www.poloniawindsor.ca/kpk/kpk/htm
33 *Pamiętnik Czterdziestolecia Parafii (Diary of the Fortieth Anniversary)*, op.cit..
34 *Polsko-Kanadyjski Klub Sportowy "Polonia" 1982-1992 (The Polish-Canadian Sports Club "Polonia" 1982-1992)*, Windsor 1992.
35 *ZHP – Wczoraj i Dziś 1910-1960 (ZHP – Yesterday and Today 1910-1969)*, Toronto 1960, p. 60.

Besides activities connected with organizational life, Polish immigrants joined their parish, which was led after Jan Andrzejewski (1918-1933) by following Parish Priests: Father Franciszek Nowak (1933-1943), Father Paweł Sargewitz (1943-1949), Father Ludwik Kociszewski (1949-1961), Father Wawrzyniec Wnuk (1961-1983), Father Piotr Sanczenko (1983-2003), Father Roman Waszkiewicz (2003-2009) and Father Zbigniew Sawicki, who presently carries out the duties of Parish Priest. Activities taken by some of these priests were of big importance for the Polish ethnic group and the local community. Father Wawrzyniec Wnuk made a lot of efforts in binding of the Polish immigrants belonging to the first wave, and those arriving after the World War II. The care to maintain the Polish identity and cultivate knowledge about the land of the ancestors showed in his involvement in the activities of the Polish Language School, which exists in the Parish since 1925. On the initiative of the Priest, in 1972, the dance group "Tatry" was formed to bring young people closer to national traditions and shape feeling of cultural ties with Poland.[36] In 1973, he initiated the beginning of the construction of Polonia Park[37], a housing estate in Windsor, and Polonia Centre, sport and recreational centre.[38] He created many charitable funds, eg. the Mikolaj Kopernik Fund, the Polish Relief Fund, the Golden Jubilee of Mitered Priest Wawrzyniec Wnuk Fund, the Wawrzyniec Wnuk Bursary for the Catholic University of Lublin. For his social work for the Canadian society and the Polish ethnic group, the Reverend Prelate Wnuk received many high honors and distinctions.

In 1965, thanks to the efforts made by Father W. Wnuk, the sisters from the Grey Ursulines came to Windsor.[39] The arrival of the sisters coincided with the resolutions of the II Vatican Council, which brought changes to Church ceremonies. In the place of Latin, the language of the nation was substituted. Accordingly, the task of the Sisters was to sustain the national language, and to cultivate Polish history and traditions. The Sisters work in aid of the local community and for the Parish. They support the activity of the Holy Trinity Church, which constitutes a sustainable mainstay of Polish identity in Windsor. They run a nursery school for children regardless of nationality and faith, and direct the work of the Polish School.[40] The activities of the Sisters also extend into a wider environment, through collaboration with Polish organizations, and Canadian community. They work with young people, not only in the Polish Language School, but also in the high schools and previously at the University of Windsor, too. The Convent of the Ursuline Sisters makes a large contribution to the prep-

36 *Tatry Song & Dance Ensemble 1972-2003*, Windsor 2003, p. 10.
37 *Celebrating the 25th Anniversary of Polonia Park*, Windsor 2005, p. 12.
38 *Diamentowy Jubileusz Kapłaństwa ks. Infułata Wawrzyńca Wnuka: 1933-1993 (The Diamond Jubilee of the Ministry of the Rev. Mitered Prelate Wawrzyniec Wnuk: 1933-1993)*, Windsor 1993, p. 12.
39 *Pamiętnik 25-lecia Pracy Sióstr Urszulanek S.J.K. w Kanadzie 1965-1990 (Diary of the 25th Anniversary of the Work of the Ursuline Sisters in Canada 1965-1990)*, Windsor 1990, p. 19.
40 *Pamiętnik 75-lecia Szkoły Języka Polskiego przy parafii św. Trójcy w Windsor (Diary of the 75th Anniversary of the Polish Language School in the Holy Trinity Parish in Windsor)*, Windsor 2000, p. 5.

aration of the exhibition (the Polish Village) during the multicultural festival, the Carrousel of the Nations, promoting Polish cultural achievements within the Canadian society. Each year the exhibition is presented with a different theme, for example: Famous Poles in the International Arena, The Contribution of Polonia to the Culture of Canada, The Dance and Music of Poland, Polish Customs and Folk Art, Poland – A Country between East and West. In the work with younger generation, the Sisters develop a feeling of pride in the cultural heritage of the Polish nation, and at the same time emphasize the importance of integration with Canadian society.

Statistics show that in years 1953-1971 Canada received about 55,000 Polish immigrants. In the same period Windsor received 1,381 immigrants of Polish origin. In 1971 there was 5,200 Poles living in Windsor. People traveling to Windsor on the basis of family reunification made up a significant proportion.

During the first half of the 1980s, Poles came to Canada mainly by way of refugee camps located in Western Europe. After the introduction of Martial Law in Poland, thanks to the regulations made by Canada, many people, who had traveled to Windsor earlier on tourist visas, were able to legalize a permanent stay within the country.

The wave of immigration from 1981-1991, known as the "Solidarity wave", amounted in Windsor to around 1,500 people. It included people with high professional qualifications and frequently with university diplomas.

The Holy Trinity Parish, through the intervention of Father Piotr Sanczenko, took on the role of guarantor, making possible travel by many people to Windsor. In order to effectively carry out the relief activities, the parish received from the Federal Government the privilege to declare itself an official sponsor-guarantor in emigration procedures. In the years 1983-1991, one thousand immigration agreements were signed as an intervention by the Holy Trinity Parish.[41]

The arrival of the large group of "Solidarity" immigrants brought significant changes to socio-cultural life of the Polish ethnic group in Windsor. The number of the Holy Trinity Parishes increased. The majority of children started their education at the Polish Language School. The newcomers' need for a financial support brought the growth of the Polish Credit Union, the financial institution raised in Windsor in 1950s.[42] New wave of Polish immigrants stimulated activities of the ethnic community. They joined socio-cultural organizations such as: the "Polonia" Sports Club, the "Tatry" Song and Dance Ensemble, the Theatrical-Vocal Group "Płomień" (established in 1995).[43]

The character of activities carried out by the members of ethnic organizations varies from the ones of the beginning of Polish settlement in the city. They go beyond the Polish community and, in some cases, go beyond the local area.

---

41   75 lat Parafii św. Trójcy 1916-1991 (75 Years of the Holy Trinity Parish 1916-1991), Windsor 1991, p. 29.
42   Nasza Credit Union (Our Credit Union), July 1997, Nr 377.
43   Grupa Teatralno-Wokalna "Płomień", 1995-2005 (The Theatrical-Vocal Group Płomień, 1995-2005), Windsor 2005, p. 5.

The Polish-Canadian Business and Professional Association, established in 1996, undertakes a number of enterprises, leading to the development of Polish-Canadian collaboration in the economic, scientific and cultural spheres. In 2000, it initiated a twin city agreement between Windsor and Lublin, which allows to maintain the cultural, educational and commercial cooperation between Polish and Canadian students and business representatives.[44]

In 2002, the Association participated in signing of the agreement between Canada and Poland, the objective of which was the development of partnerships in Central Europe. This understanding (the Official Development Assistance in Central Europe Programme – ODACE)[45] was design as a five-year programme for supporting of economic reforms and promoting technological development in Central Europe.

The new range of activities undertaken by Polish ethnic organizations is to create political lobby for Poland. It is made by the cooperation with the Provincial and Federal Representatives. In 1997, Polish ethnic group became involved with a petition to its representatives in Parliament, on the issue of the admission of Poland into NATO.[46] The Deputy Prime Minister of Canada, the Hon. Herb Gray, supported the petition and took action together with the Government of Canada, which bore fruit with the expansion of the North Atlantic Pact (1999).

In 2006, the representatives of the Polish ethnic group, together with the Federal Representative for the Windsor-Tecumseh Riding, Vice Chair of the Canada-Poland Parliamentary Friendship Group, made a visit to Poland.[47] During the meeting with the Marshal of the Senate of the Polish Republic, Bogdan Borusewicz, specific discussions were held on the subject of the abolition of visas to Canada for the citizens of Poland. The involvement of Polonia, and the Federal Representative in this matter was profitable, and has shown a big awareness of the important issues for Poland.[48] The abolition of visas gave facilities for the developing of cooperation between Lublin and Windsor, on the basis of the twin cities agreement.

An important aim of the Polish ethnic group is also, to share with the achievements made by Polish immigrants, and to support the local community. The events, such as the Polish Week organized since 2002, bring the inhabitants of the city closer to culture, the history and promote the accomplishments of Poles within the Canadian society.[49]

The ethnic organizations also participate in supporting of the local needs.[50]

---

44 *The Polish-Canadian Business and Professional Association of Windsor celebrates the 10th Anniversary 1995-2004*, Windsor 2004, p. 10.
45 www.acdi-cida.gc.ca/cida_ind.nsf/dccfe
46 Letter-Petition from Windsor Polonia to Herb Gray, 26.05.1997.
47 J. Barycki, *Wizyta posła kanadyjskiego Joe Comartina w Polsce, 19-27 lipca 2006 (Visit by Canadian Representative Joe Comartin In Poland, 19-27 July 2006)*, Windsor 2006.
48 On March 1st 2008, a temporary resident visa for the Polish citizens was abolished.
49 P. Ryniec, E. Barycka, *Polski Tydzień w Windsor 2002 (The Polish Week In Windsor 2002)*, Windsor 2002.
50 *The Polonia Centre(Windsor) Inc.* each year, designates the sum of $3,500 for the Leddy Library of the University of Windsor, and $1,000 for the Windsor Public Library. The

Creation of the Polonia Centre Academic Awards Program gives financial support to students by founding bursaries. The award of the bursaries takes place during the Harvest Festival, part of which is an Evening of Excellence Dinner.

The social involvement of Polish diaspora can be also viewed by the foundation of a vast number of charitable actions and funds carried by its members.[51]

Polish ethnic group, as an integral part of the multicultural society, has always played important role in the history of the town. Throughout the past century, they established stable and active community. Nowadays, it's easy to find in the city symbols of Polish character, proof of Polish existence. Among them the Holy Trinity Church, the Convent of the Ursuline Sisters, the Polish Hall, and the Polonia Park. Another visible symbol of Polish identity is a monument, the Astrolabe of Nicolas Copernicus[52], erected as the gift from the Canadian Polonia to the city, bequeathed on the One-hundredth Anniversary of its existence, and the Ambassador Bridge, linking the United States with Canada. One of the engineers and construction inspector was Ralph Modjeski (the son of the famous actress Helena Modrzejewska). There is also a fountain-goat, located by the shore of the Detroit River, as the gift of the twin city Lublin, on the one hundredth anniversary of the Polish settlement in Windsor.

The studies of the Polish ethnic group in Windsor permit the comment that the present-day Polonia in Windsor is a group of ambitious and hard-working people. The social advancement of Polish immigrants and individuals of Polish heritage makes them referable to the middle class of Canadian society. They do not form locally concentrated community, as they did at the beginning of the settlement in the city, but belong mainly to inhabitants of the suburbs of the city. The myth of the poor immigrant, coming to Canada in search of daily bread, is demolished. Nowadays, there are many medical doctors of different specializations, dental surgeons, lawyers, engineers, economists, artists, teachers and scientists of Polish descent.

The statistics from 2006 recorded in metropolitan area of Windsor, 4 810 people of Polish descent according to the initial identification, and 8 615 mentioned Polish origin as one of many.[53] The Polish ethnic group is the fifth in size among the ethnic groups in the city, after Italian, German, Arab and Asian.[54] The variety of undertaken activities, makes Polish diaspora an outstanding among other ethnic groups in the city.

---

money is for the purchase of books and periodicals in English about themes, connected with Polish history, economy and culture.

51 eg. The Polish Relief Fund, the Canada Saquenay Flood Relief Fund, the Polish Committee Fund, the Mikołaj Kopernik Fund, the Stanisław Grabowiecki Perpetual Fund, the Tadeusz Polewski and Ludmiła Szulgo Fund, the Millennium Fund, the Andrzej Bobola Fund, the Paul I.B. Staniszewski Bursary for the University of Windsor, the Paul I.B. Staniszewski and Tevis Staniszewski Foudation.

52 W. Makowski, 1987, *The Polish People in Canada; A Visual History*, Montreal: Tundra Books, p.99.

53 www40.statcan.gc.ca/101/cst01/demo27n-eng.htm

54 Canadian census is made in years ended with 1 and 6. The next census will be done in 2011.

References

Breton, Raymond. "Institutional Completeness of Ethnic Communities and Personal Relations of Immigrants." *American Journal of Sociology*, vol. 70, no 2 (1964).

Kmietowicz, Frank., [1984], *Polskie Siły Zbrojne w Kanadzie Podczas Drugiej Wojny Światowej*. Windsor: Komitet Windsorczyków, 1984.

Makowski, William. *The Polish People in Canada; A Visual History*. Montreal: Tundra Books, 1987.

Plaut, Jonathan V. and Larry Kulisek. *The Jews of Windsor, 1790-1990: a Historical Chronicle*. Toronto: Dundurn Press Ltd, 2007.

Plewko, Jadwiga. "Parafia św. Trójcy," in *Leksykon geograficzno – historyczny parafii i kościołów polskich w Kanadzie*. Ed. Edward Walewander. Lublin: Instytut Badań nad Polonią i Duszpasterstwem Polonijnym, 1992.

Reczyńska, Anna. *Piętno wojny, Polonia kanadyjska wobec polskich problemów lat 1939 – 1945*. Kraków: Zakład Wydawniczy "Nomos", 1997.

Reczyńska, Anna. "Diaspora Polska w Kanadzie," in *Polska Diaspora*. Ed. Adam Walaszek. Kraków: Wydawnictwo Literackie, 2001.

The Town of Sandwich. Windsor: Essex Country Historical Association, 1979.

**Migration - Ethnicity - Nation:
Cracow Studies in Culture, Society and Politics**

Edited by Dorota Praszałowicz

Vol. 1 Agnieszka Małek / Dorota Praszałowicz (eds.): Between the Old and the New World. Studies in the History of Overseas Migrations. 2012.

www.peterlang.de

Alicja Witalisz (ed.)

Migration, Narration, Communication
Cultural Exchanges in a Globalised World

Frankfurt am Main, Berlin, Bern, Bruxelles, New York, Oxford, Warszawa, Wien, 2011. 207 pp., 9 fig.
Text – Meaning – Context: Cracow Studies in English Language, Literature and Culture. Edited by Elżbieta Chrzanowska-Kluczewska and Władysław Witalisz. Vol. 1
ISBN 978-3-631-60672-8 · hb. € 44,80*

The volume offers an interdisciplinary discussion of the phenomenon of migration and mobility in the modern globalised world and their impact on multiple aspects of culture and communication. Contributors, who are literary scholars, linguists and investigators of culture, examine problems related to migration, cultural diversity and cultural globalisation.

Content: Migration · Literature Narrating the Experience of Migrants · Cultural Identity · Hybridity · Cultural Adaptation and Assimilation · Culture and Language Contacts · Linguistic Borrowing · Humour Studies

*The e-price includes German tax rate. Prices are subject to change without notice

Frankfurt am Main · Berlin · Bern · Bruxelles · New York · Oxford · Wien
Distribution: Verlag Peter Lang AG
Moosstr. 1, CH-2542 Pieterlen
Telefax 00 41 (0) 32 / 376 17 27
E-Mail info@peterlang.com

**40 Years of Academic Publishing
Homepage http://www.peterlang.com**

www.ingramcontent.com/pod-product-compliance
Ingram Content Group UK Ltd.
Pitfield, Milton Keynes, MK11 3LW, UK
UKHW022154230426
12049UKWH00004BA/95